LIVING HIGH
AND LETTING DIE

LIVING HIGH AND LETTING DIE

Our Illusion of Innocence

Peter Unger

New York   Oxford
OXFORD UNIVERSITY PRESS
1996

Oxford University Press

Oxford New York
Athens Auckland Bangkok
Calcutta Cape Town Dar es Salaam Delhi
Florence Hong Kong Istanbul Karachi
Kuala Lumpur Madras Madrid Melbourne
Mexico City Nairobi Paris Singapore
Taipei Tokyo Toronto

and associated companies in
Berlin Ibadan

Published by Oxford University Press, Inc.
198 Madison Avenue, New York, New York 10016

Oxford is a registered trademark of Oxford University Press, Inc.

Library of Congress Cataloging-in-Publication Data
Unger, Peter K.
Living high and letting die : our illusion of innocence /
Peter Unger.
p. cm.
Includes bibliographical references and index.
ISBN 0–19–507589–7; ISBN 0–19–510859–0 (pbk.)
1. Life and death, Power over. 2. Ethics. 3. Generosity.
I. Title.
BJ1469.U54 1996
170—dc20 96–1463

**All author's royalties from the sale of this book go, in equal
measure, to Oxfam America and the U.S. Committee for UNICEF.**

5 7 9 8 6

Printed in the United States of America
on acid-free paper

For my wife, Susan
our son, Andrew
my brother, Jonathan
our father, Sidney

And for my dear friend,
Keith DeRose

ACKNOWLEDGEMENTS

In the early 1970s, Peter Singer spent two consecutive academic years as a visiting assistant professor in the Philosophy Department at New York University. As he'd just recently written his now famous paper, "Famine, Affluence and Morality," I couldn't help but discuss with him that revolutionary work. As a result, I became convinced of the essential soundness of, and the enormous importance of, the essay's main ideas. In one important way, then, it's Singer's thinking that, more than any other contemporary philosopher's, influenced this present volume. And, much more recently, upon reading not just one, but two drafts of the work, he's encouraged me both to improve the book and to press on to its completion and publication. Accordingly, I'm deeply grateful to him.

While most of them still disagree with much that the volume proposes, many others helped in the writing of this book. Though unavoidably forgetting to mention some who've helped significantly, I remember to thank these folks: Jonathan Adler, José-Luis Bobadilla, Robert Hanna, Frances Howard-Snyder, Mark Johnston, Frances Kamm, David Lewis, Jeff McMahan, Tom Nagel, Derek Parfit, Bruce Russell, Peter Railton, Roy Sorensen, Sydney Shoemaker, Judith Thomson and, especially helpful, Jonathan Bennett and John Carroll.

Each reading at least two drafts of the book, three people helped me so much that I really should thank them separately: First, through much penetrating written commentary and many astute conversational remarks, Shelly Kagan got me to make the book much clearer, and saved me from numerous errors. Second, through countless conversations, Liam Murphy rightly got me to make explicit the main commitments of my views; and, more than anyone else, he's responsible for the fact that, at less than half the size of earlier versions, what's found its way into print has at least one virtue, brevity. Thirdly, while it was Singer who, in one important way, most influenced the book, so, in another, and more recently, it was Keith DeRose who had the greatest impact. Partly for that reason, but mainly because he's such a dear friend, it's to him that, along with my closest relatives, I dedicate the book.

Even with all the changes wrought on earlier work by the word processing demon in me, some sentences in chapter 4 may have survived from a paper, "Causing and Preventing Serious Harm," that appeared in *Philosophical Studies*. As that journal's publisher informed me I must do, I hereby repeat verbatim the paper's original copyright notice: © 1992 Kluwer Academic Publishers. And, I make this verbatim statement: Reprinted by permission of Kluwer Academic Publishers. Similarly, some sentences in chapter 7 may have first seen print in another paper, "Contextual Analysis in Ethics," that appeared in *Philosophy and Phenomenological Research*. For permission to reprint, without having to make any verbatim statements, I more heartily thank that journal's sensible publisher.

The book's first *several-option case* comes with a helpful diagram, the volume's only visual illustration. For that nifty drawing, I thank Jesse Prinz.

Much of the book was written in the Spring and Fall Semesters of 1993, when I was on sabbatical leave from New York University, and when I had a Research Fellowship from the National Endowment for the Humanities. As well, this project was supported by a New York University Research Challenge Fund Emergency Support Grant. For their support, I thank the NEH and NYU.

New York   P.K.U
November 1995

CONTENTS

LIVING HIGH
AND LETTING DIE

1

ILLUSIONS OF INNOCENCE:
AN INTRODUCTION

Each year millions of children die from easy to beat disease, from malnutrition, and from bad drinking water. Among these children, about 3 million die from dehydrating diarrhea. As UNICEF has made clear to millions of us well-off American adults at one time or another, with a packet of oral rehydration salts that costs about 15 cents, a child can be saved from dying soon.

By sending checks earmarked for Oral Rehydration Therapy, or ORT, to the U.S. Committee for UNICEF, we Americans can help save many of these children. Here's the full mailing address:

United States Committee for UNICEF
United Nations Children's Fund
333 East 38th Street
New York, NY 10016

Now, you can write that address on an envelope well prepared for mailing. And, in it, you can place a $100 check made out to the *U.S. Committee for UNICEF* along with a note that's easy to write:

WHERE IT WILL HELP THE MOST, USE THE ENCLOSED FUNDS FOR ORT.

So, as is reasonable to believe, you can easily mean a big difference for vulnerable children.

Toward realistically thinking about the matter, I'll use a figure far greater than just 15 cents per child saved: Not only does the U.S. Committee have overhead costs, but so does UNICEF itself; and, there's the cost of transporting the packets, and so on. Further, to live even just one more year, many children may need several saving interventions and, so, several packets. And, quite a few of those saved will die shortly thereafter, anyway, from some sadly common Third World cause. So, to be more realistic about what counts most, let's multiply the cost of the packet by 10, or, better, by *20!*

For getting one more Third World youngster to escape death and live a reasonably long life, $3 is a more realistic figure than 15 cents and, for present purposes, it will serve as well as any. Truth to tell, in the light of searching empirical investigation, even this higher figure might prove too low. But, as nothing of moral import will turn on the matter, I'll postpone a hard look at the actual cost till quite late in the book.[1] As will become evident, for a study that's most revealing that's the best course to take.

With our $3 figure in mind, we do well to entertain this proposition: If you'd contributed $100 to one of UNICEF's most efficient lifesaving programs a couple of months ago, this month there'd be over thirty fewer children who, instead of painfully dying soon, would live reasonably long lives. Nothing here's special to the months just mentioned; similar thoughts hold for most of what's been your adult life, and most of mine, too. And, more important, unless we change our behavior, similar thoughts will hold for our future. That nonmoral fact moved me to do the work in moral philosophy filling this volume. Before presenting it, a few more thoughts about the current global life-and-death situation.

1. Some Widely Available Thoughts about Many Easily Preventable Childhood Deaths

As I write these words in 1995, it's true that, in each of the past 30 years, well over 10 million children died from readily preventable

1. In the summer of 1995, I fervently sought to learn how much it really costs, where the most efficient measures get their highest yield, to get vulnerable children to become adults. Beyond reading, I phoned experts at UNICEF, the Rockefeller Foundation, the Johns Hopkins School of Hygiene and Public Health and, finally, the World Bank. As I say in the text, nothing of moral import turns on my search's findings. For

causes. And, except for a lack of money aimed at doing the job, most of the deaths could have been prevented by using any one of many means.

Before discussing a few main means, it's useful to say something about the regions where the easily preventable childhood deaths have been occurring. First, there's this well-known fact: Over ninety percent of these deaths occur in the countries of the so-called Third World. By contrast, here's something much less widely known: Though almost all these needless deaths occur in the materially poorest parts of the world, poverty itself is hardly the whole story. For a good case in point, take the poverty-ridden Indian state of Kerala. While per capita income in this state of about thirty million is notably lower than in India as a whole, life expectancy in Kerala is higher than in *any other* Indian state. And, the childhood mortality rate is *much* lower than in India as a whole.[2] Why? Without telling a long historical story, most of the answer may be put like this: In this vibrantly democratic and responsive state, Kerala's millions have food security, safe drinking water and very basic health care. By contrast, many of the richer Indians *don't* have their basic needs met, and don't have their *children's* needs met. So, while often a factor, poverty itself hardly explains why millions of kids needlessly die each year.

In one direction, I'll amplify that remark.[3] As is well known, many millions of children don't get enough to eat. These related truths are less well known: First, for each child that dies in a famine, several die from *chronic malnutrition*. Second, even if she gets over eighty percent of the calories needed by a youngster of her age for excellent health, a child who regularly gets less than ninety percent is so malnourished

---

those to whom that isn't already clear, it will be made evident, I think, by the arguments of chapter 6. Partly for that reason, it's there that I'll present the best empirical estimates I found.

2. Most of what I say about Kerala was first inspired by reading Frances Moore Lappé and Rachel Schurman, *Taking Population Seriously*, the Institute for Food and Development Policy, 1988. Almost all is well documented in a more recent book from the Institute, entirely devoted to the Indian state: Richard W. Franke and Barbara H. Chasin, *Kerala: Radical Reform as Development in an Indian State*, 1989. Still more recently, these statements are confirmed by material on pages 18–19 of the United Nations Development Programme's *Human Development Report 1993*, Oxford University Press, 1993.

3. Much of what I'll say about causes of childhood death, and about the interventions that can nullify these causes, is systematically presented in James P. Grant's *The State of the World's Children 1993*, published for UNICEF by the Oxford University Press in 1993. To a fair extent, not more, I've cross-checked this against the (somewhat independent) material I've skimmed in the more massive *World Development Report 1993*, published for the World Bank by the OUP in 1993.

that she'll have a dangerously inadequate immune system. Third, what happens to many such vulnerable children is that, because she's among the many millions who haven't been vaccinated against measles, when she gets measles she dies from it. So, fourth, each year mere measles still kills about a million Third World kids.[4]

Several means of reducing measles deaths are worth mentioning, including these: Semiannually, an underfed child can be given a powerful dose of Vitamin A, with capsules costing less than 10 cents. For that year, this will improve the child's immune system. So, if she hasn't been vaccinated, during this year she'll be better able to survive measles. What's more, from her two capsules, she'll get a big bonus: With her immune system improved, this year she'll have a better chance of beating the two diseases that take far more young lives than measles claims, pneumonia and diarrhea.

Though usually all that's needed to save a child from it is the administration of antibiotics that cost about 25 cents, pneumonia now claims about 3.5 million young lives a year, making it the leading child-killing disease. And, in the text's first paragraph, I've related the score for diarrhea. But, let's again focus on measles.

Having already said plenty about Vitamin A, I'll note that, for about $17 a head, UNICEF can vaccinate children against measles. On the positive side, the protection secured lasts a lifetime; with no need for semiannual renewal, there's no danger of failing to renew protection! What's more, at the same time each child can be vaccinated for lifetime protection against five other diseases that, taken together, each year kill about another million Third World kids: tuberculosis, whooping cough, diphtheria, tetanus and polio. Perhaps best of all, these vaccinations will be part of a worldwide immunization campaign that, over the years, is making progress toward *eliminating* these vaccine-preventable diseases, much as smallpox was eliminated only a decade or two ago. Indeed, with no incidence in the whole Western Hemisphere since 1991, polio is quite close to being eliminated; with good logistical systems in place almost everywhere, the campaign's success depends mainly on funding.[5]

---

4. But, happily, UNICEF's worldwide immunization campaign has been making great strides against measles for years. So, while just a few years ago measles claimed over 1.5 million young lives, in the past year, 1994, it claimed about 1 million.

5. In "Polio Isn't Dead Yet," *The New York Times*, June 10, 1995, Hugh Downs, the chairman of the U.S. Committee, usefully writes, "The United States spends $270 million on domestic [polio] immunization each year. For about half that amount polio could be eliminated worldwide in just five years, according to experts from Unicef and the World Health Organization. If the disease is wiped off the earth, we would no longer need to immunize American children and millions of dollars could be diverted to other pressing needs."

Finally, the vast majority of the world's very vulnerable children live in lands with UNICEF programs operating productively, including all 13 developing countries lately (1992) ranked among the world's 20 most populous nations: China, India, Indonesia, Brazil, Pakistan, Bangladesh, Nigeria, Mexico, Vietnam, Philippines, Iran, Turkey and Thailand.[6] By now, we've seen the main point: Through the likes of UNICEF, it's well within your power, in the coming months and years, to lessen serious suffering.

For even modestly well-informed readers, what I've just related doesn't come as a big surprise. All they'll have learned are some particulars pertaining to what they've learned long ago: By directing donations toward the worthy end, well-off folks can be very effective in lessening serious suffering and loss. Indeed, so well accustomed are they to this thought that, when reading the presented particulars, the worldly individuals won't make any notable response. For far fewer readers, what I've related will be something completely new. From many of them, my remarks will evoke a very notable response, even if a fairly fleeting one, about how we ought to behave: The thought occurs that each of us ought to contribute (what's for her) quite a lot to lessen early deaths; indeed, it's *seriously* wrong not to do that.

But, soon after making such a strict response, the newly aware also become well accustomed to the thought about our power. And, then, they also make the much more lenient response that almost everyone almost always makes: While it's good for us to provide vital aid, it's *not even the least bit wrong* to do *nothing* to help save distant people from painfully dying soon. (The prevalence of the lenient response is apparent from so much passive behavior: Even when unusually good folks are vividly approached to help save distant young lives, it's very few who contribute anything.[7])

Which of these two opposite responses gives the more accurate indication of what morality requires? Is it really seriously wrong not to do anything to lessen distant suffering; or, is it quite all right to do

6. The widely available table I use is presented on page 135 of *The 1993 Information Please Almanac*, Houghton Mifflin, 1993. The statement that each of these countries has a well established UNICEF program in place, and that it's currently (1995) easy for the program to work well in large parts of the nation, was told me by a U.S. Committee staffer.

7. In a typical recent year, 1993, the U.S. Committee for UNICEF mailed out, almost every month, informative appeals to over 450,000 potential donors. As a Committee staffer informed me, the prospects were folks whose recorded behavior selected them as *well above* the national average in responding to humanitarian appeals. With only a small overlap between the folks in each mailing, during the year over 4 million "charitable" Americans were vividly informed about what just a few of their dollars would mean. With each mailing, a bit less than 1% donated anything, a pattern persisting year after year.

nothing? In this book, I'll argue that the first of these thoughts is correct and that, far from being just barely false, the second conflicts strongly with the truth about morality.

2. Singer's Legacy: An Inconclusive Argument for an Importantly Correct Conclusion

While directly concerned more with famine relief than with the children's health issues just highlighted, it was Peter Singer who first thought to argue, seriously and systematically, that it's the first response that's on target.[8] Both early on and recently, he offers an argument for the proposition that it's wrong for us not to lessen distant serious suffering. The argument's first premise is this general proposition:

> If we can prevent something bad without sacrificing anything of comparable significance, we ought to do it.[9]

So that it may help yield his wanted conclusion, Singer rightly has us understand this premise in a suitably strong sense, with its consequent, "we ought to do it," entailing "it's *wrong* for us *not* to do it," not just the likes of "it's better for us to do it than not." But, in such a strong sense, many think the premise to be unacceptable. Briefly, I'll explain why that's so.[10]

Wanting his first premise to find favor, Singer offers a compelling example that's an instance of the general proposition. Using his words, and some of my own, here's that justly famous case[11]:

8. See his landmark essay, "Famine, Affluence and Morality," *Philosophy and Public Affairs*, 1972.

9. See page 169 of the original edition of his *Practical Ethics*, Cambridge University Press, 1979. Without any change, this first premise appears on page 230 in the book's Second Edition, published by the CUP in 1993.

10. Now, without departing from it's original spirit, the premise may be reformulated so that, at least at first sight, there are more appealing arguments for its importantly correct conclusion, that it's wrong for us not to lessen serious suffering, and even for the wanted stronger conclusion that it's *seriously* wrong. For example, one more appealing formulation has us replace Singer's original first premise with this proposition that, briefly, will be discussed in chapter 2, section 17:

> *Pretty Cheaply Lessening Early Death.* Other things being even nearly equal, if your behaving in a certain way will result in the number of people who *very prematurely lose their lives* being less than the number who'll do so if you don't so behave and *if even so you'll still be at least reasonably well off*, then it's seriously wrong for you not to so behave.

But, in any event, at least one of the argument's premises will be a general proposition many will think unacceptable.

11. The case first appears in "Famine, Affluence and Morality." The words I use come from the Second Edition of *Practical Ethics*.

The Shallow Pond. The path from the library at your university to the humanities lecture hall passes a shallow ornamental pond. On your way to give a lecture, you notice that a small child has fallen in and is in danger of drowning. If you wade in and pull the child out, it will mean getting your clothes muddy and either cancelling your lecture or delaying it until you can find something clean and dry to wear. If you pass by the child, then, while you'll give your lecture on time, the child will die straightaway. You pass by and, as expected, the child dies.

Now, when responding to this example, almost everyone's intuitive moral judgment is that your conduct's abominable. Does this reflect a strong obligation to aid that's quite general? Needed for Singer's first premise, the thought that it does is a pretty plausible proposition. But, also pretty plausibly, many think our response to the Shallow Pond doesn't reflect anything very general at all.

What moves them most here is the fact that, to other cases with people in great need, our intuitive responses are markedly different. Indeed, from typical thoughts about UNICEF, there's suggested:

The Envelope. In your mailbox, there's something from (the U.S. Committee for) UNICEF. After reading it through, you correctly believe that, unless you soon send in a check for $100, then, instead of each living many more years, over thirty more children will die soon. But, you throw the material in your trash basket, including the convenient return envelope provided, you send nothing, and, instead of living many years, over thirty more children soon die than would have had you sent in the requested $100.

To this example, almost everyone reacts that your conduct isn't even wrong at all. Just so, many hold that, well indicated by our disparate responses to the Shallow Pond and the Envelope, there's a big moral difference between the cases. As they pretty plausibly contend, rather than any general duty to aid folks in vital need, there are only more limited obligations, like, say, a duty to *rescue* certain people.

Since what I've just related has considerable appeal, there's no way that, by itself, any such general argument for Singer's importantly correct conclusion will convince those who'd give more weight to the response the Envelope elicits than they'd give his general reasoning's first premise, or any relevantly similar statement. So, for many years, there's been a stand-off here, with little progress on the issue.[12]

Deciding this philosophical issue amounts to the same thing as deciding between our two quite opposite responses to the thought that it's within a well-off person's power to lessen serious suffering significantly, the strict response made when first aware of that thought and the lenient response regularly made later. This disagreement between philosophers mirrors a difference, then, that many experience without the benefit of philosophy. It's important to provide the discrepancy with a rational resolution.

3. Two Approaches to Our Intuitions on Particular Cases: Preservationism and Liberationism

Toward that important end, we'll examine vigorously our moral reactions to many *particular cases*. And, we'll explore not only many cases where aiding's the salient issue, but also many other ethically interesting examples. Briefly, I'll explain why: As we've observed, a few philosophers think that, while some of our responses to aiding examples are good indications of morality's true nature, like our strict reaction to the Shallow Pond, others are nothing of the kind, like our lenient reaction to the Envelope. And, as we've also observed, many other philosophers think that (almost) all our responses to aiding examples are good indications of morality's true nature, including our response to the Envelope. Rather than being narrow or isolated positions, when intelligently maintained each flows from a broad view of the proper philosophical treatment for (almost) all of morality. Thus, the majority thinks that, or has their morally substantive writing actually guided by the proposition that, not just for aiding, but right across the board, our untutored intuitions on cases (almost) always are good indications of conduct's true moral status; by contrast, we in the minority think that, and have our morally substantive writing guided by the proposition that, right across the board, even as our responses to particular cases *often are* good indications of behavior's moral status, so, also, they *often aren't* any such thing at all.

Though few of them may hold a view that's so very pure, those in

12. For a complementary explanation of the impasse, see the subsection "The Methodological Objection," on pages 104-05 in Garrett Cullity's recent paper, "International Aid and the Scope of Kindness," *Ethics*, 1994. Taking the paper's text together with its footnotes, there's a useful overview of the discussion that, in the past couple of decades, pertains to Singer's contribution.

the majority hold a position that's a good deal like what's well called *Preservationism*: At least at first glance, our moral responses to particular cases appear to reflect accurately our deepest moral commitments, or our *Basic Moral Values*, from which the intuitive reactions primarily derive; with all these case-specific responses, or almost all, the Preservationist seeks to *preserve* these appearances. So, on this view, it's only by treating all these various responses as valuable data that we'll learn much of the true nature of these Values and, a bit less directly, the nature of morality itself. And, so, in our moral reasoning, any more general thoughts must (almost) always accommodate these reactions.

To be sure, our intuitive responses to particular cases are a very complicated motley. So, for Preservationism, any interesting principle that actually embodies our Values, and that may serve to reveal these Values, will be extremely complex. But, at the same time, the view has the psychology of moral response be about as simple as possible. For now, so much for Preservationism's methodological aspect.

Just as the view itself has it, the morally substantive aspect of Preservationism is whatever's found by employing the method at the heart of the position. So, unlike the minority view we're about to encounter, it hasn't any antecedent morally substantive aspect. For now, so much for Preservationism.[13]

By contrast with Preservationists, we in the minority hold that insight into our Values, and into morality itself, won't be achieved on an approach to cases that's anywhere near as direct, or as accommodating, as what's just been described. On our contrasting *Liberationist* view, folks' intuitive moral responses to many specific cases derive from sources far removed from our Values and, so, they fail to reflect the Values, often even pointing in the opposite direction. So, even as the Preservationist seeks (almost) always to *preserve* the appearances

---

13. Many contemporary ethicists are *pretty close* to being (pure) Preservationists, prominently including Frances M. Kamm, in papers and, more recently, in *Morality/ Mortality*, Oxford University Press, Volume 1, 1993 and Volume 2, 1996; Warren S. Quinn, in papers collected in *Morality and Action*, Cambridge University Press, 1993; and, Judith J. Thomson, in papers collected in *Rights, Restitution and Risk*, Harvard University Press, 1986 and, more recently, in *The Realm of Rights*, Harvard, 1990.

Whatever the *avowed* methodological stance, it's a radically rare ethicist who'll actually advocate, and continue to maintain, a morally substantive proposition that's strongly at odds with his reactions to more than a few cases he considers.

Of course, many gesture at the propositions presented in John Rawls' "Outline of a Decision Procedure for Ethics," *Philosophical Review*, 1951, fashionably uttering the words "reflective equilibrium". With the Liberationism this book develops, perhaps there's a step toward putting some meat on some such schematic bones; in any case, there's more than just a gesture.

promoted by these responses, the Liberationist seeks often to *liberate* us from such appearances.

Not by itself, nor even when combined with our intuitive judgments for the Envelope and for the Shallow Pond, will much of moral substance follow from the methodological aspect of Liberationism, barely sketched just above. But, that's certainly no problem with the view. To the contrary, it's the position's substantive side that, in the first place, moves Liberationists to be so skeptical of many of our case-specific responses. Just so, on the Liberationist view, a sensible methodology for treating our responses to examples will be guided by some morally substantive propositions, even as it will guide us toward further statements with moral substance. While our formulations of it are all fair game for much revision, most of the substantial moral core will be taken correctly to defeat any opposing propositions.[14]

Very briefly, here's a fallible formulation of a fair bit of Liberationism's substantive side[15]: Insofar as they need her help to have a decent chance for decent lives, a person must do a great deal for those few people, like her highly dependent children, to whom she has the most serious sort of special moral obligation. Insofar as it's compatible with that, which is often very considerably indeed, and sometimes even when it's not so compatible, she must do a lot for other innocent folks in need, so that they may have a decent chance for decent lives. For now, so much for Liberationism's morally substantive side.

Just that much substance suffices to move the Liberationist to hold that, even as (in the morally most important respects) the Envelope's conduct is *at least as bad* as the Shallow Pond's behavior, so (in those most important respects) that conduct is seriously wrong.[16] Now, even if he merely judged the Envelope's conduct to be somewhat wrong, the Liberationist would want to provide a pretty ambitious account of why our response to the case is lenient. And, since he goes much further,

14. As I'll suppose, my fellow Liberationists, including Peter Singer, are reasonably flexible here.

15. The Liberationism whose moral substance is now to be spelled out, very incompletely, is the sort I myself favor. Others, like Peter Singer, will profess somewhat different guiding substantive moral beliefs, or Values. While those differences are important in certain contexts, in the context of this inquiry they aren't.

16. The expressions just bracketed in the text are to allow for certain nice ways these matters can be complicated by considerations of our *Secondary* Basic Moral Values, which Values aren't introduced in the text till the book's second chapter. For now, don't bother with that, but just note this: Even the staunchest Liberationist can establish semantic contexts in which it's *correct to say* that only the Shallow Pond's conduct is badly wrong, and even that the Envelope's isn't wrong at all. (It's not until the book's last chapter that I'll provide the sort of semantic account that supports this note's qualification.)

the account he'll offer is so very ambitious as to run along these general lines: Not stemming from our Values, the Envelope's lenient response is generated by the work of *distortional* dispositions. But, concerning the very same moral matter, there are other cases, like the Shallow Pond, that don't encourage the working of those dispositions. Accurately reflecting our Values, and the true nature of morality, our responses to these other cases *liberate* us from the misleading appearances flowing from that distortional work.[17]

4. An Extensive Exploration of the Liberationist Approach: Overview of the Book's Chapters

While I'm most concerned with their difference regarding when it's wrong not to aid, which we'll begin to explore seriously in chapter 2, Preservationism and Liberationism also differ, I've said, as regards many other morally substantive matters. For example, the Preservationist holds that, to save others from suffering truly serious losses, like the loss of life or limb, often it's wrong to lie, and to cheat, and to steal, even though nobody will ever suffer much from your doing any of that. By contrast, the Liberationist holds that, when necessary to lessen serious suffering, then, provided nobody suffers seriously in consequence of your so doing, it's always morally good to do all those unruly things and more.[18] Of course, the Liberationist knows that, to many particular cases of stealing and suchlike, our reactions hardly support his sensibly compassionate view. In chapter 3, I'll identify the specific distortional tendency promoting our misleading responses to so many cases.

It's much harder to identify the distortional tendencies promoting responses that depart from some other substantive Liberationist

17. On a third view, our responses to *both* cases fail to reflect anything morally significant: Just as it's all right not to aid in the Envelope, so, it's also perfectly all right in the Shallow Pond. Aptly named *Negativism*, this repellently implausible position has such very great difficulties that, in these pages, I'll scarcely ever consider it. To keep the text itself free from mentions of such a hopeless view, on the few occasions when Negativism's addressed at all, the brief notices will be confined to footnotes.

18. Here, we may well distinguish between *Extreme* Liberationism and *Open* Liberationism. So, as regards stealing, for example, the Extreme view holds that, *beyond what our responses to many favorable* cases indicate, to lessen serious suffering, not only is it good to steal, but it's *wrong not* to do so. By contrast, Open Liberationism holds that it's *at least good* to steal and, while it's *open* to the (epistemic) possibility that it's wrong not to do so, it's *also open* to the possibility that it's not wrong. While I'm inclined to think that, in the end, even the Extreme view is correct, in this book it's enough to argue for Open Liberationism.

thoughts. Concerned with your *imposing truly serious losses* on folks, it's chapter 4 that first explores these matters. But, though it takes lots of work to identify even just the leading distortional culprits here, we'll still meet with considerable success. And, in chapter 5, we'll see convincing confirmation of that positive judgment.

Of course, in your life, as in mine, there won't be many situations where, to aid some fine folks, you must impose serious losses on others; most likely, there'll be none. But, almost always, you'll be in a position to help aid people just by imposing on yourself what's merely a financial loss, no serious loss at all. So, theory, fun and games aside, it's this question that truly concerns us: For such well-off folks as you and me, how costly is it, in a world with such preventable suffering as this, to lead a morally decent life? Liberationism answers that it's terribly costly, far more so than usually supposed. Based on earlier material, in chapter 6 the arguments for this are as convincing, I think, as they're uncommon.

Finally, in chapter 7 there'll be provided a semantic account of moral talk, and moral thought, that allows us to reconcile the unusual behavioral judgments I make in the book with the more ordinary moral assessments that, in almost all the contexts of my life, I'll continue to make every day. With that, Liberationism may become as plausible as might reasonably be wished.

5. The Liberationist Approach to an Unusual Family of Moral Puzzles

As a Liberationist, I make moral assessments of our conduct that, at least at first, most readers must find preposterous. So, they'll be apt to dismiss the view quickly. Trying to get them to give Liberationism a chance, this section's devoted to an unusual family of moral puzzles.

First, there's the *Ordinary Puzzle of the (Great Dead) Virginians:* Consider the accepted assessments of two famous Virginian founders of the United States, George Washington and Thomas Jefferson. They're pretty nearly as positive as Jefferson's judgments of Washington:

> In war we have produced a Washington, whose memory will be adored while liberty shall have votaries, whose name will triumph over time, and will in future ages assume its just station among the most celebrated worthies of the world. . . .[19]

19. From Jefferson's "Notes on the State of Virginia," as included in Merrill D. Peterson, ed., *Thomas Jefferson: Writings*, The Library of America, 1984, page 190. Related in the book's Chronology, the "Notes" were published in England in 1787.

He was, indeed, in every sense of the words, a wise, a good and a great man. . . . His heart was not warm in its affections; but he exactly calculated every man's value, and gave him a solid esteem proportioned to it. . . . On the whole, his character was, in its mass, perfect, in nothing bad, in few points indifferent; and it may truly be said, that never did nature and fortune combine more perfectly to make a man great, and to place him in the same constellation with whatever worthies have merited from man an everlasting re-membrance.[20]

So, we think that Washington was, at the very least, quite a good man. And, even as we also greatly admire Jefferson, we believe that, in its mass, their conduct was good.

But, a little hard thought makes the lofty assessments puzzling: During all their years of maturity, they had slaves and, in the bargain, they lived lavishly. Now, as historians indicate, it wasn't impossible for them to free their slaves and live less lavishly. About Washington's last two years, Alden writes:

He now owned 277 slaves, far more than could be usefully employed at Mount Vernon. It was possible for him, by selling many that he did not need, both to secure cash and to reduce his expenses, but he could not bring himself to resort to such a sale, certain to bring unhappiness to the slaves. He even considered the possibility of developing another plantation where the blacks not needed at Mount Vernon could be located. He also was concerned with arrangements for property when he should die. In the late summer of 1798 he had been seriously ill with a fever and had lost twenty pounds. He had rapidly regained weight and was to all appearances in very good health. Nevertheless, he was conscious that his death would come at no distant time. He drew up his will. Martha was to enjoy the use of the bulk of his estate. After her death Bushrod Washington was to have Mount Vernon, and the remainder of the estate except for special bequests was to be divided among his relatives and those of Martha, with one most important exception. He was determined to free his slaves. His personal servant, Billy Lee, was to be freed immediately upon Washington's death. His blacks and those belonging to Martha had intermarried, and he could not legally set loose her blacks during her lifetime. Accordingly, he arranged for all of their slaves to be freed at her death. His executors must provide for the aged blacks, and the young were to be supported and taught to read and write. He stipulated that certain shares of stock should be used to help finance schools.[21]

20. From Jefferson's letter of January 2, 1814 to Dr. Walter Jones; see page 1319 of *Thomas Jefferson: Writings*.

21. See pages 302–303 of John R. Alden, *George Washington*, Louisiana State University Press, 1984.

But, of course, much of that conduct is very questionable. Why didn't Washington free some of his solely owned slaves well before his death, like Billy Lee, for one? Apparently, by selling some few stocks, our first President could have provided well for them. Evidently, there's no morally satisfactory answer. And, even if George had to convince Martha by threatening her, with divorce or worse, why didn't he see to it that, long before either died, all their slaves were freed and supported? Again, no very decent answer.

In various ways, Jefferson's life differed from Washington's, but not in any ways that excuse him. For, he also could have freed his slaves without any serious suffering. To be sure, had either done that, he wouldn't have enjoyed such a lavish Virginian life. But, morally, so what? Until their deaths, both freely remained slaveholders. When that fact's combined with our positive assessments, there's the Ordinary Puzzle of the Virginians: How can someone who keeps behaving like that, year after year, be a decent person, or be someone whose *total* behavior is even all right? Apparently, in our moral assessments, there's a questionable double standard at work: For those Virginians, slaveholding won't disqualify their total conduct from having high moral status. But, for us, no such easement's available.

That's puzzling; but, the puzzle can instruct. So, next, let's note some societal differences. By contrast with our society now, in old Virginia things were like this: First, it was a common practice to hold slaves. Second, by many engaged in the practice, it was held that slaveholding wasn't a morally terrible thing. Third, through interaction with folks who behaved and thought like that, for a given Virginian social pressure made it psychologically very hard to choose to become slaveless.

At least at first, many may think those three differences do much to explain our puzzling disparity. While that thought's initially plausible, it's very inaccurate. Yet, by coming to appreciate the full extent of the inaccuracy, perhaps we'll learn something worthwhile. To show what I mean, it's useful to present a conundrum that's an expansion of the current puzzle, the *Extraordinary Puzzle of (the Great Dead Virginians and) the Imaginary Australians.* After a short Historical Preamble, I'll do some Stage Setting, and, then, we'll confront the conundrum itself.

Historical Preamble: When slavery prevailed in Virginia, it was also prevalent even in various distant parts of the world.[22] In Brazil,

22. In Orlando Patterson's monumental comparative study, *Slavery and Social Death,* Harvard University Press, 1982, see Appendix C, "The Large-Scale Slave Systems," on pages 353–364. In conjunction with the obvious truth that in (at least) some of the listed societies, more than a very few wealthy people owned slaves, the data tabulated in this long appendix yields the sentence in the text to which this note attaches.

for example, it continued for decades after it ended in the South of the United States.[23] By contrast, in still other parts of the world, like Australia, there never was any slavery.[24] End of Preamble; and onto Stage Setting: In expanding our original puzzle, I'll contrast the *actual* case of old Virginia with a *hypothetical* case that's centered on a whole contemporary society where, year after year, many still engage in slave-holding. (For no good reason, some philosophers would have us confine attention to actual cases and very mildly hypothetical cases. If I followed such a stultifying line, I'd be prevented from centering it on Australia. But, rationally, I won't.) So, I'll center the contemporary contrast case on Peter Singer's native land, Australia. End of Stage Setting.

As we'll suppose, the early Australian settlers enslaved the island's Aborigines and, even today, many wealthy Australians have slaves work on their vast ranches and farms. Still, insofar as it's possible with folks kept as slaves, these masters treat them well, providing, for example, better facilities and accommodations than at all but the finest resorts. Now, among the very most benevolent masters are one Paul Singer and one Mary Singer, each a first cousin of Peter. (Of course, Peter himself hasn't any slaves and, as we're supposing, he does all he can to end slavery.) Because they've discussed his views with him for years, Paul and Mary agree with Peter about all manner of issues their behavior might address, except for the matter of slavery. And, even on that score, his cousins' beliefs aren't all that different from Peter's. For, they believe what, at least at last, Washington and Jefferson believed: While slavery's certainly bad, it might not be all that horribly bad.[25]

23. Conveniently at hand, in Volume 2 of *The World Book Encyclopedia*, the 1988 edition, there's the article "Brazil," by J. H. Galloway, the University of Toronto. Ending the section "The age of Pedro II," on pages 594–95 are these words:

> In 1888, a law abolished slavery in Brazil and freed about 750,000 slaves. Most of them had worked on plantations, and Brazil's powerful slaveowners became angry at Pedro when they were not paid for their slaves. In 1889, Brazilian military officers supported by the plantation owners forced Pedro to give up his throne. He died in Paris two years later. In 1922, his body was brought back to Brazil. Brazilians still honor Pedro II as a national hero.

24. In the encompassing work by Patterson, there's a brief discussion of slave practices among the Maori of New Zealand, but, apparently, no mention of Australia. Certainly, there's no entry for either in the volume's apparently exhaustive index, running from page 484 to page 511. And, according to the article "Australia" in my *World Book Encyclopedia*, Australia's white settlers treated her Aborigines very much as the whites who settled in what's now the U.S. treated this country's Indians, or Native Americans. While very bad behavior, that wasn't slaveholding.

25. For evidence of Washington's mature view, refer back in the text to the passage that, placed in display, I quoted from Alden's *George Washington*. For evidence of Jefferson's most mature view, in *Thomas Jefferson: Writings*, the index entry "Slavery,

What's more, we'll suppose that, apart from their slaveholding, Paul and Mary conduct themselves in a way that's even better than the morally good way Peter behaves. For example, working extremely hard and living very modestly, each year Paul gives almost all of the huge income from his organic fruit orchards toward the saving of many young lives in the Third World, and toward lessening other serious suffering. So, what we're supposing amounts to this: *Apart* from slaveholding, the cousins' conduct is much better than almost anyone's.

At all events, what's our intuitive assessment of their total behavior? As most respond, it's rather bad. But, a couple of questions show this negative judgment to be very puzzling: Why do we judge the imaginary Australians' conduct negatively, but judge the old Virginians' positively? And, even if we can find an explanatorily adequate answer, what adequate justification can there be for such a disparity?

As for the first question, it's clear there's a lot that needs explaining: In regards to the matter of slavery, Paul's and Mary's extremely benevolent conduct is *at least somewhat better* than Washington's and Jefferson's behavior. As regards other matters, since the Australians' conduct is morally so marvelous, it's *also at least somewhat better* than the Virginians'. But, *those are all the matters there are*! So, the conduct of our imaginary Australians is *better* than the behavior of our old Virginians.

When starting to explain, we might first note this: With the old Virginians, there were other societies then also heavily involved in slaveholding. But, with the imaginary Australians, theirs is the only society where there's still slavery. Is that a good way to start? Hardly. Just ponder this apt enlargement of the hypothetical example: In addition to Australia's large society, several others, like Brazil's, persisted in slavery right up to the present time. To this expanded case, most respond just as negatively.

Our Extraordinary Puzzle accentuates what's disturbing in our Ordinary Puzzle. But, with both, what's going on? Without telling a very long story, I'll try to provide a good perspective for the book's inquiry. To begin, I'll note that, in our moral judgments, we're greatly influenced by:

Our Idea of Moral Progress. With regard to certain morally bad forms of behavior, (we have the idea that) humanity has *morally*

---

last words on, 1516" takes us to a short letter to one James Heaton, dated May 20, 1826, in which the third President laments the fact that, even as he's disapproved of it for many years, the bad practice of slavery would likely last for many more years. As Jefferson died on July 4, 1826, that letter was penned just a few weeks before his death.

progressed beyond its being even the least bit normal for anyone to engage in behavior of those forms.

Of course, slaveholding is one of these morally surpassed forms. And, much earlier still, we progressed beyond its being at all normal to support entertainments where people try to kill each other, as with the gladiators of ancient Rome. Here's a suggestion about that Idea's influence: Once a very bad form of behavior is (taken by us to be) surpassed, we'll give negative assessments to the total conduct of those (taken to be) engaged in behavior of that form *after what's **actually** (taken to be) the time of the surpassing* (unless they break with the form, soon enough, and then don't resume such bad behavior). By contrast, when someone's engagement in a bygone form is all *before* that actual time, we're open to giving her total conduct a positive assessment. It's this pervasive double-faced tendency that explains both our strangely disparate responses to many actual cases, as with our Ordinary Puzzle, and our strange reactions to many hypothetical cases, as with our Extraordinary Puzzle.

Both to make the suggestion's content clearer and to provide it with support, another far-fetched example serves well: For all of the 18th and much of the 19th century, to entertain themselves and other white folks, certain Virginian masters occasionally made one of their slaves fight to the death with the slave of another wealthy slaveholder. As we'll suppose, while Washington took care never even to so much as attend any such ghastly event, Jefferson was one of these "Neo-Roman" practitioners and, as the odds had it, some of his slaves were killed in these "backyard spectacles." To this case, we make the definite moral response that Washington's total conduct would have been good and Jefferson's bad.

Along with many others, I believe that, at least in certain respects, there's been some moral progress. And, some of it satisfies Our Idea of Moral Progress. But, I also think that the influence of that Idea is far stronger than it should be: Mainly owing to that, we'll underrate the total conduct of people who, as we suppose, engage in behavior of a form that's been surpassed; just so, we underrated Paul's and Mary's (hypothetical) total behavior. And, as regards the whole of their conduct, we overrate those who, before it was surpassed, did engage in such bad behavior; just so, we overrate Washington's and Jefferson's (actual) total conduct. And, closely related to both of those distortional tendencies, perhaps a third involves us in closely related errors.

Perhaps, right now, we're engaging in conduct that, though it's of certain morally horrible forms, is still quite normal behavior. Then, since these bad forms *haven't* been surpassed, we may be overrating our own behavior. Now, perhaps our (distant) descendants will make so much moral progress that, at some future time, humanity will surpass some of these bad behavioral forms. But, if Our Idea of Moral Progress has much the same influence then as now, which we may very well suppose, even they will overrate us. Let's pursue that thought.

Here's a form of behavior that, though we're now heavily engaged in it, might well be thought terrible by our descendants and, for that reason, might be morally surpassed by them: letting distant innocents needlessly die. So, even if it never actually happens, we may instructively suppose that, centuries hence, humanity's made just such progress as this: Whenever well-off folks learn of people in great need, they promptly move to meet the need, almost no matter what the financial cost. So, at this late date, the basic needs of almost all the world's people will be met almost all the time. Still, once in a while, a great natural disaster may befall many folks in what is, then as now, one of the world's most dangerous areas, like the cyclone-prone coast of Bangladesh. Whether through demanding to be taxed more by their governments, or through contributing to nongovernmental organizations, or whatever, very many millions of the world's more fortunate folks make sure such beleaguered people don't ever undergo more serious suffering than a big cyclone causally necessitates. What's more, should any of these descendants find herself facing such preventable suffering as now actually obtains, she'd devote almost all her energy, and resources, toward lessening the suffering. To do any less would be as unthinkable for her as having slaves. Finally, in making moral judgments, they'll be just as affected as we by Our Idea of Moral Progress. Just as we overrate Washington and Jefferson, cutting them slack in the matter of slaveholding, they'll overrate you and me, cutting us slack in the matter of allowing much needless suffering.

From this discussion, two Liberationist lessons emerge, one pretty specific, the other far more general. Specifically, as we've seen one distortional tendency evoke misleading responses, both to hypothetical examples and even to actual cases, it won't be surprising to see, in other chapters, the operation of others. More generally, this thought places our whole inquiry in an appropriately humbling perspective: However much we increase our awareness of morality, it may hardly ever seem that our currently very consequential conduct is even mildly wrong.

6. Morality, Rationality and Truth: On the Importance of Our Basic Moral Values

Starting in the next chapter, I'll try hard to make a strong case for Liberationism. Before that, it's useful to place to the side large matters that, in moments of confusion, might be thought greatly to affect my inquiry. By focusing on two of the very largest of those matters, and two that are most representative, in this section I'll try to show how usefully, and how safely, that may be done.

The first concerns the relation between morality and rationality. For millennia, philosophers have been concerned to show a strong connection between these two normative conceptions. In some instances, their belief has been that, unless morality has the backing of rationality, reasonable people, like them, and us, won't engage in morally decent behavior. But, since there's nothing to this thought, I needn't here inquire into the relation between morality and rationality. Briefly, I'll try to show that.

Consider the *Rival Heirs*, a case closely based on one from James Rachels[26]: You and your four-year-old cousin, a distant relation whom you've previously seen only twice, are the only heirs of the bachelor uncle, very old and very rich, to whom you're both related. Now, the old man has only a few months left. And, as his will states, if both of you are alive when he dies, then you'll inherit only one million dollars and the cousin, to whom the uncle's much more closely related, will inherit fully nine; but, if the order of deaths is first your cousin, and then your uncle, you'll inherit all of ten million dollars. Right now, you see that it's this cousin of yours who, even as she's the only other person anywhere about, is on the verge of drowning in a nearby shallow pond. As it happens, you can easily arrange for things to look like you were then elsewhere; so, if you let the child drown, you can get away with it completely. And, since you'd take a drug that would leave you with no memories of the incident at all, you'd never feel even the slightest guilt. So, in a short time, you'd then enjoy ten million dollars, not just one.

As is very clear, your letting the child drown is extremely immoral behavior. But, it might be asked, is it *irrational* behavior? Now, some philosophers will hold that it's also irrational. By contrast, others will

26. I refer to the case of Jones, in his, "Active and Passive Euthanasia," *The New England Journal of Medicine*, 1975. Reprinted in several places, especially useful is an anthology edited by J. Fischer and M. Ravizza, *Ethics: Problems and Principles*, Harcourt Brace Jovanovich, 1992. There, the example appears on page 114. Rachels uses the case to discuss very different questions.

hold that, on at least one sense of "rationality," your conduct *isn't* irrational: You care for this very distant cousin little more than for a perfect stranger; largely owing to the "wonder" drug, there won't be any significantly bad effects on your life; nine million ain't hay, and so on.

For the sake of the exposition, let's suppose that, as new arguments all conspire to show, the second group of philosophers is *completely* correct: Even in accordance with *the only* sense of "rationality", and of cognate terms, that highly immoral conduct is only very rational behavior and, further, your saving the child must be highly irrational. For good measure, let's suppose that, plenty reasonably enough, you've become quite certain of all that. With these strong suppositions firmly in mind, how many readers would let such a little rival drown?

Since I'm sure my readers are decent people, I'm also sure of this: Very few will be even so much as strongly disposed to behave in such a morally outrageous manner; fewer still would actually do it. So, for being a potent guide for our conduct, morality certainly doesn't need any help from whatever authority we may accord rationality. For my main purposes, it's quite enough to learn a lot about which conduct is really morally all right and, in contrast, which is morally horrible behavior. If the former also has rationality's backing, that's fine; but, if not, it's no big deal.

Properly placing to the side the very interesting question of how rationality relates to morality, I'll turn to the equally interesting question of how truth relates to morality. Now, various philosophers have been concerned to show that there are many significant moral truths and that, far from reducible to even the wisest people's most basic moral commitments, they're as fully objective as any truths. Truth to tell, I myself believe in such robust moral propositions. But, what I'll now be concerned to show is just that, given this inquiry's purposes, it's a distracting digression to investigate the issue.

Why do objectivists offer arguments for our metaethical position? Ranging from sheer intellectual impulses to religious convictions, the motivation behind the endeavors is very varied. But, it's just this worrisome one I'd best discuss here and now: What would happen if we believed there weren't any substantial moral truths? Mightn't all hell break loose? Rather than feeling constrained by our deepest moral commitments, mightn't even we decent folk be free to do just what we please, or what's to our advantage? For, if the Values don't point to some reality beyond themselves, then there's nothing to have us comport with them rather than even our most self-centered desires. And, then, there won't be much more point to learning about our Values than, say, our most refined preferences in food.

Though those thoughts have a certain appeal, they're deeply confused. Recall the Rival Heirs and, this time, suppose you've come to think there aren't any objective moral truths. Will that free you up to let your little rival drown? Not a chance; when clear that there's a great conflict between some conduct and our Values, we avoid it like the plague.

None of this is to deny the philosophical importance of investigating the relations among morality, truth and rationality; it's just to say that, whatever holds for those abstruse matters, investigating our Values may help us engage in more decent behavior. Just so, when speaking of certain moral propositions as being true, it's quite well that I'll address many who abjure such Realistic talk; in terms of their favorite treatment of moral discourse, they'll understand me, I'm sure, both easily and well.

7. An Introductory Summary: Morality, Methodology and Main Motivation

Ever since my first acquaintance with him, and his ideas, more than twenty years ago, I've thought Peter Singer correct when saying that it's far from all right for folks like me to let distant innocents suffer seriously. So, I've long been moved to supplement his arguments with others that, for the progress of much time and hard work, might be better. But, as we've lately observed, however good some such general reasoning may be, it won't ever do much, by itself, to convince many philosophers, let alone many other folks: If we can trust nearly all our intuitions on the cases, as it often appears, we'll go with them instead, especially as that will be very much less costly. So, as a first step in effecting behavioral change, I've had to embark on what may fairly be called, I suppose, an extremely ambitious endeavor, comprising not only a lot of substantive ethics, but also much informal moral psychology and, to boot, much scrutiny of philosophical methodology.

After years of working on this endeavor, there's the Liberationist volume now in your hands. As is my hope, after reading the book some will agree that, between the whole Liberationist approach and anything else on offer, there's no real contest. If that happens, then perhaps one or two people, with communicative talent far greater than mine, will engage in some aptly effective verbal behavior. Perhaps partly as a result of that, the nonverbal conduct of many may change so greatly for the better that, without much further delay, so many millions of folks won't needlessly suffer so terribly.

2

LIVING HIGH AND LETTING DIE: A PUZZLE ABOUT BEHAVIOR TOWARD PEOPLE IN GREAT NEED

Let's explore a puzzle about our behavior toward people in great need. Centrally, it concerns our untutored reactions to two cases, the two *puzzle cases*. For the cases to pose a puzzle, they must be similar in many ways even while they differ in many others. For the puzzle to pack a punch, the cases should be pretty simple and realistic. And, there should be a strong contrast between our intuitive responses to the cases. Now, one of our two puzzle cases will be the Envelope. For a case to pair with it, there should be an example that, though similar to the Shallow Pond in many respects, goes well beyond it in a few. For instance, in the Shallow Pond there's *very little cost* to you, the case's agent; so, in a newly instructive contrast case, there'll be very *considerable* cost to you.

1. A Puzzle about Behavior toward People in Great Need

With those thoughts in mind, this is the first of our cases:

> *The Vintage Sedan.* Not truly rich, your one luxury in life is a vintage Mercedes sedan that, with much time, attention and

money, you've restored to mint condition. In particular, you're pleased by the auto's fine leather seating. One day, you stop at the intersection of two small country roads, both lightly travelled. Hearing a voice screaming for help, you get out and see a man who's wounded and covered with a lot of his blood. Assuring you that his wound's confined to one of his legs, the man also informs you that he was a medical student for two full years. And, despite his expulsion for cheating on his second year final exams, which explains his indigent status since, he's knowledgeably tied his shirt near the wound so as to stop the flow. So, there's no urgent danger of losing his life, you're informed, but there's great danger of losing his limb. This can be prevented, however, if you drive him to a rural hospital fifty miles away. "How did the wound occur?" you ask. An avid bird-watcher, he admits that he trespassed on a nearby field and, in carelessly leaving, cut himself on rusty barbed wire. Now, if you'd aid this trespasser, you must lay him across your fine back seat. But, then, your fine upholstery will be soaked through with blood, and restoring the car will cost over five thousand dollars. So, you drive away. Picked up the next day by another driver, he survives but loses the wounded leg.

Except for your behavior, the example's as realistic as it's simple.

Even including the specification of your behavior, our other case is pretty realistic and extremely simple; for convenience, I'll again display it:

The Envelope. In your mailbox, there's something from (the U.S. Committee for) UNICEF. After reading it through, you correctly believe that, unless you soon send in a check for $100, then, instead of each living many more years, over thirty more children will die soon. But, you throw the material in your trash basket, including the convenient return envelope provided, you send nothing, and, instead of living many years, over thirty more children soon die than would have had you sent in the requested $100.

Taken together, these contrast cases will promote the chapter's primary puzzle.

Toward having the puzzle be instructive, I'll make two stipulations for understanding the examples. The first is this: Beyond what's explicitly stated in each case's presentation, or what's clearly implied by it, there aren't ever any bad consequences of your conduct for anyone and, what's more, there's nothing else that's morally objectionable about it.[1] In effect, this means we're to understand a proposed scenario so that it is as boring as possible. Easily applied by all, in short the stipulation is: *Be boring!*

Also easily effected, the other stipulation concerns an agent's motivation, and its relation to her behavior: As much as can make sense, the agent's motivation in one contrast case, and its relation to her conduct there, is like that in the other. Not chasing perfection, here it's easy to assume a motivational parallel that's strong enough to prove instructive: Far from being moved by any malice toward the needy, in both our puzzle cases, your main motivation is simply your concern to maintain your nice asset position. So, even as it's just this that, in the Envelope, mainly moves you to donate nothing, it's also just this that, in the Sedan, similarly moves you to offer no aid.

Better than ever, we can ask these two key questions: What's our intuitive moral assessment of your conduct in the Vintage Sedan? And, what's our untutored moral judgment of your behavior in the Envelope? As we react, in the Sedan your behavior was very seriously wrong. And, we respond, in the Envelope your conduct wasn't even mildly wrong. This wide divergence presents a puzzle: Between the cases, is there a difference that adequately grounds these divergent intuitive assessments?

Since at least five obvious factors favor the proposition that the Envelope's conduct was *worse* than the Sedan's, at the outset the prospects look bleak: First, even just financially, in the Vintage Sedan the cost to the agent is *over fifty times* that in the Envelope; and, with *non*financial cost also considered, the difference is greater still. Second, in the Sedan, the reasonably expected consequences of your conduct, and also the actual consequences, were that *only one* person suffered a serious loss; but, in the Envelope, they were that *over thirty* people suffered seriously. Third, in the Sedan the *greatest loss suffered*

1. To understand our cases according to this usefully simplifying stipulation, we should have a good idea of what's to count as clearly implied by the statement of an example. Toward that end, perhaps even just a few words may prove very helpful. First, some fairly general words: To be clearly implied by such a statement, a proposition needn't be logically entailed by the statement. Nor need it be entailed even by a conjunction of the statement and a group of logical, mathematical, analytical or purely conceptual truths. Rather, it's enough that the proposition be entailed by a conjunction of the statement with others that are each commonly known to be true. Second, some more specific words: With both our puzzle cases, it's only in a *very boringly balanced* way that we're to think of the case's relevantly vulnerable people. Thus, even as we're not to think of anyone who might be saved as someone who'll go on to discover an effective cure for AIDS, we're also not to think of anyone as a future despot who'll go on to produce much serious suffering.

by anybody was the loss of a *leg*; but, in the Envelope the *least loss* suffered was *far greater* than that.[2] Fourth, because he was a mature and well-educated individual, the Sedan's serious loser was *largely responsible* for his own serious situation; but, being just little children, none of the Envelope's serious losers was *at all responsible* for her bad situation. And, fifth, the Sedan's man suffered his loss owing to his objectionable trespassing behavior; but, nothing like that's in the Envelope.

Now, I don't say these five are the only factors bearing on the morality of your conduct in the two cases. Still, with the differential flowing from them as tremendous as what we've just seen, it seems they're almost bound to prevail. So, for Preservationists seeking sense for both a lenient judgment of the Envelope's conduct and a harsh one of the Sedan's, there's a mighty long row to hoe.[3]

2. An Overview of the Chapter: Distinguishing the Primary from the Secondary Basic Moral Values

In the next section, we'll start the hard work of investigating the "apparently promising" differences between the puzzle cases. Here, I'll provide an overview of how it will proceed and where it may lead.

There are enormously many differences, of course, between the two examples: Only one of them involves a Mercedes automobile. On the other side, only the Envelope involves the postal system. But, as is evident, very nearly all of these enormously many differences haven't any chance of helping to ground a stricter judgment for the Sedan's behavior than the Envelope's. So, the job at hand may well be manage-

---

2. Among other reasons, this accommodates the friends of John Taurek's wildly incorrect paper, but highly stimulating essay, "Should the Numbers Count?," *Philosophy and Public Affairs,* 1977. But, as even some of the earliest replies to it show, no accommodation is really necessary; flawed only by some minor errors, a reasonably successful reply is Derek Parfit's "Innumerate Ethics," *Philosophy and Public Affairs,* 1978. So, my making this accommodation is an act of philosophical supererogation.

3. For the moment, suppose that, as the five factors indicate, your conduct in the Envelope was at least as bad as in the Sedan. From a purely logical point of view, there's naught to choose between the two salient ways of adjusting our moral thinking: (1) *The Negativist Response.* While continuing to hold that your conduct in the Envelope *wasn't* wrong, we may hold that, despite initial appearances, your conduct in the Sedan *also wasn't* wrong. (2) *The Liberationist Response.* While continuing to hold that your conduct in the Sedan *was wrong,* we may hold that, despite initial appearances, your conduct in the Envelope *also was wrong.* But, since we've more than just logic to go on, we can see the Liberationist Response is far superior. So, unless there's a sound way to hoe that mighty long row, we should conclude, with Liberationism, that the Envelope's conduct was very seriously wrong.

able. First, we'll try to look at genuine differences one by one. But, sometimes we'll confront thoughts that, though they might first appear to locate differential factors, really don't find any. With some of these thoughts, the fault's that the idea doesn't really fasten on any factor at all. With others, the fault's that the factor's really present in both puzzle cases, not just the one where it's obvious.

Going beyond all such confusions, we'll note some factors that do differentiate between our puzzle cases. Each time that happens, we'll ask: Does *this* difference do much to favor a harsh judgment only for the Sedan's conduct, and not for the Envelope's? In trying to answer, each time we'll consult our two main guides. On the one hand, we'll note our *moral intuitions on particular cases.* On the other, we'll note the deliverance of what I'll call our *general moral common sense,* since this second sensibility is directed at matters at least somewhat more general than the first's proper objects. Pitched at a level somewhere between the extremely general considerations dominating the tenets of traditional moral theories, on one hand, and the quite fine-grained ones often dominating the particular cases philosophers present, on the other, it's at this moderately general level of discursive thought, I commonsensibly surmise, that we'll most often respond in ways reflecting our Values and, less directly, morality itself. Not yet having much confirmation, that's now just a sensible working hypothesis. At all events, after seeing what both these guides say about each of nine notable differences, we'll ask: Does any combination of the differences ground a harsh judgment just for the Sedan?

Increasingly, we'll see that, for the most part, the deliverance from our two guides will agree. Occasionally, however, we'll see disagreement. What will explain that discrepancy? Though we won't arrive at a fully complete answer, we'll see a partial explanation full enough to be instructive: Even while the imperilled folks peopling certain cases have absolutely vital needs to be 'met, since their dire needs *aren't conspicuous* to you, the examples' agent, our intuitive response has your conduct as quite all right. Rather than anything with much moral weight, it's this that largely promotes the lenient response to the Envelope's behavior. Correspondingly, our harsh response to the Sedan's conduct is largely promoted by a serious need that's so salient.[4]

To avoid many confusions, a few remarks should suffice: Generally, what's most conspicuous to you is what most fully attracts, and what most fully holds, your attention. Often, what's very conspicuous

---

4. As I'll use the term "salience" in this book, it will mean the same as the more colloquial but more laborious term, "conspicuousness". So, on my use of it, "salience" *won't* mean the same as "*deserved* conspicuousness."

to you is distinct from what you perceive clearly and fully. Thus, while we may clearly and fully perceive them, the needs of a shabby person lying in one of New York City's gloomiest streets *aren't* very conspicuous to us. But, when someone's nicely groomed and dressed, and he's in a setting where no such troubles are expected, then, generally, his serious need is conspicuous.

As matters progress, these points about salience will become increasingly clear: When it's present in spades, as with the Vintage Sedan, then, generally, we'll judge harshly our agent's unhelpful behavior; when it's wholly absent, as with the Envelope, then, generally, we'll judge the agent's conduct leniently.

When the intuitive moral responses to cases are so largely determined by such sheer salience to the examples' agent(s), do they accurately reflect our Values? Straightforwardly, Preservationism's answer is that they do. By contrast, the best Liberationist answer isn't straightforward. Briefly, I'll explain.

At times, some people's great needs may be highly salient to you and, partly for that reason, it's then *obvious* to you that (without doing anything the least bit morally suspect) you can save the folks from suffering serious loss. Then, to you, it may be *obvious* that your letting them suffer *conflicts very sharply* with your Basic Moral Values (and, so, with the very heart of morality). To highlight this, let's say that, for you then, there's an Obvious Sharp Conflict. Now, since you're actually a quite decent person, when there's such an Obvious Sharp Conflict, generally it will be *hard* for you, psychologically, *not* to help meet people's great needs, even if you must incur a cost that's quite considerable. So, then, usually you won't behave in the way stipulated in the Vintage Sedan; rather, you'll behave helpfully.

In sharp contrast with that, there's this: When you let there be more folks who suffer serious loss by failing to contribute to the likes of UNICEF, then, even to you yourself, it's *far* from obvious that your conduct conflicts sharply with your Values, and with much of morality; indeed, as it usually appears, there *isn't* any such conflict. To highlight this contrasting situation, let's say that, for you *then*, there's No Apparent Conflict. Now, even though you're a decent person, when there's No Apparent Conflict, generally it will be *all too easy* for you, psychologically, not to help meet people's great needs. So, then, as with most decent folks, you'll behave in the unhelpful way stipulated for the Envelope.

With the difference between there being an Obvious Sharp Conflict and there being No Apparent Conflict, we've noted a contrast between the Envelope and the Sedan that *isn't* always morally irrelevant. Indeed, perhaps particularly when thinking whether to praise or to damn some conduct, *sometimes* it's appropriate to give this difference *great* weight. But, until the last chapter, in most of this book's pages, even the mere mention of the difference would be misplaced. For, here the aim is to become clearer about what really are the Basic Moral Values and, perhaps less directly, what's really morally most significant. And, since that's our aim, it's useful to *abstract away from* questions of what psychological difficulty there may be for us, in one case or another, to behave in a morally acceptable manner. Thus, until the book's last chapter, I'll set contexts where, as is there perfectly proper, no weight at all will be given to such considerations.

For a good perspective on this methodological proposal, it's useful to compare the Liberationist's thoughts about the Envelope's behavior to a reasonably probing abolitionist's thoughts, addressed to an ordinary "good Southerner" some years before the Civil War. No Jefferson he, our Southerner thinks that, especially as it's practiced by so many nice enough folks all around him, slaveholding isn't so much as wrong. Now, without seeking to dole out blame, our abolitionist may compare a typical white slaveholder's conduct with respect to his black slaves and, say, the conduct of a white person who, without any good reason for assaulting anyone, punches another white hard on the jaw, rendering his hapless victim unconscious for a few minutes. (Perhaps, because he abstained from alcoholic beverages, and said as much, the victim refused to drink, say, to the puncher's favorite Virginian county.) As the abolitionist might painstakingly point out, first focusing on one contrast between the two behaviors, then another, and another, and another, in the morally most important respects, that bad assaulting behavior *wasn't as bad* as the much more common slaveholding behavior.

Paralleling the difference in psychological difficulty noted for the Envelope and the Sedan, there's a difference in the slaveholding conduct and the assaulting behavior. For the ordinary Old Southerners, there's No Apparent Conflict between common slaveholding conduct and the Basic Moral Values, whereas, even for them, there's an Obvious Sharp Conflict between the gratuitous punching conduct and the Values; and so on, and so forth. For both parties to the discussion, *that's* common knowledge right from the outset. Indeed, attempting to focus the discussion on any *such* difference is, really, just a move to opt out of any serious discussion of the moral status of the slaveholding. Now, what that abolitionist was doing with such controlling conduct as was then widespread, this Liberationist author is doing, or is going to try to do, with such unhelpful conduct as the Envelope's currently common behavior. So, as decently sensible readers will see, it's inappropriate to focus on the thought that there's an Obvious Sharp Conflict only with the Sedan, and not with the Envelope; for, that will be just a move to opt out of seriously discussing the moral status of such vitally unhelpful conduct that, with No Apparent Conflict, is now so commonly exemplified. Not perfect, the parallel between the abolitionist and the Liberationist is plenty strong enough for seeing the sense in my modest proposal.

By now, I've made all the section's main points. So, it's with hesitation that, in what remains, I try to say something of interest to readers who enjoy, as I do, making philosophical distinctions, and enjoy exploring what utility may derive therefrom. Hesitantly, I'll offer a distinction between our *Primary* and our *Secondary* Basic Moral Values, a contrast that may have only heuristic value.

I'll begin with some remarks about the Primary Values: Among them is, plainly, a value to the effect that (like any well-behaved person) you not contribute to the serious suffering of an innocent other, neither its initiation nor its continuation. In the Envelope, your conduct *didn't* conflict, apparently, with this obviously important Value; so vast is the sea of suffering in the world and so resolutely efficient are UNICEF's health-promoting programs that, even if you'd made as large a donation as you could possibly afford, there *still wouldn't* have been *anyone,* apparently, whose serious suffering *you'd* have averted, or even lessened much. Concerning an equally "ground level" moral matter, is there some *other* Primary Value the Envelope's conduct *did* contravene? Well, there's none that's obvious.

But, as Liberationists may suggest, perhaps the Envelope's conduct conflicts with an *unobvious* Value, near enough, a Primary Value to the effect that, about as much as you possibly can manage, you *lessen the number of (the world's) innocent others who suffer seriously.* Though it encompasses, apparently, your relations with many millions of needy people, this unobvious Value might be *just as central* to your Values as the obvious one so prominent in the previous paragraph.

As I'll trust, that's a useful start toward indicating the domain of the Primary Values. Perhaps a helpful indication of this domain can be given, briefly and roughly, along these more general lines: Knowing everything you ought about what's really the case morally, and knowing all that's relevant to your situation, it's in the domain of the Primary Values that you look when, being as morally well motivated as anyone could wish, you deliberate about what you morally ought to do. So, motivation needn't be a stranger to the Primary Values' domain: When someone has his conduct conflict with what morality *obvi-*

ously requires and, so, with what even a *modestly* cognizant moral agent *knows* it requires, then, (at least) for being motivated so poorly, the person's behavior does badly by his good Primary Values.

Well, then, what's in the domain of the Secondary Values? Here's a step toward an answer: As has long been recognized, part of morality concerns our *epistemic* responsibilities. Here, morality concerns what we *ought* to know about the *nonmoral facts* of our situation. A simple example: In an area frequented by little kids, when you park your car quickly, without taking care to know the space is free of kids, then, even if you cause no harm, there's *something morally wrong* with your behavior. Now, another step: Far less well recognized, another part of morality concerns what we ought to know about our *Values* and, perhaps less directly, about what's really *morally* the case. Again, suppose it's true that central to the Primary Values is a Value to the effect that, roughly, you have the number of innocents seriously suffering be as small as you can manage. Then, even though it may be hard to do, it may be that you ought to know that. And, should you fail to know it, you've failed your Secondary Values.

Further, our Secondary Values concern how our conduct *ought to be moved by* our knowing what's really the case morally. Generally, in an area of conduct, one must first do well by the epistemic aspect of these Values, just introduced, before one's in a position to do well by their motivational aspect, now introduced: In the area of slaveholding conduct, during their mature years Washington and Jefferson did well, apparently, by the epistemic aspect of the Secondary Values. This put them in at least some sort of position to do well, in this area, by the motivational aspect of these Values (and, so, to do well by the Primary Values). But, they did badly by this other aspect; and, so, they contravened the Primary Values.

In the area of the Envelope's conduct, the Liberationist suggests, we do badly even by the epistemic aspect of the Secondary Values. So, we're far from doing even modestly well by their motivational aspect (and, so, by the Primary Values). By abstracting away from questions of how well we may do by our Secondary Values, we can learn about our Primary Values. So, until the last chapter, I'll set contexts where weight's rightly given only to how well an agent does by the Primary Values. At that late stage, it will turn out, I'll do well to give the Secondary Values pride of place.

Both the Primary and the Secondary Values are concerned with motivational matters. What the Secondary Values alone concern is, I'll say, the *unobvious* things someone ought to know about her Values and *those* motivational matters most closely connected with *those* things. Now, this notion of the Secondary Values may harbor, irremediably, much arbitrariness: (1) Through causing doubts as to what's really the case in certain moral matters, a person's social setting may make it hard for her to know much about the matters and, so, she may know far less than what, at bottom, she ought to know. (2) Insofar as she knows what's what morally about the matter, the setting may make it hard for her to be moved much by what she does know and, so, she may be moved far less than what, at bottom, she ought to be moved. For both reasons, (1) and (2), someone may fail to behave decently. Of a particular failure, we may ask: Did it derive (mainly) from a failure of awareness; or did it derive (mainly) from a failure of will? Often, it may be arbitrary to *favor either* factor, (1) *or* (2), and *also* arbitrary to say they're *equally* responsible. So, with the offered contrast, I don't pretend to mark a deep difference.

Recall this leading question: When they reflect little more than the sheer conspicuousness, to this or that agent, of folks' great needs, how well do our case-specific responses reflect our Basic Moral Values? In terms of my heuristic distinction, the Liberationist answers: When that's what they do, then, properly placing aside Secondary matters, our intuitions on the cases promote a badly distorted conception of our *Primary* Values. In line with that useful answer, the chapter's inquiry will lead to this Liberationist solution of its central puzzle: According to the Primary Values, the Envelope's behavior is at least as badly wrong as the Sedan's. But, first, the Preservationist gets a good run for the money.

3. Physical Proximity, Social Proximity, Informative Directness and Experiential Impact

What might ground judging negatively only the Sedan's behavior, and not the Envelope's? Four of the most easily noted differences cut no moral mustard.

Easily noted is the difference in *physical distance*. In the Vintage Sedan, the wounded student was only a few feet away; in the Envelope, even the nearest child was many miles from you. But, unlike many physical forces, the strength of a moral force doesn't diminish with distance. Surely, our moral common sense tells us that much. What do our intuitions on cases urge?

As with other differential factors, with physical distance *two* sorts of example are most relevant: Being greatly like the Envelope in many respects, in one sort there'll be a *small* distance between those in need and whoever might aid them. Being greatly like the Sedan, in the other there'll be a far greater distance. To be terribly thorough, for each factor I'd have an apt example of *both* its most relevant sorts. Mercifully, with most factors, I won't have both, but just one. But, to show what could be done with each, with physical distance I'll go both ways. First, I'll present this "Envelopey" case:

> *The Bungalow Compound.* Not being truly rich, you own only a one-twelfth share in a small bungalow that's part of a beach resort compound in an exotic but poor country, say, Haiti. Long since there's been much strife in the land, right now it's your month to enjoy the bungalow, and you're there on your annual vacation. In your mailbox, there's an envelope from UNICEF asking for money to help save children's lives in the town nearest you, whichever one that is. In your very typical case, quite a few such needy kids are all within a few blocks and, just over the compound wall, some are only a few feet away. As the appeal makes clear, your $100 will mean the difference between long life and early death for nearby children. But, of course, each month such appeals are sent to many bungalows in many Haitian resort compounds. You contribute nothing and, so, more nearby children die soon than if you'd sent $100.

As most respond to this case, your behavior isn't so much as wrong at all.[5] Next, a "Sedanish" example:

> *The CB Radios.* Instead of coming upon the erstwhile student at a crossroads, you hear from him on the CB radio that's in your fine sedan. Along with the rest of his story, the trespasser informs you, by talking into his own much cheaper CB radio, that he's stranded there with an old jalopy, which can't even be started and which, to

5. Throughout this work, my statements about how "most respond" are to be understood like this: Informally and intermittently, I've asked many students, colleagues and friends for their intuitive moral assessments of the agent's behavior in a case I've had them just encounter. Even as this has been unsystematic, so, at any given point, I'll use reports about how "most respond" to a certain case mainly as a guide for proceeding in what then appears a fruitful direction. Without ever placing great weight on any one of the reports, it may be surprisingly impressive to feel the weight of them all taken together.

Trying to be more systematic, I asked a research psychologist at my home university to read an early draft of the book, with an eye to designing some telling experiments. Good enough to start with that, he asked graduate students to take on the project, and its onerous chores, as a doctoral dissertation; but, he found no takers. Having limited energy, I've left the matter there.

boot, is out of gas. Citing landmarks to each other, he truthfully says you're just ten miles from where he's stranded. He asks you to pick him up and take him to a hospital, where his leg can be saved. Thinking about an upholstery bill for over $5000, you drive in another direction. As a foreseen result of that, he loses his leg, though not his life.

As most react to this other case, your behavior was seriously wrong.

In the Bungalow Compound, you were only a short distance from the needy children; in the CB Radios, you were ten miles from the needy trespasser. Thus, our responses to relevant cases jibe with the deliverance from our more general moral common sense. So much for physical proximity.

Often, physical distance correlates with what we might call *social distance*. Following the instruction to be boring, we've thus supposed that the Sedan's trespasser was your compatriot and, so, he was socially somewhat close. As we've also supposed, the Envelope's children are all foreigners, all socially more distant. Can that difference matter much? Since all those children become dead little kids, our common sense says, "Certainly not." What do we get from examples?

As usual from now on, I'll hit the issue from just one side. Here, we'll confront a Sedanish example:

> *The Long Drive.* Rather than going for a short drive, you're spend-ing the whole summer driving from your home, in the United States, to the far tip of South America and back. So, it's somewhere in Bolivia, say, that you stop where two country roads cross. There you confront an erstwhile Bolivian medical student who tells you of his situation, in Spanish, a language you know well. As you soon learn, he wants you to drive him to a hospital, where his leg can be saved. Thinking also of your upholstery, you drive elsewhere and, as a result, he loses a leg.

To the Long Drive, almost all respond that your behavior was abomi-nable.

Perhaps it's only within certain limits that social proximity's mor-ally irrelevant. But, insofar as they're plausible, such limits will leave so very much leeway as to be entirely irrelevant to our puzzle: Where those in need are socially *very* close to you, like your closest family members, there may be a very strong moral reason for you to meet *their* dire needs. But, in the Sedan, it wasn't your father, or your sister, or your son whose leg was at stake. Indeed, as we've been boringly supposing, the trespasser was a complete stranger to you. So much for social proximity.

A third difference concerns how the agent learns of the great need he can help meet. In the Sedan, much is learned by your direct perception of the wounded man. In the Envelope, the information is acquired far more indirectly, by your reading something that was produced by someone who herself collated reports, and so on. In this differential factor of *informative directness,* will there be much to favor a Preservationist solution? Well, when their information is only indirectly acquired, sometimes people aren't very sure of things, or they aren't very reasonable in being sure. But, nothing remotely like that's going on in the Envelope. So, our common sense now tells us this: Since you're quite certain of what will happen if you don't contribute to UNICEF, and since you're quite reasonable in being so certain, the fact that your information's indirectly acquired is morally insignificant. What's more, our responses to relevant cases often agree, as with our severe reaction to the CB Radios.

A fourth difference, *experiential impact,* often goes along with informative directness: In the Vintage Sedan, both the needy man himself and the condition of his great need entered into your own experience. But, that's not so in the Envelope. About this difference, common sense is clear: While the need may seem more compelling in the Sedan than with folks behind a wall, there's no moral weight here. And, our reactions to cases can agree with that good common sense: In the CB Radios, the man's awful plight doesn't enter your experience. Even the sounds you hear aren't the real deal: electronics had as much to do with your audition as he. And, suppose the trespasser had signalled you in morse code, with nonvocal "dots" and "dashes." It would still be seriously wrong to favor your leather over his leg.

Having considered four differences, we haven't moved one inch along the row to be hoed for a comfortably Preservationist solution. Might we fare better by looking in quite another direction?

4. The Thought of the Disastrous Further Future

When thinking about cases like the Envelope, many often have this *thought of the disastrous further future:* "If I help prevent some of these young children from dying soon, then, years from now, they'll produce yet more children, worsening the population explosion that, more than anywhere else, goes on precisely where there are so many imperilled children. If I donate to UNICEF, I'll just help create a situation, in the further future, when there'll be disastrously more little kids painfully dying. So, it's actually *better* to throw away the envelope. At the very least, it's not wrong."

As we'll soon see, this thought of the disastrous further future is a fallacious rationalization, at odds with the great bulk of available evidence.[6] More to the present point, even if the thought were true, it wouldn't help with our puzzle: Just as we wisely followed the instruction to be boring, so there's no clear implication, from the statement of our puzzle cases, to any disastrously large future population. And, when responding to cases, we directly comply with that instruction.

Recall the Long Drive. Now, you're right there at the crossroads with the Bolivian and, all of a sudden, you're thinking mainly of how your conduct can bear on the further future: "If I take this guy to the hospital, then, as he'll long continue to have both his legs, he'll long be a reasonably attractive guy and, even worse, a very mobile fellow. Whether in wedlock or not, he then may well father far too many little Bolivians. But, if he'll have only one leg, he probably won't contribute nearly as much, if anything at all, to a disastrous dying of Bolivians many years hence. Playing the odds well and thinking also of the *further* future, it's *better* to let him lose a leg. At the least, if I do that, I won't behave badly." Finally, we'll suppose that, moved mainly by those thoughts, you drive away and let him suffer the loss. Now, was *that* in the example to which we recently responded? Certainly not. And, if it *were* in our original specification, our response would still be severely negative.[7]

Since it doesn't bear on our puzzle, we needn't examine the data bearing on population in the further future. But, since the matter's of broad importance, it's important to know this: The available evidence strongly supports the thought that *decreasing* childhood mortality *stabilizes* population! To be sure, the increasingly widespread availability of modern contraceptives is partly responsible for the recent big decreases in how fast the world's population is growing, as many studies show. This is one reason, even if perhaps not the most important

6. For an excellent analysis of population issues that's accessible even to laymen like me, I'm grateful for Amartya Sen's lucid essay, "Population: Delusion and Reality," *The New York Review of Books,* September 22, 1994. As Sen there does much to make clear, our thought of the disastrous further future is little better than an hysterical fantasy.

7. More directly, a variant case chimes in with the same results: Suppose that, because he has a very large wound, our Bolivian's very life is greatly in danger. For him to live, you must take him to a hospital. Thinking about population problems and the further future, you drive away and let him die. As we intuitively react, your conduct's morally outrageous.

reason, to support the International Planned Parenthood Federation, or IPPF.[8] For us, that effective group's most relevant address is:

International Planned Parenthood Federation,
Western Hemisphere Region, Inc.
902 Broadway - 10th Floor
New York, NY 10010

Still, for population to stabilize, much more is needed than any fine group like that will provide.

What's also needed can be seen from many perspectives. For continuity, I'll again focus on the Indian state of Kerala: Since the Total Fertility Rate's already down to 1.9, or even lower, population won't just stabilize there; it will decline! Beyond widespread availability of contraceptive means, there are other reasons that fully 80% of Keralan couples actually use family planning measures: Because they know the *childhood mortality rate there is very low,* Keralans can be confident that, without having many kids, they'll have some surviving children. And, since they know the community will make sure their basic needs are met, Keralans know that, even without children to rely on, their *life expectancy is high.* And, since the *female literacy rate is very high,* marking much respect for women's interests, it's no surprise that in Kerala there's a population success story.[9] Not only does the thought of the

8. What's just been mentioned is only one of the good reasons to support IPPF. Here are others: First, with maternal mortality still standing at about 500,000 women a year, IPPF is cutting down the number and, so, lessening the number of children, still in the millions, who each year become motherless. Second, in IPPF clinics, many Third Worlders receive the basic health care they need. Right now I'll stop with this third point: Perhaps the greatest of all IPPF affiliates, Colombia's PROFAMILIA supports some clinics for men only. Owing to that, the terribly macho attitudes of many Colombian men have become much less macho, a big benefit to many Colombian women. At all events, in Colombia there's occurring a population success story.

9. Presented in literally graphic form, this paragraph's facts, and other fascinating data, cover page 49 of *The State of the World's Children 1995,* just off the press from the OUP at the time of this writing. For other fascinating facts, see Sen's essay, "Population: Delusion and Reality." As careful readers will note, presenting data from India's Ministry of Home Affairs, on page 70 of his paper, Sen's Table 2 shows Kerala to have even a slightly lower TFR, 1.8 rather than 1.9. But, of course, anything under 2.0 is happily remarkable.

Much more than living in a region with a high per capita income, and very much more than living in one where a liberal religion prevails, it's the factors I've just stressed that are important in determining the numbers of children that the region's women will bear. Just so, and very well worth noting, of all the world's pretty populous places, it's Italy, where even the Pope himself resides, that has the lowest Total Fertility Rate. With a TFR of just 1.3, Italy's set for a *big* decline in population!

disastrous further future bypass our puzzle, but it's also undermined by the evidence. So much for that unhappy thought.

5. Unique Potential Saviors and Multiple Potential Saviors

To many people, the most promising difference between our contrast cases is this: In the Vintage Sedan, you're the only one who can get the trespasser's leg saved; using jargon to highlight that, you're his *unique potential savior*. But, in the Envelope, there are more than enough well-off people to get the distant children saved; in kindred jargon, they're all the children's *multiple potential saviors:* "Because you're his unique potential savior, mightn't you have a great responsibility toward the trespasser? That may be why, in the Sedan, your behavior was wrong. Because you're only one of their multiple potential saviors, you might not have much responsibility toward the Envelope's children. This may be why, in that case, your behavior wasn't wrong."

But, to our moral common sense, that's nonsense: You knew full well that, even though they *could* do so, almost all the other well-off folks *wouldn't* aid the needy children. You knew that, for all they'd do, there'd still be kids in dire need. So, while many others behaved very badly, you did, too.

Often, that much of our moral common sense is reflected in our intuitions on particular cases. Building on the preceding section, one case in point is:

> *The Wealthy Drivers.* In addition to you, there are three other drivers in the area with CB radios, all four of you hearing the pleas from the wounded trespasser. Even this much quickly develops on the air: Each of the others is less than five miles from the erstwhile student, while you're fully ten miles from him. And, each of the others is far wealthier than you. But, as each of the three complain, she doesn't want to get involved. So, none of you help the wounded man. Since those who can aid him don't, he loses his injured leg.

With multiple potential saviors, none is unique. But, as most react, even your conduct was badly wrong.

In closing the section, I'll note this: By pretty high epistemic standards, in the Wealthy Drivers you knew your help was needed. But, by *much higher* epistemic standards, in the Envelope you knew that (since the likes of UNICEF get far less than can be put to vital use), your money was needed.

6. The Thought of the Governments

When thinking of the likes of the Envelope, many entertain the *thought of the governments:* "Toward aiding the distant needy children, a person like me, who's hardly a billionaire, can do hardly anything. But, through taxation of both people like me and also billionaires, our government can do a great deal. Indeed, so wealthy is our country that the government can do just about everything that's most needed. What's more, if ours joined with the governments of other wealthy nations, like France and Germany and Japan, then, for any one of the very many well-off people in all the wealthy nations, the financial burden would be very easily affordable. And, since making one's tax payments is a routine affair, the whole business would be nearly automatic. Just so, these governments really ought to stop so many children from dying young. And, since they really ought to do the job, it's all right for me not to volunteer." What are we to make of this common line of thought?

Well, whatever it precisely means, I suppose those governments ought to contribute, annually, the tens of billions of dollars that, annually, would ensure that only a tiny fraction of the world's poorest children suffer seriously. And, whatever it means, it's even true that their conduct is seriously wrong. But, what's the relevance of that to assessing your own behavior, and mine? There isn't any. For we know full well that, for all the governments will do, each year millions of Third World kids will die from easily preventable causes. And, knowing that, we can make use of the previous section.

In the morally important respects, in the Envelope your situation is the same as in the Wealthy Drivers: Since it was harder for you to help, and since the real cost to you would have been greater, it's credible that, in the Wealthy Drivers, your conduct wasn't *as bad* as the others' behavior. Even so, your conduct also was very bad. Similarly, in the Envelope it was harder for you to do much for distant needy children than it was for the wealthy governments, and perhaps the cost to you was greater. So, it's also credible that, in the Envelope, your behavior wasn't *as bad* as the wealthy governments' conduct. Yet further, it's also credible that the behavior of these wealthy governments wasn't *as bad* as the conduct of the German government, under Hitler, in the 1940s. So much for the thought of the governments.

7. The Multitude and the Single Individual

When thinking of the Envelope, we may feel overwhelmed by the enormous multitude of seriously needy people: "In the face of that vast multitude, I'm almost impotent." With this feeling of futility, is there something to distinguish between the Envelope and the Sedan? At first, it may seem so: "In the Sedan, there was just a *single individual* in need; in the Envelope, there were *so many altogether in a vast multitude.* Though I had to help the single individual, mayn't I simply leave be such a vast multitude?"

But, just as were each of the world's most badly endangered children, the trespasser was also one of the very many greatly needy people in the world. And, while there are certain perspectives from which he'll seem an especially singular figure, that's also true of every last one of the needy children. So, in point of even mathematical fact, neither thoughts of the multitude nor thoughts of particular individuals can mark any distinction at all between our puzzle cases. So much for those confused thoughts.

8. The Continuing Mess and the Cleaned Scene

Related to thoughts of the multitude, there's the *thought of the continuing mess:* "Even if I do send the $100 to UNICEF, there'll still be many children very prematurely dying. Indeed, *no matter what I do,* there'll still be, for very many years, very many children dying from easily preventable causes." In this thought, is there something to distinguish between our puzzle cases? At first, it may seem so: "Unlike the Envelope's distant children, the Sedan's trespasser presented me with a particular distinct problem. If only I got him to the hospital, the problem would have been completely resolved. Starting with just such a problem, I'd finish with nothing less than a completely *cleaned scene.* How very different that is from the *continuing mess* involving all the distant children!"

But, this appearance also is illusory: Just as much as any distant child's diarrheal dehydration, the trespasser's infected leg was part of the "continuing mess in the world." As has long been true, and as will long be remain true, the world has many people with infected legs, many of whom will lose them. If distant children were part of a "continuing mess," *so was the trespasser.* No more than the Envelope does the Sedan offer the chance to have the world be a cleaned scene. So much for this confusion.

9. Emergencies and Chronic Horrors

Rather than any genuine differences between our puzzle cases, in the previous few sections we've seen only some confusions. It's high time to observe a real difference between the Envelope and the Vintage Sedan: In the Vintage Sedan, there's an *emergency*, while in the Envelope there's none. But, does that mean any moral ground for favoring the Envelope's conduct?

Our moral common sense speaks negatively. First, on the Vintage Sedan: Shared with many other emergencies, what are the main points to note about the bad bird-watching incident? Well, until recently, the erstwhile student was doing reasonably all right; at least, his main needs were regularly met. And, that was also true of the other people in his area. Then, all of a sudden, things got worse for him, and, for the first time in a long time, he had a big need on the verge of not being met. Next, the Envelope: The distant little children always were in at least pretty bad straits. And, in their part of the world, for a long time many people's great needs weren't met and, consequently, those many suffered seriously. But, then, even as there's no emergency in the Envelope, that situation's *far worse* than almost any emergency; to highlight this, we may say that, in the Envelope, there's a *chronic horror*.

Of course, their living in a chronic horror is no reason to think that, by contrast with the previously fortunate trespasser, it was all right to do nothing for long-suffering children. Indeed, such a thought's so preposterous that, indirectly, it points to a *sixth* factor favoring *stricter* judgment for the Envelope: During the very few years they've had before dying, those children were among the worst off people in the world, while the trespasser had quite a few years of a reasonably good life. (And, insofar as the exam-cheater's life was less than very happy, that was due mainly to his own bad behavior.) So, it's just for the Envelope's unhelpful conduct that *justice* wants an especially strict judgment. At all events, from our moral common sense, there's no good news for Preservationism.

Before remarking on our intuitive responses to particular emergency cases, I should say something about how, during the past 35 years, the world's chronic horrors have become less horrible, though there's still a long way to go. For the big picture, most of what's wanted comes when seeing the worldwide progress, from 1960 onward, in four basic categories[10]:

10. For 1960, 1970, 1980, and 1990, I use the figures graphically presented on page 55 of *The State of the World's Children 1995*. For the estimated average year in the range 1990–1995, the latest reliable estimate, I use the three figures found in *World*

	1960	1970	1980	1990	1990–95
Life expectancy in years	46	53	58	62	64.4
Under-five deaths per 1000 births	216	168	138	107	86
Average births per woman (TFR)	6.0	5.7	4.4	3.8	3.1
Percentage of 6–11-year-olds in school	48	58	69	77	NA

(As population's been increasing most in the Third World, the more recent the numbers, the more they're determined by events there. So, there's been *more* progress *there* than these figures indicate.)

Especially as this section features emergencies, for a more fine-grained picture I turn to the cyclone-prone country of Bangladesh, where about 15 million people, out of about 115 million, live in the vulnerable coastal region. The victim of 7 of the century's 10 worst cyclones, in the past 25 years 3 big ones struck Bangladesh. When 1970's big cyclone struck the unprepared country, the windstorm killed about *3 million,* about 2.5 million succumbing, in the storm's devastating aftermath, to waterborne disease. Far beyond just helping to prompt the writing of Singer's "Famine, Affluence and Morality," this disaster "sparked the founding of Oxfam America," about 25 years after the original Oxfam was founded in Oxford, England.[11] With help from such foreign non-governmental organizations (NGOs), and with hard work by Bangladeshi groups and individuals, by 1991 a lot was done to make the country's people less vulnerable to killing winds; when a big cyclone hit Bangladesh that year, only(!?) about *130 thousand* folks were killed, a dramatic improvement.[12] But, come to

---

Population Prospects: The 1994 Revision, Population Division of the United Nations Secretariat, United Nations, New York, 1995. As a reliable estimate for more recent school enrollment is *not* available to me now, there's the "NA".

11. The quoted phrase, and much of the information about Bangladesh and cyclones here related, is from Fauzia Ahmed, "Cyclone Shelters Saving Lives," *Oxfam America News,* Summer 1994, page 5.

12. For those skeptical of what's to be found in such obscure places as *Oxfam America News,* I'll cite a piece in "the paper of record." From Sanjoy Hazarika, "New

think of it, a great many poor folks still had to bury their children, or their parents, or their spouses, or their siblings, or their best friends. So, with continued support from far and near, Bangladeshis continued to work hard. So, by 1994 those Third Worlders had built 900 cleverly designed cyclone shelters, each able to protect thousands of people. Expressing a misleadingly *high* estimate, I'll end the paragraph with the first sentence of the piece in *Oxfam America News* so recently cited, with only the italics being my creation: On May 2, a 180 mph cyclone pummeled southeastern coastal Bangladesh, claiming just *under 200* lives.[13] Though it looks like there's a misprint, that's as well ordered as it's well warranted.

For ever so many years, really, but, especially in more recent years, most in the world's poorest countries, including Bangladesh, have lives that are actively effective, socially committed, and part of a palpable upward trend; their lives are clearly well worth living. When thinking whether to help these materially poor folks, so that more and more of them will bury fewer and fewer of their children, it's useful to have that in mind.

Just as UNICEF works effectively both to make chronic horrors less horrible and to address emergency situations, OXFAM, as Oxfam America is popularly known, is also effective across the board. Now, the 1994 cyclone left about 500,000 Bangladeshis homeless, many of

---

Storm Warning System Saved Many in Bangladesh," *The New York Times*, May 5, 1994, I offer this sentence, "A major cyclone in 1991 killed an estimated 131,000 persons, wiping out entire villages and islands and leaving human corpses littering the countryside." As Oxfam's main source in Bangladesh, the Bangladesh Rural Advancement Committee, is closer to the ground than the *Times'* main source, apparently just the Bangladesh Government, their *News'* estimate for the 1991 toll, 138,000, is probably closer to the actual number of people killed then.

13. This is well in line with what's in the Hazarika piece, *loc. cit.*, a Special to *The New York Times*. Here's its first sentence: "The comparatively low death toll in the huge storm that whipped across parts of southeastern Bangladesh on Monday night with winds of up to 180 miles an hour was attributed today to a combination of modern technology and simple steps that led to the evacuation of hundreds of thousands of villagers to high ground and storm shelters." Next, here's a scrap from later in the piece: ". . . according to Bangladesh Government officials, took the lives of 167. . . ." Finally, the piece's real kicker comes with its final sentence: "Most of the victims in the storm Monday were not Bangladeshis but Muslim refugees from Myanmar, formerly Burma, who had fled an army crackdown against followers of Islam in that country." So, without those unlikely and unlucky foreigners, the toll would have been *under 100*.

To my mind, far better than anything the *Times* offers on Bangladesh and its cyclones, there's a marvelous, and marvelously short, video on this amazing true story, called "Shelter," available from Oxfam America. Americans willing to make a contribution to OXFAM can get Shelter by calling this toll-free number: **1 - 800 - OXFAM-US**, easily dialed as **1 - 800 - 693 - 2687**.

whom still need help; so, in 1995 there's still something of an emergency even there. And, as every several months the group must address a brand new emergency, I think you should know how to help the good group aid many folks newly in great need. All you need do is make out a sizeable check to *Oxfam America* and mail it to this address:

Oxfam America
26 West Street
Boston, MA 02111

With this added to the U.S. Committee's address and IPPF's, you now know more than enough, I think, about how to be an effectively helpful person.

In closing the section mercifully, I'll help you escape from the Real World, by taking you back to the Philosophy Room: Regarding *emergencies,* what's to be found in our responses to the cases? For good instruction in our happy Room, I'll contrive a case where, first, there *is* an emergency, and, second, you *can* help folks in dire need, but, third, people's dire needs are *inconspicuous* to you:

> *The Emergency Envelope.* UNICEF informs you of the terrible effects of a recent hurricane on, say, Haiti: Now, there are many additional Haitian kids who, without outside help, will soon die. By Haitian standards, these are upper middle-class children. While they were doing quite well before the hurricane, now, they, too, are in mortal danger. So, if you don't soon send $100 to a special fund set up by UNICEF, within the next few weeks, not only will more poor Haitian kids die, but so will more of these others. Even so, you send nothing and, in consequence, that happens.

As most respond to this case, you didn't do anything so much as wrong. So much for emergency.

10. Urgency

Often, it's especially important to act when matters are *urgent.* Along with that idea, there comes this line of thought: "When someone will lose life or limb *very soon* unless you help him, it's morally *required* that you aid. But, if there's lots of time before anything much happens, aiding isn't morally required. Mightn't this be ground for judging the Envelope's conduct more leniently than the Sedan's?"

It's plenty obvious that, in the Vintage Sedan, there's plenty of urgency: If you don't soon take him to the hospital, the trespasser will soon lose a leg. And, it appears that, in the Envelope, there's no urgency: Even if you put $100 in the mailbox just a minute from now, it will take at least a couple of weeks for that to translate into life-saving aid for anyone. What's more, if you don't send anything right away, you can do it later, say, next month. Soon or not so soon, just as many will be vitally aided.

In these thoughts of a contrast, however, there's illusion and confusion. This isn't to deny that, in many cases, it's important both to act promptly and to have one's conduct determined by a clear sense of who's in the most imminent danger. Rather, it's to say that, even as the Sedan's a case with morally important urgency, so is the Envelope.

Toward seeing that, I'll present two cases that really do differ in morally important urgency. For both, we'll make these suppositions: In room A, there's a man tied down with rope and, next to him, a time bomb's set to go off in just an hour. Unless he's untied and released from the room, its explosion will kill him. The same for room B, but the time is 24 hours. You can save either man, but not both.

For the first case, we'll go on to make the most natural further assumptions: After you save the man in A, not only will there still be time for someone to save the man in B, but, during the extra 23 hours, B's man enjoys *extra chances* for rescue that A's could never have.

For the second case, we'll make more unusual assumptions: As you know with absolute certainty, beyond what you'll do soon, there *aren't any* extra chances even for the man in B. So, simply and surely, you're to choose who'll live and who'll die.

In the first case, clearly you must save the man in A. But, what of the second case? Well, in some sense, perhaps it's still true that A's man's in a more urgent situation than B's. But, still, there's little reason to favor aiding him.

What have we learned? Well, at least for the most part, what moral weight attaches to urgency is due to the lesser chances of avoiding serious loss that, normally but not inevitably, are found in situations where there's little time to save the day. But, between the Sedan and the Envelope, there's never any such difference in the chances. Since that's not easy to see, I'll try to make enlightening remarks.

There's a continual flow of aid from some of the world's well-off folks to many of the most seriously needy. At it's far end, every day there are thousands of children on the very brink of death. Today, their vital need is *very* urgent. In the case of over 30,000 of these kids, this will be proven by the fact that, even as their need won't be met today, by tomorrow they'll be dead. Of course, just as urgent are the needs of thousands of others who, only through receiving today some *very* timely ORT, won't be dead tomorrow or, happily, any time soon. To be sure, there are many more thousands of children whose vital needs today *aren't so very* urgent: For over 30,000 of these, in just two days, their needs *will be* that urgent. And, for over 30,000 *others*, in just three days they'll have such terribly urgent needs; and so on. Just so, for over thirty thousand still other needy youngsters, their last day alive with danger will be in 30 days, or 31, that is, just a month from now.

Consider these "monthers." In some sense, it may be true that, over the next month, their needs will become more and more urgent. But, since we can be *certain* that, if you don't donate to UNICEF soon, more of these "monthers" will die, what moral relevance can *any such* increase in urgency have for your behavior? Clearly, none at all. By contrast, what matters is that, very soon, you begin to lessen the number of children who die a month from now and that, then, you help lessen the number who die shortly after that, and so on. So, facts like its taking a month for your mailed check to have a vital impact aren't morally significant. To think otherwise is like thinking that, in our second case with the two rooms, saving the man in A is morally much better than saving B's man.

In morally relevant respects, each greatly needy child is like a man in a room, tied down with a rope, with a time bomb set to explode. Some children's bombs are set to go off around noon tomorrow; others' are set for five days hence; still others' are set for a month from now. But, since it's certain that, for all everyone else will do, even in a month's time, many of the children *still won't* have their ropes untied, in these different settings there's precious little moral weight. Because the ways of the world are slow to improve, for quite a while remarks like these will be quite true. And, *that's* more certain than that you yourself will be alive a day from now. So, our moral common sense delivers the message: As for morally weighty urgency, there's plenty in the Sedan *and* in the Envelope.

Hoping you won't forget that main thought, I'll present this less important idea: When not mixed with factors that help it promote the salience of vital needs, often urgency doesn't even influence our responses to particular cases. To see that, it's best to confront a case with *all sorts* of urgency, some as weighty as it's easily overlooked, and lots as slight as it's blatantly obvious:

The Super Express Fund. The most bizarre thing in your mail today is an appeal from the SEF: By calling a certain number and using any major credit card, you can donate $500 to the SEF right away, night or day. The effect of such a prompt donation will be that one more child will receive ORT this very day and, in consequence, won't soon die. Of course, the SEF's appeal makes clear the reason that it will cost so much to provide ORT to just one child: Upon hearing from you, your credit card donation is attended to personally, directly, and completely. So, moments after your call, a certain ORT packet is rushed to the nearest international airport, speeded to the next jet bound for Africa, and so on. Eventually, in a remote region, a paramedic rushes from a speeding vehicle. After examining several moribund children, he chooses one that, certainly, is today on the very brink of death. Then, he rapidly mixes the solution and administers it to just that most urgently needy little child. But, you don't ever make such a call and, in consequence, one more child soon dies than if you'd made the requested donation.

As everyone responds, you didn't do wrong. So, for now, we've learned enough about urgency.

11. Causally Focused Aid and Causally Amorphous Aid

From discussing thoughts bound to occur to many, I turn to some esoteric distinctions. Perhaps the most notable concerns *causally focused* aid and, by contrast, *causally amorphous* aid. First, a few words about causally focused aid: If you'd provided aid to the trespasser in the Vintage Sedan, your helpful behavior would've been causally focused on that particular needy person. In an enlarged but parallel case, you might helpfully take, in your large vintage Mercedes bus, fully thirty greatly needy trespassers to a hospital. In the *Vintage Bus*, the aid you'd provide would be causally focused on *each one* of those thirty people. Next, causally amorphous aid: In the Envelope, even if you'd behaved helpfully, there'd never be *anyone* for whom *you'd* have made the difference between suffering a serious loss and suffering none; there'd never be a child of whom it would be true that, had you sent in $100, she wouldn't have died prematurely. Rather, on one end of a causal chain, there are many donors contributing together and, on the other, there are all the people saved by the large effort they together support. The more support given, the more folks saved, and that's all she wrote.[14] Does this favor the Envelope's conduct?

As our moral common sense directs, there's no chance of that. Rather, since there's nothing morally objectionable about proceeding to aid greatly needy folks amorphously, no moral weight attaches to the precise character of the causal relations between the well-off and those whom, whether collectively or not, they might help save. Morally, the important thing is that the vulnerable don't suffer. And, with a well aimed case, our intuitive reactions confirm that decent deliverance:

> *The Special Relations Fund.* You receive material from a group that assures you they'll find a moribund little child that your money, if you contribute, will prevent from dying prematurely. Since very many moribund little kids are out there, this won't be terribly difficult, or costly, but neither will it be very cheap and easy to have your vital aid be causally focused: So, if you donate $100 to the SRF, while only one less child will die soon, the group will ensure that your donation makes the big difference for the one child. But, you send nothing and, in consequence, one more child soon dies than if you'd made the requested donation.

Here, it's clear that any aid will be causally focused. But, as all respond, your conduct wasn't the least bit wrong. So, on our reactions to cases, this esoteric factor doesn't have any great effect.

12. Satisfying Nice Semantic Conditions

Before noticing another esoteric distinction, I'd like to discuss a family of quite ordinary ideas that's closely related to, but that's not quite the same as, the one just considered. Just as the common concepts are well placed under the head *satisfying nice semantic conditions,* so the family's most salient notion prompts this suggestion: "When you can *save* folks from much suffering, it's wrong not to aid. But, perhaps, if you'll merely *help to prevent* folks from suffering seriously, you needn't help. Mightn't that ground a big difference between our puzzle cases?"

---

14. On one logico-metaphysical view, there can't be casually amorphous relations. Though it appears false, it just might be true. If so, then this distinction marks no real difference. But, of course, it might well be false. And, since I should see if Liberationism prevails even on a "worst case scenario," I'll suppose that, in the Envelope, any aid would be causally amorphous.

Hardly. First, by contrast with the Shallow Pond, had you been helpful in the Vintage Sedan, a doctor's services would still be needed to save the leg; so, in strict truth, the very most we could have said for you would be that, then, *you and a doctor* would have saved the leg. Second, and much more importantly, there's this: Whatever their precise character, these semantic niceties don't matter morally; at any rate, abandoning the wounded man was wrong.

About other members of *saving's* family, the same points hold true. For example, when you've the chance to be only a partial enabler of someone who might save a needy person, but you're needed, then, just as surely as the one who has the chance to star as the saver, you must play your supporting role. Certainly, our moral common sense tells us that.

Plenty well enough, we can also see the point by way of apt examples. As with many cases where a great need is conspicuous, this happens with:

> *The Indian Sewer.* While vacationing in India, you come upon a child who's on the verge of drowning in the waters of a sewer. When the child fell in, she knocked away the bar propping up the sewer's trapdoor grating, which is also now down in the sewer. So, the heavy door's now closed. For the child to be saved, three able adults are needed. One person, who's both strong and agile, must go down into the sewer and bring up the child. Being strong but not agile, you can't do that. Still, there's someone else there who can. For the agile man to play the central role in a rescue, two others must hold open the filthy, strangely-shaped grating, one holding it by one edge and the other by another. A third person is able and willing to hold one of these edges and, so, it's now all up to you. But, not wanting to soil your new suit, you walk away and, so, the child drowns.

As all strongly react, your behavior was monstrous. Now, recall the Shallow Pond, where you had a chance to *save* someone from suffering a serious loss. Was your behavior in the Indian Sewer any better? Very widespread is the comparative intuition on the cases: Your behavior in this new example is just as abominable as in that old one.

Of course, in the Envelope, you never had even the chance to fill any such fairly fulfilling supporting role as the one just noted; rather, you had, at most, only the chance to *contribute to enabling others* to save children. But, it's only a confusion to think that could give you even the slightest moral license.

Underlying the confusion, sometimes there may be the idea that, much as with writing poetry, for example, what we do for needy people constitutes personally fulfilling projects. To fulfill ourselves, each of us wants to write her own poems, or to grow her own garden, or whatever: If I'm just a pretty fair poet, not greatly talented, a poem written mainly by a great poet, with just marginal input from me, might well be much better than any I'd write by myself, or with only some help. But, quite rationally, my attitude is that it's not enough for there be excellent poems in whose writing I had only a marginal role. By contrast with poetry, however, toward *people in serious trouble,* it's crazy to have an attitude that's even *remotely like that,* and for our conduct toward them to be determined by any such attitude.

13. Epistemic Focus

Analogous to the distinction between aid that's causally focused and aid that's causally amorphous, there's a distinction between *epistemically* focused aid and *epistemically* amorphous aid: Even if you donated the $100 requested in the Envelope, and even if you thereby helped save some people, you *wouldn't know which* folks you helped save from an early death, or even aided at all. In the Vintage Sedan, by contrast, if you took the trespasser to the hospital and his leg was saved, you'd know whom you aided.[15] Can this favor the Envelope's behavior? Our common sense says that, morally, it doesn't matter whether you come to know whose dire needs you help meet. And, our reactions to cases can chime in nicely.

Though I resolved not to cover you with cases, here I'll bother to go both ways. First, here's an Envelopey case that's very like other recent examples:

> *The Very Special Relations Fund.* Not only does the VSRF make sure your $200 will go to save the life of a certain particular child, but it makes sure you'll get to know which kid that is. By providing you with her name and a picture of the child saved, you'll know precisely which child's life just your donation served to spare. Still,

15. Even here, some possible philosophers deny there's any real difference between the cases; skeptics about knowledge hold that, since we don't ever know anything, you'll never know anything about the fate of the trespasser. But, this can be passed over. And, from now on, I won't bother with philosophical views that deny an apparent difference between our two cases is a real one.

you don't send anything and, in consequence, one more child soon dies than if you'd made the requested donation.

To this epistemically focused case, we respond that your conduct was all right. Indeed, with lenient responses in mind, many *actually* refrained from donating to groups enormously like the VSRF. And, here's a suitable Sedanish example:

> *The Vintage Boat.* Your one real luxury in life is a vintage power boat. In particular, you're very happy with the fine wood trim of the handsome old boat. Now, there's been a big shipwreck in the waters off the coast where your boat's docked. From the pier, in plain view several hundred are struggling. Though both Coast Guard boats and private boats are already on their way to the people, more boats are needed. Indeed, the more private boats out and back soon, the more people will be saved. But, it's also plain that, if you go out, still, owing to all the melee, nobody will ever know which people will have been benefited by *you*. Indeed, for each of the folks whom you might bring in, it will be true to say this: For all anyone will ever know, she'd have been brought in by *another* boat, in which case some *other* person, whom some other boat rescued, would've perished. On the other hand, this you do know: While there's no risk at all to you, if you go out, your boat's wood trim will get badly damaged, and you'll have to pay for expensive repairs. So, you leave your boat in dock and, in consequence, a few more plainly struggling folks soon die.

As almost all respond to this epistemically amorphous case, your conduct was seriously wrong.

It's worth noting, briefly, an extended form of this distinction: In the Vintage Sedan, even *beforehand* you know whom you'll aid, if only you bother to provide the aid there relevant; but, in the Envelope, you *certainly wouldn't* know *beforehand* whom you'll aid. Can *that* mean much for a comfortably Preservationist solution? Again, our moral common sense speaks negatively. As with the Vintage Boat, reactions to many cases can confirm that decent deliverance. So much for epistemic focus.

14. Money, Goods and Services

In the Sedan, to provide apt aid you must perform a *service* for a needy person. Moreover, one of your *goods* would be needed in the performance of the service, namely, your vintage car. By contrast, in the Envelope all you must contribute is *money*; and, beyond the trivial effort needed to mail the money, the monetary cost is all you'd incur. Can this difference favor the Envelope's behavior?

Often, the difference between mere money and, on the other side, actual goods and services, has a psychological impact on us: When there's a call for our money, generally we think of what's going on as just charity. And, when thinking this, it seems all right to decline. But, at least in blatantly urgent situations, when there's a call for services, or one of our especially apt goods, a fair number of us think we must rise to the occasion. Does this difference have much moral relevance?

On this point, our moral common sense is clear: It doesn't matter whether it's money, or goods, or services, or whatever, that's needed from you to lessen serious suffering. There isn't a stronger moral call on you when it's your goods or services that are needed aid than when it's just your money.

In everyday life, that's confirmed by our reactions to very many cases: When disasters strike, like earthquakes, hurricanes, or floods, organizations work to aid the imperilled victims. On many of us, these groups often call only for our money. But, on some, they call for goods or services: For example, one good group may suggest that, since you're well placed in the pharmaceutical industry, you might make calls to your associates, asking them to donate medicines needed by victims of last week's disaster. But, plenty often, in these ordinary cases, the needs *aren't salient* to the agent approached and, then, our uncritical reactions are lenient. So, plenty often, the fact that what's needed is an agent's services, or her goods, doesn't affect even our responses to cases.

15. Combinations of These Differentiating Factors

Though no single one of the most notable factors differentiating the puzzle cases can carry much moral weight, mightn't certain *combinations* of them carry great weight? If that's so, then our puzzle might have, after all, a comfortably Preservationist solution. But, it's not so.

To get a good grip on the matter, we'll list explicitly the notable differential factors. Besides sheer conspicuousness, we've noted nine. In the order of their first appearance, and "viewed from the side of the Vintage Sedan," they are: (1) physical proximity, (2) social proximity, (3) informational directness, (4) experiential impact, (5) unique potential savior, (6) emergency, (7) causal focus, (8) epistemic focus, and (9) goods and services.[16] What does our general moral common sense say about those nine factors? Just as it's already done, it keeps telling us, about every single one, that it's *morally irrelevant*. Quite as clearly, this common sense says the same thing about any more complex difference the simpler ones combine to form, namely, that *it's* morally irrelevant.[17]

Concerning this question of their combination, what do our untutored responses to examples tell us about the nine listed factors? For relevantly interesting data, we're to look only at cases, of course, where people's great needs are inconspicuous to the cases' agents. For, if there's one thing we're *not* concerned now to explore, it's the extent to which our nine factors can combine to promote sheer conspicuousness of people's terrible troubles.

Now, it might be very difficult to confront a case that, at once, both included all nine "Sedanish" features and had only such great needs to meet as were quite inconspicuous. But, however that may be, it doesn't much matter. For, even with decidedly fewer than all nine, we can get the right idea quite clearly enough and, from the examples we've already confronted, we've already done that. So, for the energetic reader, I'll leave the exercise of constructing a complex case of the sort lately indicated. For the less energetic, there's the note appended to this very sentence.[18]

16. We've also discussed, of course, some candidates for being additional differential factors that proved unsuccessful. In the order discussed, and this time "viewed from the Envelope's side," they are: (a) worsening the further future—both factually false and contrary to our main stipulation, (b) leaving matters to the wealthy governments—at best just a modestly interesting instance of multiple potential saviors, (c) aiding only a very small part of an enormous multitude, as opposed to aiding a particular needy individual—a mere ethical illusion, (d) making only a decrease in the continuing mess rather than cleaning the scene—an even crazier illusion, (e) lacking important urgency—another illusion, and (f) failing to satisfy a nice semantic condition—not a genuinely differential factor, since, with a doctor's work needed, in the Sedan you couldn't really save someone's leg.

17. Perhaps, I may note a purely logical point: Those favoring stricter judgment for the Sedan aren't the only ones who can talk about combinations. Just as well, it can be done by those favoring a stricter judgment for the Envelope. But, since our common sense so clearly says that there's nothing substantial in any of this, it's silly to make a big deal about this logical symmetry.

18. In section 6 of the next chapter, "Combination of Factors and Limited Conspicuousness," I work up a complex case with all the Sedan's listed factors, and with salience of need kept low. The example, the African Earthquake, has an obvious *variant* that's directly relevant to the present question. And, to this variant, we'll respond that unhelpful conduct isn't wrong.

16. Highly Subjective Morality and Our Actual Moral Values

In our Primary Values, how much weight's accorded to psychologically powerful salience? Of course, there may be great weight given to certain things *often associated* with it: Often, the people whose needs are most conspicuous to you are your closest relatives and friends. And, someone might have extra strong moral reason to meet the great needs of folks who, socially and personally, are extremely close to her. But, even as it remains when their needs become very obscure to you, as can occur when you travel, such extra reason won't derive, of course, from the salience of these folks' needs. So, we've yet to see any reason to think that moral weight's given to conspicuousness of need itself.

In at least two ways, we can see that the reverse is true. First, consider the choice between certainly saving ninety-nine strangers whose dire needs are highly salient to you and, on the other side, certainly saving a hundred whose equally dire needs are very *inconspicuous*. As our Primary Values direct, you ought to save the hundred. Second, consider the choice between an attempt that has a 90% chance of success in saving a stranger whose dire need is highly salient to you and, on the other side, an attempt that has a 91% chance of success in saving one whose equal need is very inconspicuous. Here, our main Values direct you to make the attempt with the slightly greater chance of success.

According to the Values of certain possible people, and maybe even a few actual people, you'll be directed oppositely. Then, *just because* their dire needs are more conspicuous, you ought to favor saving *fewer* people over more folks; and, *just because* his dire need's more conspicuous, you ought to favor making the *less likely* attempt to meet someone's dire need. Those possible Values may be well called *Highly Subjective* Primary Values.

According to such Highly Subjective Values, conspicuousness to a particular agent is a factor that, in and of itself, has substantial moral weight. But, as we've just clearly seen, that's enormously different from our Primary Values. So, now, that fact will surprise few. What may remain surprising is an implication of the fact: In our Primary Values, nothing favors the Envelope's conduct over the Sedan's.

No doubt, our discussion's furthered our appreciation of the implication. Even so, there remains much resistance to thinking the Envelope's conduct is wrong. Accordingly, in the chapter's final sections,

I'll make an attempt, to be further pursued in later chapters, rationally to reduce this persistent resistance.

17. Resistance to the Puzzle's Liberationist Solution: The View That Ethics Is Highly Demanding

Here's one main line of persistent resistance: By contrast with judging the Sedan's conduct severely, if we do that with the Envelope's, then, since we can't reject certain boring truths we all know full well, we'll have to accept a certain general position that's very strict and demanding. Composed partly of purely moral propositions and partly of propositions relating moral ideas to our actual circumstances, it may be called the *View that Ethics is Highly Demanding*, and it may be seen to have these implications: To behave in a way that's not seriously wrong, a well-off person, like you and me, must contribute to vitally effective groups, like OXFAM and UNICEF, most of the money and property she now has, and most of what comes her way for the foreseeable future.

Is there much substance in this line of resistance? To answer well, we'll proceed systematically. And, for that, we'll distinguish two statements that, if true, can each undermine the line. One is categorical:

(1) The View that Ethics is Highly Demanding is the correct view of our moral situation.

And, the other is a conditional proposition:

(2) (Even) if this View isn't correct, a strict judgment for the Envelope (still) won't do any more toward committing us to the View than will a strict judgment for the Vintage Sedan.

Much later, in chapter 6, I'll argue for the View that Ethics is Highly Demanding.[19] But, at this early stage, we'll learn most by focusing on the conditional. So, I'll argue that, if a strict judgment for the Sedan *doesn't* commit us to anything very costly, then neither does a strict judgment for the Envelope.

19. Even while the View that Ethics is Highly Demanding allows few exceptions to the sort of transfer of wealth just indicated, none will give you any substantial license to pursue your own happiness, or your own (nonmoral) fulfillment: Insofar as it gets you to be more helpful to those in direst need, as with earning more money to be given toward saving children's lives, not only may you spend money on yourself, but you

Now, even before looking for any such argument, we know that its conditional conclusion must be correct. How so? Well, we've *stipulated* that, to the cases' agent, the helpful conduct requested in the Sedan is *over fifty times* as costly as in the Envelope. Still, observing details can be instructive.

Often, it's good to treat morality as an infinity of moral *principles*, or *precepts,* each entailing infinitely many others, more and more specific. On that approach, I'll first present this relatively general principle:

> *Lessening (the Number of People Suffering) Serious Loss.* Other things being even nearly equal, if your behaving in a certain way will result in the number of people who suffer serious loss being less than the number who'll suffer that seriously if you don't so behave (and if you won't thereby treat another being at all badly or ever cause another any loss at all), then it's seriously wrong for you not to so behave.[20]

To indicate the scope I mean the maxim to have, I'll make some remarks about the intended range of "serious loss." First, some positive paradigms: Even if it happens painlessly, when someone loses her life very prematurely, she suffers a serious loss. And, if someone loses even just a foot, much less a leg, she also suffers seriously. And, it also happens when, without losing any of his parts, someone loses his eyesight. Next, some losses less than serious: There's your losing just a tooth. And, there are financial losses from which you can recover. Anyway, this precept clearly applies to both puzzle cases.

Clearly, this maxim makes no provision for financial costs to the agent. And, so, many will resist the idea that it's a genuine moral principle. By the book's end, we'll see that such cares for costs conflict with any truly decent moral thinking. But, now, it's good to see how they can be accommodated.

How might it be ensured that, even when followed fully, a precept won't ever mean a terribly burdensome cost? Of course, we must see to

---

positively must do that. And, insofar as it's needed to meet your strictest special moral obligations, as with getting your child a costly life-saving operation, you must do that. In some detail, we'll discuss this in chapter 6 when, based on material from chapters that precede it, I'll argue that morality's far more demanding than we commonly suppose.

20. It's with thoughts about the causally amorphous aid you might have provided in the Envelope that I bother to formulate precepts, like this one, with rather lengthy locutions.

it that, *in the principle itself,* there's a logical guarantee to that effect. So, I'll do that straightaway and, to save space, I'll make other obvious changes when going from Lessening Serious Loss to this more specific precept:

> *Pretty Cheaply Lessening Early Death.* Other things being even nearly equal, if your behaving in a certain way will result in the number of people who *very prematurely lose their lives* being less than the number who'll do so if you don't so behave and *if even so you'll still be at least reasonably well off,* then it's seriously wrong for you not to so behave.[21]

Before moving to a yet more appealingly lenient specific maxim, we'll notice two points about this one: First, complying with it can't have you be less than reasonably well off! And, second, while the Envelope's conduct gets a severe judgment from the precept, *not* so the Sedan!

Few truly rich folks, if any at all, will fully comply with Pretty Cheaply Lessening Early Death. So, for any particular billionaire, the cost of compliance will be very great: If the toll's not taken all at once, then a decently progressive sequence will soon turn any into someone who's just reasonably well off.[22] So, for a maxim that's appealing even to the very rich, we must have a precept that's a lot like:

> *Very Cheaply Lessening Early Death.* Other things being even nearly equal, if your behaving in a certain way will result in the number of people who very prematurely lose their lives being less than the number who'll do so if you don't so behave and if even so you'll still be both (a) at least reasonably well off *and (b) very nearly as well off as you ever were,* then it's seriously wrong for you not to so behave.

Even for rich folks, this precept's full observance can't ever be very costly. And, since you're not very poor, you'll see clearly that, while it yields a strict judgment for the Envelope's conduct, it doesn't yield any for the Sedan's![23] So, it's very clearly indeed that we see the soundness of the section's main point: If a strict judgment for the Sedan doesn't commit us to anything onerous, then a strict judgment for the Enve-

---

21. For economy, I haven't again inscribed the long bracketed clause, "(and if you won't thereby treat another being at all badly or ever cause another any loss at all)." But, as context makes clear, its thought's in all the section's precepts.

22. Though many may find this to be excessively demanding on rich folks, I think the maxim really doesn't make any excessive demand. But, biding my time till chapter 6, I won't argue that now.

23. While not poor, it may be that you're not rich, either. Then, there'll be at least two reasons why this precept doesn't yield a strict judgment for your conduct in the

lope is *fully compatible* with a View that Ethics is Highly *Undemanding!*[24]

18. Further Resistance: Different Sorts of Situation and the Accumulation of Behavior

A good closing for the chapter can come from considering this other line of resistance: "In the Vintage Sedan, *the sort* of situation I encountered was a very *unusual* sort, and a quite *rare* sort. And, so, if I'd behaved well in the Sedan, then, pretty surely, I'd be off a certain moral hook for a good long while. By contrast, *the sort* of situation I faced in the Envelope was a very *common* sort of situation, a sort that's all too *frequent*; so, all too surely, I'll face a situation of *this other* sort again pretty soon. So, even if I'd behaved well in the Envelope, I wouldn't be off this other moral hook for long at all. Though hard to detail, that's a weighty moral difference between the cases." What's more, it seems this line may be furthered by a thought that, as was made clear by this text's very first page, we should all endorse: The fact that, in the Envelope, you failed to respond to an *appeal* has only minuscule moral weight. So, the line then continues like this: "With the sort of situation where I'll help save lives by contributing to UNICEF, there's hardly ever any stopping. But, nothing remotely like that holds for the sort in the Sedan. So, between the two cases, there's a huge moral difference."

Though it has a certain appeal, in this line there's really nothing more than in, say, the thought that people in a vast multitude are quite different from single individuals, that is, there's nothing whatsoever. But, since it's not obvious, I'll take pains to explain: Right at the line's start, we find the assumption that, in the Vintage Sedan, there actually is something that's *the one and only sort* of situation you encountered. But, that's as far from the truth as can be; for, in truth, you there encountered a situation of, or belonging to, *enormously many sorts*. For example, you confronted a situation of the sort *situations involving*

Sedan. Of course, one has been in play for a fair while: Unlike in the Envelope, in the Sedan there was never any question of any life being lost. Independent of that, another reason's this: Unlike when you're out only $100, when you're out over $5000, it's probably fair to say you *aren't* very nearly as well off as you ever were.

24. As I hope you're coming to agree, at least for us in a world like this, any decent morality must be, at the very least, a *Pretty Highly* Demanding Ethics. And, while in chapter 6 I'll advance a View that's even much more ambitious than that, in the section now closing, all I needed to do, and all I aimed to do, was something extremely unambitious.

vintage automobiles and, for another, *situations where there's the chance for someone to take another to a hospital*, and, for a third, *situations where someone's dire need is conspicuous to you.* Compounding errors, moments later there was made the equally defective assumption that, in the Envelope, there's something that's *the one and only sort* of situation you there encountered.

An appreciation of those twin troubles has us ask a properly pointed question: Perhaps rather rarely instanced, (and perhaps *not* rarely instanced) is there a *sort of situation* that (even as it *is* instanced by the Sedan and *not* by the Envelope) *can* ground strict judgment for the Sedan, but *can't* for the Envelope? At first glance, this question may seem to introduce new issues. But, for a simple reason, it really doesn't: If some such *sort* can effect this grounding, then certain *factors* must be similarly potent, namely, those serving to distinguish such a potent sort from less potent sorts. So, the question fails to locate anything we haven't already worked to investigate.

So far, the section's discussion has been very general and abstract. For a fuller sense of its main point, I'll illustrate with material more specific and concrete: Suppose that, though far from rich, you've already donated fully a fourth of your income this year to support effective programs conducted by OXFAM, UNICEF, and IPPF. Largely, you did this by responding quite positively to the many appeals that, during the year, you've received from the organizations. (As I'll bother to observe, unless you're "one in a million," this supposition is *wildly* false. Yet, because we've made it, we're set to hear a helpfully concrete little story.[25]) Near the year's end, it's now late December. Before the year's over, there appears in your mail, complete with material about ORT and a return envelope, yet another appeal from UNICEF. Throwing up your hands, you think this: "Even forgetting about the thousands I've given to OXFAM and IPPF this year, I've already sent UNICEF itself thousands of dollars. Now, I don't want to be a Scrooge, you understand; but, holy moly, enough is enough!" With that exasperating thought in mind, you throw away the most recent material.

Of course, there's another half to this little story: Later the same day, you go for a drive in your vintage Mercedes sedan. At a rural

25. While quite a few give a lot to elite institutions, and while many give much to local religious groups, hardly anyone gives even a fortieth of her annual income toward anything even remotely as important, ethically, as those programs. Just so, each year well-off Americans give far more to Harvard University than to all three mentioned groups combined, UNICEF and OXFAM and IPPF; and far more to Yale than all three combined; and they also give more even to my less elite home institution, NYU, than to all combined. Owing to facts like these, what's in the text is a gross understatement.

crossroads, you come upon a trespasser, evidently a harmless bird-watcher, with a badly wounded leg. After hearing his elaborate appeal, you throw up your hands and have the same thoughts as a few hours before. Finishing with another token of "Now, I don't want to be a Scrooge, you understand; but, holy moly, enough is enough!," you drive away and he loses a leg.

For your conduct in this two-scene story, what are our intuitive moral assessments? For the scene where you tossed UNICEF's envelope in the trash, our response is lenient. But, for your conduct in the second scene, our response is strict. Of course, in a slightly different form, that's just our old puzzle.

As I've suggested, some may try to ground the divergent responses along a certain "sortal" line: "In the story's first part, I confronted a situation of *the same sort* I already often encountered this year. So, taking together all the situations of *that* sort, I'll have behaved quite well during the whole year. But, in the story's second part, I confronted a situation of a *new* sort. Now, taking together all the situations of this second sort, we find that, since there's only one of them, for my letting the trespasser lose his leg, I'll have acted very badly, during the whole year, in *all those* situations."

At this point, the absurdity of these sortal thoughts becomes clear quickly: In both the story's first part and its second, there was a situation belonging to enormously many sorts. Now, with the "Envelopey" situation faced first, it's only certain of its *morally irrelevant* sorts that do much to promote your quickly grouping it with other situations, for example, the sort *situations where you receive appeals from organizations that aid the vitally needy*. But, for accurate moral assessment, it's only certain *other* of its sorts that are relevant, for example, the sort *situations where behaving helpfully has no morally bad aspects and results in fewer folks suffering serious loss*. Of course, the Sedanish situation second in the story *doesn't* belong to the morally *irrelevant* sort just noted for its Envelopey predecessor, nor to ever so many *other* such irrelevant sorts. But, so what? It *does* belong to the ethically *relevant* sort lately noted. Indeed, (with our Secondary Values' domain rightly remaining to the side), as this chapter's work has helped show, *all* its morally relevant sorts are *also* instanced by its Envelopey predecessor.

Like the points surviving scrutiny in previous sections, the few here surviving support only a Liberationist solution to the chapter's puzzle, not a Preservationist answer. But, even now, many will think the Envelope's conduct isn't wrong at all, much less seriously so. With that in mind, in the next chapter I seek a deeper understanding of such commonly, but perhaps terribly, unhelpful behavior.

3

LIVING HIGH, STEALING AND LETTING DIE: THE MAIN TRUTH OF SOME RELATED PUZZLES

While supporting the previous chapter's main points, in this one I'll extend inquiry to other morally substantive matters. So, I'll argue for a main conclusion that, in one important way, is more ambitious than the previous chapter's: Toward aiding folks in great need, it concerns what you might do not merely with what's yours, but, more ambitiously, with what's rightfully another's.

So that it packs a notable punch, the proposition to be argued concerns what may be called *simple appropriating:* When you simply appropriate what's another's, then, whether or not you steal it, you don't get her consent to take it and, what's more, you don't compensate her for the loss imposed. To the same punch-packing purpose, our proposition will concern your taking what's of considerable financial, or economic, value: Much more valuable than most rubber bands, and most nickels, here you'll be taking the likes of ships and rare antiques, and monetary sums much greater than one dollar. But, so that matters may remain manageable, the new conclusion concerns only appropriations where there is far less than any truly serious loss.

So that the punch-packed argument may be cogent, I'll see to it that, in another way, our new conclusion's less ambitious than the previous chapter's main moral result: Rather than saying anything about what you morally *must* do for the greatly needy (with what's another's), it will only go so far as to say what it's morally *good* for you to do for them.

Though the chapter's first several sections won't yield much new insight, they'll lead to where we'll see Liberationism break lots of new ground. There, we'll explain why it is that, in promoting your reactions to many examples, the conspicuousness of others' great needs works so powerfully. Roughly, the account will run like this: Usually, you're very much in the grip of a doubly misleading sort of moral thinking, fallacious *futility thinking*. On one side of this habitually confusing coin, when so gripped you're greatly influenced by a consideration that's morally irrelevant: the vastness of the serious losses that will be suffered even after you do your utmost to lessen such suffering. And, on the other side, when so gripped you're only slightly influenced, or perhaps even influenced not at all, by a consideration that's morally weighty: the lessening in serious suffering you can effect. So it is that, usually, you erroneously think that, since you can make only a small dent in the vast mass of all the serious suffering, there's no strong moral reason for you to take what's another's, or even to give what's your own, to lessening the serious suffering. But, usually isn't always: Aptly called "positive highly subjective factors," there are opposite influences, like the salience to you of some folks' great needs, that can, and that sometimes do, liberate you from the grip of your fallacious futility thinking; (while I've just mentioned the most familiar of these positive highly subjective factors, in due course we'll also notice some others.) And, when you're thus liberated, you can see that, to lessen serious suffering, there is strong moral reason for you to engage in helpful behavior: Important for the chapter, you then can see that, to lessen serious suffering, it's good to take what's rightfully another's; important for the whole book, you can see that, to that serious end, it's badly wrong not to give what's your own.

1. A Puzzle about Taking What's Rightfully Another's

For this discussion to be as engaging as the previous chapter's, we'll again begin with a pair of pretty simple and realistic cases. Just so, here's one of the new examples:

> *The Yacht.* You're employed on the waterfront estate of a billionaire. Through binoculars, you see a woman out in the waves, already in danger of drowning. And, in under an hour, a hurri-

cane will pass through the area. So, there's this: If you go to aid her soon, she'll be saved; if not, she'll soon die. But, there's also this: To aid her, you must use a motor yacht worth many millions of dollars. And, if you go, then, on the return trip, to avoid complete wreckage by the hurricane, you must pass through a channel where the yacht will suffer a few million dollars damage. Since the boat's the billionaire's and you don't have his permission to do this, it's against the law. And, being far from rich, you can't help much with the repair bill that, even after insurance, will be over a million bucks. Still, you take the yacht and save the woman.

And, here's the other:

The Account. You're one of many accountants who work in the large firm among whose clients is a certain billionaire. As you know, he gives a lot to several fashionable charities, but does hardly anything to aid the world's neediest people. Today, you've the rare chance to decrease, by only a million dollars, the billionaire's huge account. Partly because it can be done without ever being noticed, for the billionaire this won't ever mean even as much as mild annoyance. What's more, via a sequence of many small anonymous contributions, the million will all go to UNICEF and, as a result, ten thousand fewer children will die in the next few months. Now, largely because you've long been in the habit of giving most of your own money to UNICEF, you'll never be in a position to reimburse the magnate to any significant degree. Still, you shift the funds and, in consequence, ten thousand more children don't die soon but live long.

Of course, we'll make the same stipulations as with the previous chapter's two puzzle cases: We'll *be boring* and we'll suppose that, in these cases, your main motives are as parallel as can boringly be.[1]

What's our intuitive judgment of your conduct in the Account? And, what's our untutored assessment of your conduct in the Yacht? As most react, in the Account your behavior was wrong. By contrast, most respond that in the Yacht your conduct wasn't wrong and, what's more, it was even good behavior. Much as our previously noted responses greatly favored the Sedan's conduct over the Envelope's, these reactions favor the Yacht's behavior over the Account's.

---

1. Though not central to our inquiry, it's worth noting this difference between the two pair of parallel motives: Both in the Envelope and in the Vintage Sedan, your main motivation was to maintain your own asset position, which is rather egoistic. By contrast, both in the Yacht and in the Account, your main motivation is entirely altruistic.

But, our more general moral common sense doesn't do anything like that: With your behavior in the Account meaning the difference between a reasonably long life and a tragically short one for ten thousand children and, on the other hand, with its never meaning anything very bad for anyone, the Account's conduct is very good behavior, at least as good as the Yacht's. Again, we confront an intriguing puzzle.

As you'll recall, the Sedan's needy person not only got himself into his bad fix, but he did it by behaving in a way that was recklessly irresponsible as regards his own person and morally objectionable as regards (the rightfully owned property of) someone else. By complicating it a bit, it's easy to have the Yacht be another case where the needy person leaves a lot to be desired. For irresponsible recklessness, these suppositions suffice: Like everyone else for many miles around, the Yacht's imperiled woman recently heard clear hurricane warnings on reliable broadcasts; but, unlike everyone else, she was moved by the thought that, if she went well out on the waves, she'd have a thrilling experience and, with a bit of luck, she'd live to tell a thrilling tale. For objectionable behavior, this more than suffices: Seeking great speed, the daredevil left her own "sail-fish" at home, roughly, a surfboard fixed up with a sail, and she took out the faster one she stole from your rich employer. So, ironically, it's his board that's floating hopelessly beyond her reach.

Even when the Yacht's intriguingly enlarged, from both our standard sources for moral messages the deliverance remains the same: Your conduct was good.[2] Still, in our discussion, I won't refer much to this complicated version of the Yacht. Rather, so that things are easily kept clear, we'll have in mind just the original, simple version of the case.

At all events, the chapter's central conundrum concerns this challenging question: Is there any adequate ground for both a *positive* judgment of the Yacht's appropriation and also a *negative* assessment of the one in the Account? As in the previous chapter, we'll sensibly restrict the search to what's given weight by our *Primary* Values. Especially with that in mind, we'll eventually see this puzzle's true answer to be a thoroughly Liberationist solution.

---

2. Had she murdered the tycoon's children, or maybe even anyone's children, then many would react differently and, perhaps, that might be apt. But, though she wrongly stole from the very person on whom, in order for her life to continue, you must inflict a further loss, still, in this case the badness of her behavior was far too slight to affect substantially the moral situation. Evidently, that's reflected in our reactions to the example.

2. Stealing and Just Taking

When an accountant, your behavior involved *stealing,* but when a "yachtkeeper," you *just took* the yacht, and there wasn't stealing. Relying on that distinction, some may attempt a quick Preservationist solution: "When there's just the taking of what's another's and not stealing, then perhaps there's not even a presumption that the conduct's wrong. But, when there's the stealing of what's another's, then, at the least, there's a strong presumption that the behavior's wrong. So, *because he stole,* and nothing overrode the presumption it was wrong, the accountant's conduct was wrong. And, *because he didn't steal,* and there wasn't anything else bad about the yachtkeeper's behavior, his conduct wasn't wrong."

But, for reasons as simple as they're basic, that fails to make even the slightest bit of progress toward providing our present puzzle with a sensible solution: To begin, let's make the simplistic but useful supposition that something's being a case of stealing *entails* that it's a *wrongful* taking of what's not one's own. But, then, we don't yet have even the slightest clue why it is that, in the Account, your taking of the funds is *properly* regarded as a *wrongful* taking of what's another's and, so, why *that* taking is a case of *stealing.* Nor do we have we even the least idea why it is that, in the Yacht, your taking of the valuable vessel *isn't* properly regarded as a wrongful taking and, so, why *this other* taking *isn't* a case of stealing. So, doing nothing to reveal ground supporting the divergent intuitions on our two cases, a reference to stealing fosters, at most, just a trivial reformulation of the puzzle they pose: Why should we take only the accountant's conduct, and not the yachtkeeper's, to be a *wrongful* taking?

At this point, some will notice this natural reply: If the tycoon should find out what you did with a million of his dollars, he'd *greatly mind* what you did. By contrast, if the magnate learned what you did with his Yacht, he *wouldn't* much mind. Like the mentions of stealing, this uncovers no moral ground. One logically deeper than the other, I'll note two reasons why that's so.

The less deep reason can be viewed from two sides. On one, we see this: In the Yacht, the magnate might be *abnormally heartless;* then, even if he learned the whole situation, he'd greatly mind what you did. But, even so, our reaction's as positive as with the original Yacht. On the other side, there's this: In the Account, the magnate might be *extraordinarily compassionate;* then, if he learned of that whole situation, he wouldn't mind what you did. But, even so, our reaction's negative, even if not quite so negative, perhaps, as with the original Account. So, we've as much to explain as ever.

That brings us to the logically deeper reason: For the natural answer to make much sense, we must assume that the usual difference in minding, which we'll find with any normal tycoon, is explained by another difference in a normal person's psychology: Just as we ourselves are set to do, a normal magnate's set to regard the yachtkeeper's behavior as a morally good taking. And, just like us, a normal mogul's set to regard the accountant's behavior as a wrongful taking. So, in giving the natural answer, we've just taken the question of grounding our own responses to the cases and made it into a question about another's perfectly parallel responses. Of course, that's no way to make progress.

A few moments ago, we supposed that stealing always involves taking that's wrongful. But, actually, that's not so. Indeed, sometimes stealing's very good. Not only does our moral common sense deliver this correct idea, but, often enough, so do our responses to cases. For a useful example, here's:

> *The Key.* A tycoon owns a valuable antique key. In a nearby town, a bomb's set to explode in a few hours and, if it does, dozens of people will die. But, if the key is used, then a certain door will be opened and the bomb, which is behind it, will be defused. Now, even though the tycoon is aware of this, he's so greatly concerned about the great prospective damage to, and devaluation of, his antique that he won't part with the key. A gifted pickpocket, you can take the key from him and, thus, make sure the bomb's soon defused. Though the ensuing damage to the uninsurable antique will lessen its value by over a million dollars, you take his key, use it as needed, and, in consequence, dozens are saved from dying soon.

While it's absolutely clear that, in the Key, you *stole* something valuable, still, most rightly react that your conduct was fine behavior. So, why is there a negative response to the Account, but a positive response to the Key? But, of course, that's just another version of our puzzle!

3. The Account's Additional Morally Suspect Features

Another attempt to provide a quick Preservationist solution draws on this other difference: Absent from the Yacht's conduct, the Account's has morally objectionable features quite additional to appropriating what's rightfully another's. Now, at least for the most part, the Account's *additional morally suspect features* fall under two broad heads. First, in the Account there's the likes of fraud and, relatedly, your failure to meet your professional responsibilities. Second, as is properly boring, the Account's conduct was covert; by contrast, the Yacht's was out in the open and, also properly boring, you were willing to face the consequences of the overt behavior. Don't these additional morally suspect features ground a negative assessment for the Account, with their absence allowing the Yacht a positive assessment?

As can be seen clearly, that attempt is badly misconceived.[3] First, let's look to our moral common sense: Even if just one child's life is at stake, it far outweighs those moral considerations. And, with "ten thousand innocent lives hanging on what you do," the contrary suggestion's perfectly absurd. Next, we'll look to our untutored intuitions on the cases. And, even as the relevant examples fall into two distinct classes, by looking at just one case from each class, we'll see ample returns.

First, we'll confront a "Yachtish" case whose conduct's morally suspect in a whole slew of ways, each logically distinct from the fact that there's appropriating behavior:

> *The Small Marina.* In a small marina are the motor yachts of three billionaires. On a nearby beach, you spy a woman in the waves and learn of an upcoming hurricane. Rushing to the marina, you find a guard with an automatic weapon. Pointing out the endangered woman, you ask him to use one of the yachts. But, as he insists that only someone with an authorization slip signed by a yacht's owner can use it, that's to no avail. Spying slips on a nearby table, you tell the guard you have one and you just need to look in your attaché case for a minute. Your hand being quicker than his eye, you distract him with your complicated case, you filch one of the slips and, unnoticed, you deftly forge a tycoon's signature that's familiar to you. Handing the guard the slip, you take out that mogul's yacht. How could you do that so easily? Well, you're a professional calligrapher and handwriting analyst, often consulted to authenticate documents. In fact, for help with his collection of rare papers, that billionaire's often consulted you. Always giving you a check signed in your presence, he's paid you handsomely; for he's greatly valued your promise to be completely honest in all matters

3. Before beginning this task, I'll note something that may be of more than just philosophical value: In trying to declare a moral distinction between the accountant's duties to his firm's clients and the yachtkeeper's duties to his employer, there's more snobbery than substance. In time, we may be less snobbish in our thoughts about those not highly placed on society's status ladder.

regarding him. Knowing you'll easily land him with a bill for over a million bucks, you take his yacht and save the woman.

Here, your conduct's *loaded* with morally suspect features. Yet, most respond that it was good.

Next, an "Accounty" case that *lacks* the original's additional morally suspect features. Since the case must be complex, I'll present it in two steps. In the first, there's conduct lacking the morally suspect features, like fraud, falling under our first head:

> *The Moderately Complex Account.* Not a professional in an accounting firm, you're a graduate student in economics who knows a lot about accounting, computers, and so on. You're in these offices only because you're delivering sandwiches from the deli where you work part-time. Living modestly, you give fully a third of your meager income to UNICEF. Just now, you can shift a million bucks from a billionaire's account to UNICEF. Flicking a few buttons, you do that.

In the second step, there's conduct that, as it's also open, falls under both heads:

> *The Complex Account.* Everything here is as above except for this: Even as you push the last button, you make this accurate Announcement to many: You've moved a million dollars out of the huge account of the billionaire, J. P. Plentymoney, in such a way that, over the next month, bit by anonymous bit, it will find its way into accounts of UNICEF, OXFAM, CARE and seven other similarly effective groups. As you've determined, each of the ten will receive *at least one* dollar, but, beyond just a dollar, not even you can know how much is received by any one group. With no proper way for Plentymoney to retrieve more than ten bucks of the million, and not making a big fuss about just ten bucks, the magnate swallows the loss of a million.

With the Complex Account, there are none of the original Account's additional morally suspect features. Yet, as most react to it, your behavior was wrong. So, from both sides of the matter, we've seen that what generates divergent responses to the two puzzle cases isn't such suspect features.

Since we react positively to the Small Marina and negatively to the Complex Account, that pair presents a puzzle that's even more perplexing than the one chosen for focus: First, in the Small Marina your conduct had *more* morally suspicious features than in the Account. And, second, your openly honest appropriation in the Complex Account had several morally *good* features absent from the Account's behavior. So, why didn't I make this yet more perplexing problem the focus of the chapter? Well, much simpler and more realistic, the puzzle actually selected is easier to grasp and, once grasped, easier to keep clearly in mind. And, for a protracted inquiry, that's important. But, then, I should send this signal: If the puzzle chosen has a Liberationist solution, so do others, each far more comprehensive.

4. Proper Property, Mere Money and Conversion

In the Yacht you took property properly so-called, or *proper property*. But, in the Account, you *didn't* take any; rather, you took only the "financial equivalent," or *mere money*.[4] To make this distinction clear, a few words should suffice: Not only certain minted coins, but also certain pieces of paper currency have notable features that are only rarely found, and that make the monetary items highly prized by collectors. If you're a collector, then those you possess will be both some of your money and also some of your proper property. So, unlike "what's sitting in your bank accounts," and what's in most cash registers, that money isn't mere money.

This distinction separates the Yacht from the Account. But, can it favor the Yacht's behavior? Reflection shows the suggestion's preposterous: It certainly *isn't less* bad to take someone's proper property from her; indeed, often the reverse is true. After all, even a billionaire's likely to care strongly about just a few of his many costly possessions: While caring little about his hunting lodge, his concern for his yacht may extend well beyond considerations of its financial value. And, no matter how much money's thrown at the repair project, it takes time to make a badly damaged ship seaworthy again, meaning *more* of a loss for its anxious owner.

Related but distinct is this distinction: In the Yacht, what was taken was *directly used* to prevent serious loss. By contrast, in the Account

---

4. Though not obvious, the distinction applies to many ordinary monetary items: Suppose you have a very extensive collection of U.S. dimes, including importantly different dimes minted in each of the last hundred years. Those minted in the last two years are common and, for that reason, each may be worth only ten cents. Still, just as the rare old dimes in your collection are your proper property, so are these common new dimes. By contrast, the three common dimes in my pocket are mere money.

nothing remotely like that happened.[5] Even with all of it done just electronically and symbolically, the Account's transferred funds were used only very indirectly to lessen the loss of life: The money stolen was used only to *buy other* things, like ORT packets, that were of *much more direct* use in the saving of needy people. Conveniently, we'll say that there then was the *conversion* of what was appropriated to something that was of much more direct use in meeting great needs. However it's best expressed, will this difference favor the Yacht's behavior? Our moral common sense says there's no moral significance there: When innocent lives are at stake, to take only what can be used directly, and not what must be converted, is no more than a horrible fetish.

For both distinctions, our responses to cases can confirm the accurate commonsense judgments. To see this best, we'll confront cases of two sorts. First, there'll be a case where, like the Account, there's the taking of mere money and its conversion. But, unlike the Account and like the Yacht, in this case the great need is highly conspicuous to you:

> *The Large Deposit.* To pay certain large bills for him, like those he gets after throwing one of his multimillion-dollar "flotilla" parties, you're empowered by your tycoon to write large checks on his huge account. Indeed, it's been several times that, part for rent and part as a security deposit, you've written such checks to a certain "sealord," who rents several grand motor yachts. One day, you spy a woman in the waves who's in mortal danger. Since the tycoon's taken his own Yacht to sea, the only way to save her is with one of the sealord's yachts. Now, because he has a loaded gun in hand, you can't overpower him. What you can do is write a check for a couple of million dollars, a little for an hour's rent of a vessel and almost all for a deposit against damages. Using a rented yacht, you save the woman's life and, just as you knew would happen, you make your magnate lose over a million dollars of the large deposit.

As most respond here, your behavior was good.

Second, there'll be a case where, like the Yacht, there's the taking of proper property and its direct use. But, unlike the Yacht and like the Account, the great need is inconspicuous to you:

5. What happened in the Account was very different from the direct use of mere money to lessen serious loss: Suppose that you appropriate a lot of paper currency, that's mere money, because it's all the easily ignitable stuff available in the cabin where folks are about to freeze to death. Then, to provide them with vitally needed warmth, you use the flaming paper to ignite some twigs, thus to ignite some branches, thus to ignite some logs. Directly enough, you use the mere money to save the people.

The Yacht Ferry. While the billionaire spends much of the winter at his waterfront estate, and on his yacht, it's now summer. For the next three months, neither he nor anyone reporting to him will be concerned with the whereabouts of the yacht; it will just be assumed the ship's in its dock. Now, during these months, if you take the yacht, you can "sail" it to the main port of an impoverished country, where hundreds of thousands are prematurely dying. After sailing for a week to the distant land, you can use the yacht to ferry needed supplies from a central dock, through very rocky straits, to a remote harbor that's much nearer a few thousand desperate people in dire need. If you ferry the supplies, then, while the vast majority of them will die anyway, at least you'll prevent several hundred from dying, though you'll also greatly damage the yacht by taking it through the straits with all the rocks. Still, you take it upon yourself to do all that and, thus, to make your employer face a repair bill for over a million dollars.

As most respond here, your behavior was wrong. So, from complementary cases comes an endorsement of what we've heard from moral common sense. Clearly, nothing here helps the Preservationist.

5. Appropriation and the Doctrine of Double Effect

Some philosophers endorse a thought called the *Doctrine of Double Effect,* or DDE. As even most of them agree, it's hard to be clear about the content of the Doctrine.[6] And, so, there are various versions of it. But, in our discussion, it's enough to consider the bare bones of just one: Just so, we'll take the DDE to entail at least this: (1) As (part of) a *means necessary for* preventing loss from befalling some, you might harm others. (2) By contrast, not as (part of) any such needed means, but *only as a fully foreseen result of, or side-effect of,* preventing loss from befalling some, you might harm others. (3) Other things being at least very nearly equal, harming behavior of that first (means-end) sort is morally more objectionable than harming of that second (foreseen-result) sort. At all events, some may think the Doctrine marks a differ-

---

6. Two recent examples are Thomas Nagel, *The View from Nowhere,* Oxford University Press, 1986, pages 179–80 and Warren S. Quinn, "Actions, Intentions and Consequences: The Doctrine of Double Effect," *Philosophy and Public Affairs,* 1989. To my mind, the most incisive discussion of this topic is in Jonathan Bennett, *The Act Itself,* Oxford University Press, 1995. Unlike Nagel and Quinn, Bennett thinks no moral stock should be placed in any such doctrine, and I'm inclined to agree.

ence useful for a Preservationist solution to our puzzle: As part of what's needed to help prevent 10,000 from dying, in the Account you harm a billionaire. But, in the Yacht, though it's fully foreseen, the loss imposed is a mere side-effect of your saving someone's life.

Now, *even if* the DDE might *sometimes* carry a great deal of moral weight, which I doubt, in the cases *now* at hand it can't carry any at all. About this, our moral common sense is perfectly clear. And, rather than along any line the DDE might draw, our untutored reactions to several most germane cases go in an *opposite* direction. For a good example, just recall the Yacht Ferry. There, the damage to the magnate's vessel wasn't (any part of) a needed means to the vital end. Rather, though you fully foresaw that great damage, it was a mere side-effect of your saving lives by ferrying vitally needed supplies. So, if the DDE does apply in the current discussion, it classes the Yacht Ferry with the Yacht, not with the Account: The Doctrine would have it that, like with Yacht but not the Account, in the Yacht Ferry it's all right to impose a loss. But, unlike with the Yacht and just like with the Account, with the Yacht Ferry we react negatively. So much for the Doctrine of Double Effect.

6. Combination of Factors and Limited Conspicuousness

In the previous chapter, we considered the idea that, perhaps only when they're taken in combination, some salient differences between the Envelope and the Sedan might provide some badly wanted moral ground. Here, we'll consider the idea that, perhaps only when *they're* taken in combination, some salient differences between the Yacht and the Account might provide some *related* badly wanted ground.

As we saw before, such an idea of combination didn't reveal any ground for favoring the Envelope's conduct over the Sedan's. So, the prospects are bleak for our finding, in a parallel idea of combination, a comfortably Preservationist solution to our present puzzle. But, especially as we were a bit short with combinations before, let's now give the matter a good run for the money.

Viewing things "from the Yacht's side," the factors to be canvassed include all those we noted as absent in the Envelope but present in the Sedan: (1) physical proximity, (2) social proximity (that's not *very* great), (3) informational directness, (4) experiential impact, (5) unique potential savior, (6) emergency, (7) causal focus, (8) epistemic focus, and (9) (goods and) services. And, they also include a couple that might well have been noted as distinguishing the Sedan from its puzzle partner, namely, (10) proper property (not mere money) and (11) direct use (not conversion). Finally, and by contrast, we noted three features of the Yacht that *didn't* occur in the Sedan, namely, (12) just taking (not stealing), (13) no "additional morally suspect features" and (14) means-end (not merely foreseen result).

With all 14 features present in the Yacht, we responded that your appropriation was morally good behavior. With none present in the Account, we responded negatively. When these individually irrelevant factors are present together, do they yield a complex greatly favoring the Yacht's conduct? To our moral common sense, an affirmative answer is crazy: In both cases, what matters morally is that, on the one side, innocent life is at stake and, on the other, there's no great harm done.

Since our response to an apt combination case is instructive, I'll present one exhibiting 13 of the 14 listed features, all but (12) just taking (not stealing). A variant of a case of Jonathan Bennett's, I'll provide a complex case, starting with this background material[7]: A graduate student of anthropology, when doing the fieldwork for your dissertation, you lived in a very remote peaceful African village. Except for you, the village remains unknown outside its area. But, your knowledge of the village is intimate and thorough: Not lacking any basic necessity, your villagers don't live in a chronic horror. But, in the large part of Africa also containing thousands of other hamlets, recently there's been a severe earthquake, wreaking havoc on them all. In many villages, including yours, while many of the folks are still alive, they need vital aid soon. Luckily, you were one of the few who wasn't injured at all; you're fit enough to seek help for your village. To be sure, on your portable radio, you learn of thousands of similarly suffering hamlets. Yet, along a lengthy and barely passable road, you make a trek to an African airport, the first step in seeking help for your favorite village. With that background, here's:

> *The African Earthquake.* Right after flying back to the Northern metropolis that's the site of your university, you try all sorts of legal ways to get vital supplies to your village. But, while a drug company makes the vitally needed medicines available free of

7. Not involving stealing nor even any appropriation, but only concerning what you might do with your own resources, Bennett's nice example of a badly needed African well is presented at page 89ff. of his "Morality and Consequences," in S. McMurrin, ed., *The Tanner Lectures on Human Values,* II, University of Utah Press, 1981.

charge, you can't come close to getting the needed transportation legally. Being resolute, you simply take the private jet of a billionaire. Landing it in a field near your village, you get the medicines to its folks in time to save many, but, as you knew would happen, the jet's so damaged its owner must swallow a repair bill for over a million dollars.

As most respond to this complex case, your behavior was wrong.

With fully 13 of the Yacht's 14 noted factors present, why is there a negative response? Well, though your villagers' great needs at first were very salient to you, when you learned of so many similarly suffering folks, with your radio, those needs were no longer so salient. Thus, although so many noted factors were present together, they failed to promote suitably sustained salience and, so, they didn't much affect our intuitive responses. So much for thoughts of combination.

7. The Influence of Conspicuousness Explained: Overcoming Our Fallacious Futility Thinking

Why are we strongly influenced by the extent to which folks' great needs are conspicuous to you, our agent? Details aside, I'll suggest the general form of a Liberationist explanation.

Even while conspicuousness is a highly subjective psychological factor, it's hardly the most morally misleading of those that strongly affect us. Far more misleading are those *negative* factors, equally subjective, whose habitual effect is to have us ignore vital needs that *aren't* salient to us. So, these badly misleading factors serve to promote fallacious forms of moral thinking, prominently including what I'll call *futility thinking*. By liberating us from the grip of the bad thinking, salience allows our moral responses to reflect our Values. So, there's reason to call it a *positive* highly subjective factor.

Of that general form, I'll begin an account that, while never much more than sketchy, does provide some substantive details. Followed by qualifying commentary, it divides nicely in two Parts.

In *Part One*, we take futility thinking's pattern to have these five steps:

(1) First, when *all* you know is that others are in great need, you (correctly) think there's *strong* moral reason for you to help them. (So, you think that, with what's yours, it's seriously wrong not to do that; and, you think that, with what's another's, it's good to do it.)

(2) But, second, often you also know that, no matter *what* you do, very many of the greatly needy people *still* won't have their needs met and, so, *they'll all suffer anyway.*

(3) Third, often your most *powerfully operative* thought about the needy is, then, one that *primarily presents* the individuals as *members of just such a hopelessly overwhelming* group.

(4) Fourth, even behavior that's *successful* in meeting some of the people's great needs then *seems to be futile*; it seems like successfully removing a mere drop of trouble from a whole sea of suffering.

(5) So, fifth and finally, you (incorrectly) think there *isn't* strong moral reason for you to help meet any of the great needs. (So, you think that, with what's yours, it's not wrong not to do that; and, you think that, with what's another's, it's wrong to do it.)

In *Part Two*, we see how there may be something to upset the pattern just roughly related: When some folks' great needs are *highly conspicuous to you*, often you're liberated from futility thinking's grip. And, when that occurs, often *your most powerfully operative* thought primarily presents *those* folks as *greatly needy people*, not as members of such an overwhelming group. And, when that happens, behavior that meets their great needs *doesn't* seem futile. And, then, your last thought about the matter is just the same as your first: You (correctly) think there's *strong* moral reason for you to help them.

Qualifying commentary on this Bipartite Account. To be helpful, I cast the account in a certain rough form. It was presented as (a) extremely general regarding the people to whom it applies, and (b) heavily temporal regarding the order of thoughts expressed in five steps, and (c) supremely selective regarding what positive (subjective) factor might liberate us from the grip of futility thinking. Though such simplification was helpful, it can later lead to misunderstanding. To prevent that, I'll qualify the account.

(a) Generality of Application. In the account's first step, I may have made it appear that, when mature members of our society typically behave, often we know there are only a few greatly needy people whom we can help. But, of course, that's not our epistemic situation; rather, we know there are very many such people. Now, it's easy to dispel the appearance of naivete, as the counter-factual below helps show.

(b) Times of Thoughts. All too easily, my words can be taken as ascribing a temporal order to our futility thinking, from the first step through the fifth. But, the common situation can be understood, often at least as well, in terms of a counterfactual presentation, such as the rough one that starts with a sentence like this: If *all* you knew was that others were in great need, and you didn't even have any idea that, no matter *what* you did, very many of them *still* wouldn't have their needs met, then you'd (correctly) think that there'd be *strong* moral reason for you to help.

(c) Selectivity of Positive Factor. In Part Two, I spoke only of how thoughts of conspicuous great need liberate us from futility thinking; if only by omission, I did a bit to suggest that's the only (positive highly subjective) factor that does that. But, the psychological situation isn't so simple and, indeed, it's worth spending a full section on noticing some of the complexity.

8. Beyond Conspicuousness: Dramatic Trouble and Other Potent Positive Subjective Factors

Even if not as commonly operative as conspicuousness, other highly subjective factors also break the hold of futility thinking. Indeed, with the Key, we've already encountered one: As many people were all coming and going beyond your ken, quite unpredictably, in that case there wasn't any particular person whose great need (to have a bomb defused) was even the least bit salient to you. Yet, our reaction was that, in stealing the key, you behaved well. To make the point still clearer, I present a cousin of the Key:

> *The Key Call.* Not having even the least sense of right and wrong, some utter lunatics placed time-bombs in 10 of the world's 100 busiest airports. Though nobody outside their small circle knows which 10 busy airfields are imperilled, many people, including you yourself, know certain related facts: All 10 bombs are set to explode in the next 24 hours, though not all at once, and each explosion will kill several people. And, while nobody else can do anything about the terrible situation, you can do something: If you steal an intransigent billionaire's antique gold key, you can open a certain door. While that must so badly damage the key as to decrease its value by over a million bucks, you'll get to see a certain note. The note will tell you precisely where one of the bombs is located. (For example, it might say that, at Chicago's O'Hare, one of the bombs is in temporary storage locker #2318.) By calling the authorities of the airport specified in the note, you can quickly get that one bomb rendered harmless. So, you take the key and you make a call. While many are violently killed at several busy airports

anyway, you prevent several from being blown to smithereens at one.

Here, it's completely clear no one's need was at all salient to you; still, we react positively.

Though not having salient great needs, the Key Call's endangered folks were in *dramatic trouble*. Unlike kids on death's door due to boring old measles, these folks were at risk in a way that, to us normal folks, was exciting. Since it featured folks in dramatic great trouble, the Key Call helped us break through our habitual futility thinking. For those at risk from the bombs, whoever they might be, our most operative thought *isn't* that they're members of a hopelessly overwhelming group. So, we think there was strong moral reason for you to help and, so, to the Key Call, our response is positive.

Whatever some might have been thinking about salience of great need, it's perfectly plain that *dramatic* trouble is a morally irrelevant factor: When people's great trouble is as boring and undramatic as can be, there's just as much moral reason to help them as when it's exciting and dramatic. For those interested in sound moral thinking, that point's importance can't be exaggerated.

To appreciate fully the point just emphasized, it's useful sharply to separate dramatic trouble from trouble that's *evilly produced*. For, some might think that, in reacting positively to the Key Call's stealing, we're affected by the fact that you help people in evilly produced trouble. And, these might then think that, since the Account's people were in only *naturally produced* trouble, there's much stronger moral reason to steal in the Key Call than in the Account and, so, the difference in our responses to the two cases is an accurate reflection of morality.

By this stage of the inquiry, few will place much trust in thoughts like those. Still, it's worth making clear how badly confused they are: Beyond all cases where trouble's made by utter lunatics, and where it's just *crazily* produced, there are many where dramatic trouble's the product of only *unthinking natural objects*. And, in cases like this, it's absolutely clear the trouble isn't evilly produced:

> *The Explosive Meteor.* Near a densely populated area, a small but explosive meteor has fallen to earth. If not rendered harmless within the hour, its explosion will violently kill several folks living in the crowded area. In order for that to be prevented, you must soon operate on the meteor with a costly Ejector, an industrial machine belonging to a billionaire. Since he knows that this will

damage it greatly, and cost him over a million bucks, the tycoon won't let you use the device. With little time left, you seize the Ejector from the frail old mogul and you eject the explosive natural object into a deep uninhabited canyon, so that nobody's seriously harmed. Making the mogul pay a big repair bill, you prevent several from being fatally blown sky high.

To such an evidently nonmalignant case, our response is positive.[8]

With that in mind, few won't appreciate fully the truth that there's no moral importance in whether someone's serious trouble is dramatic, or exciting. Yet, this highly subjective factor greatly influences our moral responses to many cases. But, then, is it plausible to think that this is the only positive subjective factor we've observed and that, against appearances, conspicuousness of great need isn't another? No; it's not. So, we've strong support for the thought that, lacking moral significance, salience is just another positive highly subjective factor.

Even if not as often as either conspicuousness or dramatic trouble, other highly subjective factors also can break the hold of our futility thinking. Here's a bit about one I'll call *descriptive segregation:* From the rest of all the world's greatly needy people, certain descriptions can effectively separate, in your mind, manageably small groups. Some are relevantly personal; for example, one relating just the greatly needy folks now in the small hometown of *your* childhood. By contrast, others are nonpersonal; for example, a report of the very few folks who're the last ever imperilled by a noncommunicable disease that, though it's killed many millions, now can be stopped from claiming even one more life.

Before closing the section, this should be made clear: Just as there are positive subjective factors other than salience, so there are negative

8. Complementing this, in the literature there are cogent considerations to the effect that conduct well aimed at trouble that's evilly produced isn't to be much favored over that well aimed at trouble that's only very naturally produced.

Here's one: If you go to the left, you'll save ten folks from being killed by a horrible hit man. If you go to your right, you'll save eleven innocents from being killed by a naturally occurring rock-slide. Of course, you can't go both ways in time to do any good on the side you don't go to first. As almost all agree, it's morally better for you to go to the right.

Here's another: If you go to the left, there's a 75% chance that you'll save an innocent from being killed by a malicious villain. If you go to the right, there's a 76% chance that you'll succeed in saving one from being killed by a naturally occurring rock-slide. Again, it's better to go to the right.

For a discussion of considerations like these, see pages 109-110 of Samuel Scheffler's *The Rejection of Consequentialism*, Oxford University Press, 1982, where he remarks on some ideas related to him by T. M. Scanlon, and offers his own ideas.

subjective factors, and bad forms of thinking, other than futility think-ing. So, futility thinking isn't the only thing promoting our distorted responses to the Account, and to the Envelope. Relatedly, there's the work done by what may be called our *repeatability thinking*.[9] Taken up in the next chapter, another may be a distortional tendency well called *projective separating*. Often, these negative factors may work in combi-nation. But, I'll suggest that, plenty safely enough, a clear exposition's furthered, here and now, by not detailing the other distorters: Since futility thinking's *enough* to explain, well *enough*, the responses we've been exploring, making such a simplifying supposition here is, really, as safe as it's reader-friendly.

9. In a Perennially Decent World: The Absence and the Presence of Futility Thinking

At this point, we'll profit most, I believe, from confronting certain highly hypothetical thoughts. To prepare for that, I'll stress some sad aspects of what actually prevails: For ever so long, each year millions of children painfully died on our planet. Second, and unlike just a cen-tury ago, now most of the horror can be readily prevented. But, third, a great deal of what's so preventable *isn't* prevented. Finally, for years to come, this sad situation will continue. So, it may be usefully fair to say that, in our era, at least, this is a *perennially rotten* world.

For a stark contrast, let's imaginatively suppose *our* planet's now a *perennially decent* world: Though there may be great inequalities, it's in at least decent circumstances that, for well over seventy years, almost all the world's billions live. For the exercise to be instructive, we'll also suppose that, still and all, we'll have the very same habits of intuitive moral thinking that, in actual fact, are those in force.

With those two suppositions, we're set to see some remarkable responses to interesting cases. While various emergency cases elicit notable reactions, it's more instructive, I think, to confront a few far-fetched cases where folks live in a chronic horror. So, here's the first example in a short sequence of just such "perennially decent" cases:

9. Habitually, it may seem that, if lessening serious suffering, about as much as you can, will require you to do difficult things of a certain salient sort repeatedly, time after time after time, there's no *strong* moral reason for you to do *anything* of *such* a hard sort. With that appearance holding sway, it will seem that there's no strong reason to give away any of what's yours and, certainly, there's none strong enough to license taking, and then giving, what's not yours.

The Newly Discovered Village. Somewhere in the deepest recesses of the great Amazon rain forest, there's a terribly remote village of fifty folks, with ten in vital need. For many years it's been isolated from the "civilized world." While investigating rare tropical wildlife, you've just newly discovered the village. Directly, you learn that its folks have long lived in a chronic horror: Lacking medicine long available in the civilized world, for centuries many ancestors of the present villagers have painfully died prematurely, quite as ten of these folks are about to do, in about a month's time. So, you go to get help. But, as it's been many decades since anyone's gotten the villagers' disease, nobody believes your plea for them. Anyhow, to save the villagers from dying soon, you must divert a million dollars from a billionaire's account and, using the money, rush them the needed medicine. So, you take the million and save the ten.

As most respond here, your conduct was good.[10]

What explains our positive response to this stealing? Before giving the Liberationist answer, we'll encounter another example: In the *Three Newly Discovered Villages*, you discover not one but three such villages, each with ten folks in such easily countered peril. While you can save the ten in any of these villages, you can't save the folks in more than one. Selecting a hamlet at random, when going back for help you steal a million dollars, the most you can manage, and you save the randomly selected ten. Again, most respond positively.

Whatever explains our positive response to the Newly Discovered Village must also do that for the Three Villages. So, there can't be much gained by hypothesizing that, in the first case, what prompts a positive judgment is the thought that you'd there prevent all, or most, of the needless serious suffering on earth. For, in the Three Villages, even after you'd done your utmost to lessen suffering, *most* of the relevant folks would *still* suffer the loss of their lives. Well, then, what explains our positive response to the Three Villages?

10. What are only very minor variants of the case just displayed show how very liberating is the thought of living in a perennially decent world. For example, suppose that you're just one of several agents who are each in a position to divert a different magnate's million and, by so doing, to send aid to the ten in the Newly Discovered Village. And, on top of that, suppose that each of you faces a great deal of *uncertainty*: For all you know, *all* the others will steal a million; and, if even as much as just one of them steals a million, your doing so won't help prevent any loss at all. But, also, for all you know, *none* of them will steal; and, then, your stealing will be greatly needed. Faced with this uncertainty, you divert a million dollars, you send jets to the Amazon, but, as it happens, your stealing wasn't needed. Still, as most respond, your conduct was good.

As I'll suggest, most of what's wanted comes with this Liberationist proposition: There's *not so very much* affliction that will occur anyway, no matter what you do, as to make your success seem like a mere drop from an ocean of misery. In our jargon, those cases don't prompt your futility thinking. So, not only *is* there strong moral reason in the Three Villages, but it also *seems* there's strong moral reason to steal a million bucks and save ten lives.

How good is that Liberationist explanation? With our sequence's last case, we'll see it may be quite good: In the *Three Hundred Newly Discovered Villages,* you discover just so many hurting hamlets in the deepest Amazon, each with ten in peril. Again, you can save only the ten in one. Randomly selecting a hamlet, by stealing a million bucks, you save the town's ten; but, within the month, nearly 3000 others die of the disease.[11] Especially when it's the *first case confronted* of our sequence's salient sort, to its stealing behavior most respond negatively. By Liberationists, that's expected: With about 3000 soon dying no matter what you do, just ten lives doesn't seem like much, not nearly enough to call for stealing substantial sums.

10. The Liberationist Solution of This Puzzle and What It Means for Related Puzzles

By now, we've seen enough to embrace the idea that, for resolving our puzzle about taking what's rightfully another's, we want a Liberationist solution: Even as the Yacht's conduct is good behavior, so is the Account's. And, we've also seen enough to think the same holds for more comprehensive puzzles, like the one encountered in section 3: Not only is the Small Marina's conduct good behavior, but so is the conduct in the Complex Account. More generally, much of what the chapter's shown can be put like this: When needed to lessen the serious suffering of innocent enough people, it's morally *good* to engage in what's typically *objectionable* conduct, like lying, promise-breaking, cheating, stealing, and so on.

11. With nearly 3000 youngsters dying in the month, some might say that, with this example, we've left the realm of perennially decent worlds. If one wants to use those words in that very restrictive way, that's quite all right with me; none of my points depend on any less restrictive usage. Though not important do so, I'll say something for a less restrictive use of "perennially decent world." In a typical month in the actual world, over a million children needlessly die and, of course, 3000 is just a small fraction of just one percent of a million. While I could say other supportive things, it would be wasteful to dwell on this matter.

Toward making morally important changes in our behavior, that's not nearly as important, of course, as the fact that this chapter's main lessons greatly raise confidence in the Liberationist solution to the previous chapter's main puzzle: Not only is the Sedan's conduct horrible, but so is the Envelope's.

4

BETWEEN SOME ROCKS
AND SOME HARD PLACES:
ON CAUSING AND PREVENTING
SERIOUS LOSS

In order to lessen the number of people who'll die very prematurely, you needn't cause anyone any serious loss, and you certainly needn't cause anybody to lose her life. Indeed, all you need do is send money to UNICEF, or to OXFAM, or, for that matter, to CARE, whose address you also now know:

CARE
151 Ellis Street, N.E.
Atlanta, GA 30303

From this chapter's first paragraph, most get what, for the bulk of our adult lives, is the most important moral message we need.

As inquisitive philosophers, however, we're interested in going beyond what helps us to see the great moral importance of following that advice. Indeed, with our discussion of stealing and other appropriations, in the prior chapter we did a fair amount, though not a great amount, toward satisfying our interest in extensively searching moral inquiry. But, so far, the discussion's been limited to cases where, to lessen serious suffering overall, you had to impose on others only slight losses and, certainly, not any serious loss. In the present chapter, we'll go well beyond that limitation.

Seeking further domains in which Liberationism might prove enlightening, I'll address the question of what you ought to do in the event, however unlikely, of facing an *ethically serious causal conflict*: Between a rock and a hard place, there you can lessen the serious losses that befall folks overall only if you increase, perhaps upward from none at all, the serious losses for some innocent others. About this question, too, I'll argue for some ambitious Liberationist propositions. While that's important for the whole Liberationist case, my main concern is to prepare for a close Liberationist look, in chapter 6, at how costly it is, for well-off folks in a perennially rotten world, to lead morally decent lives.

Here's why work on the present task can be useful for that central inquiry, best attempted only later: Often, it's much harder to account for our responses to cases of ethically serious causal conflict than to do that for the reactions we've already explained. The reason for that may be expressed, roughly but well enough, like this: In explaining our reactions to the previous two chapters' examples, we did well just by disclosing the work done by the negative subjective factor(s) of our fallacious futility thinking, and by observing how some positive subjective factors can break the grip of futility thinking. By contrast, when responding to cases of ethically serious causal conflicts, not only are we affected by factors of those two sorts, but we're powerfully misled by many other distortional factors.

Because they're both so numerous and very varied, we won't try to identify all of, or even most of, these other factors. Rather, we'll concentrate on observing those few that are most centrally powerful. As it will develop, when those observations are effectively employed, that's enough to make credible this chapter's Liberationist conclusions about the infliction of serious losses on others. And, looking yet further ahead, this will be the situation: Through an appreciation of distorting factors we'll soon see to be central, we'll be best able to comprehend, in chapter 6, how costly it is for us to live morally decent lives. That's why the work we'll now do bears strongly on the book's central moral propositions.

Before developing the chapter's argument, which rightly will be highly indirect, I ought to voice some sensibly cautionary thoughts: With almost all ordinary people, like you and me, it almost never happens that, for folks' serious suffering to be lessened overall, we must make some folks suffer seriously. So, in our everyday lives, we *shouldn't* bring serious losses to others. With that in mind, we may be as bold in our moral inquiry as we are harmless in our social behavior.

1. A Puzzle about Causing and Preventing Serious Loss

Among cases where you face serious causal conflicts, the most straightforward are those where you'll cause serious loss to befall some folks while, at the same time, you'll prevent serious loss from befalling others. As I'll conveniently refer to them, these are the cases of *causing and preventing serious loss.*

By presenting two of these cases, I aim to pose another instructive puzzle. Here's one:

> *The Foot.* In the park outside your window, there's a man reading the sports pages. In homes bordering the park, there are sixty neighbors who, just because they were bitten by certain rats and through no fault of their own, have contracted a fatal disease. Now, if you *do nothing about* the situation, your *first* option, then, in a couple of days, these sixty will die from their disease. So, on this first option, you'll let the sixty die. Still, you have *precisely one other option*: Because he has a certain very rare body chemistry, a life-saving antidote can be made from only a foot's worth of the reader in the park. (Now, you may first ask this man to give up a foot for the neighbors. But, saying that he's no hero, he'll decline.) On this other option, after rendering the reader unconscious, you push a button and, with your trusty laser knife, you slice off one of the man's feet, say, his left foot. After liquefying the free foot, you inject a sixtieth of the product into each of the neighbors. So, on your second option, you'll save sixty and you'll make one have just a single foot for the rest of his own long life. On reflection, you choose this second option and, in consequence, the sixty are prevented from dying.

And, the other's a minor variant of some well-known cases[1]:

---

1. Among the famous cases, it's Judith Thomson's *Bystander at the Switch* to which my Trolley is most similar. For that case, see her paper, "The Trolley Problem," *The Yale Law Journal*, 1985; in Fischer and Ravizza's anthology, it appears on page 281. Bystander at the Switch is similar to a case Thomson presented years earlier, namely, case (6) in her "Killing, Letting Die, and the Trolley Problem," *The Monist*, 1976, appearing on pages 70–71 in the noted anthology. As Thomson clearly acknowledges, it's Philippa Foot who's the mother of, or by now maybe the grandmother of, the many trolley cases

The Trolley. By sheer accident, an empty trolley, nobody aboard, is starting to roll down a certain track. Now, if you *do nothing about* the situation, your *first* option, then, very soon, it will run over and kill six innocents who, through no fault of their own, are trapped down the line. (They've been tied down by a mustachioed villain.) So, on your first option, you'll let the six die. Still, you have *precisely one other option*: If you push a remote control button, then you'll change the position of a certain switch-track and, before it gets to the six, the trolley will roll onto another line. Now, on this other line, there's another who's similarly trapped and, if switched, the trolley will roll over her. So, on your second option, you'll save six lives and you'll take one. On reflection, you choose this second option and, in consequence, the six are prevented from dying.

As with our prior pairs of puzzle cases, we'll understand these, too, in conformity with our instructions to be boring and to take motivation, insofar as is possible, to be parallel. What's more, with these new cases, as well as others soon upcoming, it's almost automatically that we'll also suppose that, to you, the agent, the needs of all the featured folks are highly salient, and their trouble is very dramatic.

As most respond to the Foot, your conduct was seriously wrong. But, consistent with what's found in the literature, to the Trolley most respond that your conduct's good behavior. So, going by our responses to the cases, the Foot's conduct is far worse than the Trolley's.

Now, let's hear from our moral common sense: What's morally most weighty is how much you (knowingly) lessened, and how much you (knowingly) increased, the serious losses suffered. As far as lessening goes, you did much better in the Foot, where you saved fully sixty, than in the Trolley, with only six saved. And, as far as increasing goes, again it's much better in the Foot, where you made someone lose just a foot, than in the fatal Trolley. Regarding this sensibility's weightiest factors, then, since the Foot's conduct fares *enormously much better* than the Trolley's, it certainly isn't worse.

To be sure, there also are these differences: In the Foot you're *using* the sports fan in a way that's *seriously harmful to him,* and in the Trolley you *aren't* using the person you kill, not in any way at all. So, by

---

in the literature. Foot's first trolley case appeared, I believe, in her "The Problem of Abortion and the Doctrine of the Double Effect," *Oxford Review,* 1967. Aptly, Foot's piece is the lead paper in the anthology. But, even as my Trolley case ultimately derives from that stimulating thinker, my case of the Foot is, I think, completely independent of Professor Foot.

contrast with the silly attempt to invoke such a thing in chapter 3, here it's *not silly* to invoke a Doctrine of Double Effect. But, though that might do *something* for the Trolley's conduct, our common sense allows, it won't do very much, not near as much as what's here wanted: In *both* cases, you *knew full well* what serious losses your conduct would mean for innocent people; just as you *knew full well* that in the Foot your conduct would mean an innocent person's losing *one of his feet* (in the process of saving many others' lives), you also *knew full well* that in the Trolley your conduct would mean an innocent person's losing *his very life* (in the process of saving some others' lives).

The puzzle posed by the Foot and the Trolley parallels the central puzzles of the previous chapters. Again, Preservationists will shrug their shoulders at the puzzle. Since such complacency thwarts hard work, it's again unlikely we'll learn much by following that lead. At all events, by the end of the chapter, we'll see good reason to embrace the Liberationist solution to its puzzle: Just as the Trolley's conduct is good, so is the conduct in the Foot.

2. The Method of Several Options

As with almost all the examples in the literature, in both the Trolley and the Foot, the agent has only two options. And, as with virtually all the literature's *two-option cases,* in both the Trolley and the Foot, one of the options is *passive,* where the agent "does nothing about the situation." In the past few years, I've devised many radically new two-option cases. As my experience with even the most novel of them indicates, it's likely that the insight to be gained from such limited cases will itself forever remain quite limited. So, there's reason to explore some *several-option cases,* examples where an agent has more than two options, and where she must have at least two active options.

In the area of causing and preventing serious loss, while I've always managed to keep the number well below ten, I've constructed many cases with three options, many with four, and many with more. No friend of complexity, I've explored more complex cases only when simpler ones promoted many more problems than insights. So, with a diagram for the example, it's in that spirit that I exhibit[2]:

2. When thinking about a several-option case, often I've found it useful to draw a diagram for the example, whether on scratch-paper, or on a blackboard, or whatever. With some of the several-option cases upcoming, I encourage the reader to do that.

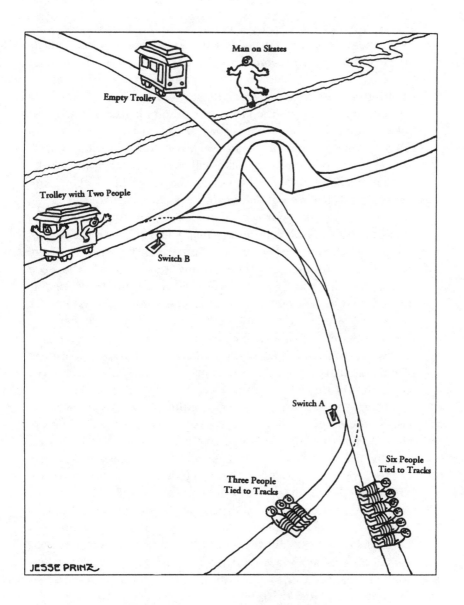

Man on Skates

Empty Trolley

Trolley with Two People

Switch B

Switch A

Six People
Tied to Tracks

Three People
Tied to Tracks

JESSE PRINZ

Diagram for the Switches and Skates

The Switches and Skates. By sheer accident, an empty trolley, no-body aboard, is starting to roll down a certain track. Now, if you *do nothing about* the situation, your *first* option, then, in a couple of minutes, it will run over and kill six innocents who, through no fault of their own, are trapped down the line. (So, on your first option, you'll let the six die.) Regarding their plight, you have *three other* options: On your *second option*, if you push a remote control button, you'll change the position of a switch-track, switch A, and, before it gets to the six, the trolley will go onto another line, on the left-hand side of switch A's fork. On that line, three other inno-cents are trapped and, if you change switch A, the trolley will roll over them. (So, on your second option, you'll save six lives and you'll take three.) On your *third option*, you'll flip a remote control toggle and change the position of another switch, switch B. Then, a very light trolley that's rolling along another track, the Feed Track, will shift onto B's lower fork. As two pretty heavy people are trapped in this light trolley, after going down this lower fork the vehicle won't only collide with the onrushing empty trolley, but, owing to the combined weight of its unwilling passengers, the collision will derail the first trolley and both trolleys will go into an uninhabited area. Still, the two trapped passengers will die in the collision. On the other hand, if you don't change switch B, the lightweight trolley will go along B's upper fork and, then, it will bypass the empty trolley, and its two passengers won't die soon. (So, on your third option, you'll save six lives and you'll take two.) Finally, you have a *fourth option*: Further up the track, near where the trolley's starting to move, there's a path crossing the main track and, on it, there's a very heavy man on roller skates. If you turn a remote control dial, you'll start up the skates, you'll send him in front of the trolley, and he'll be a trolley-stopper. But, the man will be crushed to death by the trolley he then stops. (So, on your fourth option, you'll save six lives and you'll take one.) On reflec-tion, you choose this fourth option and, in consequence, the six are prevented from dying.

To this moderately complex case, most react that your conduct was good behavior.

In this four-option example, you *used* someone much *more harm-fully* than you used the Foot's sports fan. But, unlike with the Foot, with the Switches and Skates our intuition is quite the positive judg-ment our moral common sense delivers. This greatly enhances the puzzle of the Trolley and the Foot and, though not so greatly, it suggests that the puzzle's solution lies along Liberationist lines.

3. The Deletion and Addition of Options Spells the Fall of Preservationism

Already, you may be somewhat interested in what I'll call the *Method of Several Options*. In this section, I want to generate more interest in this fruitful method.

By deleting from the four-option Switches and Skates both its middle options, we get a two-option case that's intriguingly similar to some well-known examples.[3] So, now, we'll "pretend to forget" the Switches and Skates and, "starting from scratch," we'll think of only:

> *The Heavy Skater.* By sheer accident, an empty trolley, nobody aboard, is starting to roll down a certain track. Now, if you *do nothing about* the situation, your *first* option, then, in a couple of minutes, it will run over and kill six innocents who, through no fault of their own, are trapped down the line (just beyond an "elbow" in the track). (So, on your first option, you'll let the six die.) Regarding their plight, you have *one other* option: Further up the track, near where the trolley's starting to move, there's a path crossing the main track and, on it, there's a very heavy man on roller skates. If you turn a remote control dial, you'll start up the skates, you'll send him in front of the trolley, and he'll be a trolley-stopper. But, the man will be crushed to death by the trolley he then stops. (So, on your second option, you'll save six lives and you'll take one.) On reflection, you choose this second option and, in consequence, the six are prevented from dying.

Especially when there's no thought of the likes of the Switches and Skates, most make the very negative response that, in the Heavy Skater, your conduct was terribly wrong.

---

3. Perhaps most notably, there is Thomson's *Fat Man* that, like her Bystander at the Switch, is presented in her "The Trolley Problem." With just a number, not a name, years earlier the same example, or an extraordinarily similar scenario, is presented as case (7) in her "Killing, Letting Die and the Trolley Problem." For sources for both papers, see this chapter's first note.

An IMPORTANT METHODOLOGICAL MESSAGE. Though there was reason to bring up the matter long before, here's the best place to note the effect of the *order in which cases are presented* on our responses to the cases. Long examined by psychologists, but longer ignored by philosophers, the response someone makes to a given example can be greatly influenced by (her memory of) responses made to cases previously encountered. And, since folks want their responses to seem consistent, often the influence is greatest when the present case seems "essentially the same" as the just previous example. Here, the present two-option case seems essentially the same as the just previous four-option example; so, our having responded positively to the Switches and Skates greatly influences us to respond positively, as well, to the Heavy Skater. So, for a negative response to the two-option case, there's a strong tendency for the reader to overcome. Many will overcome it, but many others won't. By the same token, had readers confronted the Heavy Skater *first*, there'd be a strong tendency, overcome by many but not by many others, to respond *negatively*, as well, to the four-option Switches and Skates. So, to get decent data, I've given different people different presentational orders.[4] **End of the MESSAGE.**[5]

Despite such obfuscation as comes from presentational order, the results found here are plenty clear enough to be striking: When we take the Heavy Skater and *add* those two "middle" options, we obtain, of course, the Switches and Skates. And, to this "expanded" case, we respond that, quite beyond being all right, your sending in the big guy is good! Conversely, when we take the Switches and Skates and *delete* the two middle options, we obtain the Heavy Skater. And, to this "contracted" case, we react that, far from being good, sending in the big guy is seriously wrong![6] What sense can we make of this strangely enormous disparity in our responses to the cases?

4. This is one reason I tried to join forces with an experimental psychologist. For a note about that, see chapter 2's note 7.

5. At all events, the discrepant phenomena stemming from different presentational order are an embarrassment to Preservationism. Of course, if this were the Preservationist's worst problem, her view wouldn't be in such bad shape. But, as we've already seen several times over, and as we'll soon see much more clearly, the Preservationist has far, far worse problems.

6. Though it certainly doesn't obtain with all ethically sensitive respondents, a fair number, myself included, find these fluctuating reactions to obtain, time after time, despite the effects of presentational order. In this respect, our experience here is quite like what we've had with many (only) moderately effective optical illusions.

Not just according to our moral common sense, but, to any good sense, it's absolutely absurd to think there's *any* moral difference between the one case's conduct and the other's. If possible, it's even more absurd to think there's such an *enormous* difference. As my experience has made clear, this is a staggering blow to Preservationism and, barring the use of gratuitous or *ad hoc* repairs, it's all but fatal to the view. With no wish to drag you through very many words, I'll try briefly to explain.

Nothing could be further from an isolated instance than the awful disparity we've just confronted. Just so, there are an *infinite number* of case-pairs that each promote the same surprise: To the two-option case, our intuitive reaction's that the loss-lessening conduct's badly wrong. And, to the several-option counterpart case, our response, to the very same behavior as before, is that the conduct is morally good! Nor is this an infinity that's generated within narrow limits; to the contrary, these startling case-pairs comprise an indefinitely wide variety of morally interesting examples. (For very different case-pairs in the enormously wide infinity, the reader need only go further into the book.) So, what the Preservationist must claim is (not merely that there's a big moral difference between your conduct in our two displayed cases, where there seems to be none, but) that there's a *big* moral difference in *each of an enormously wide infinity* of case-pairs, in each of which there *seems to be no* moral difference at all.

Though it's now just barely possible, for Preservationism things directly go from extremely bad to even worse. As with every case-pair in our enormously wide infinity, nothing less than this happens with the troublesome couple I selected to display: In addition to the (discrepant) responses noted, well called *first-order* intuitions on the cases, there's another moral intuition on the two examples. Most marked with those who initially see the cases at once, side by side, it's a *comparative* assessment of their conduct, well called a *second-order* intuition on the examples[7]: To the pair taken together, all react that the Heavy Skater's conduct is *morally the same as* the Switches and Skates'.

With presentational order's effect properly placed aside, the total pattern of moral responses to these examples, including both first- and

7. Along with some ideas indicating its fruitful use, this nomenclature is introduced in "First-Order Intuitions and Second-Order Intuitions," which is section 6 of chapter 3 of my *Identity, Consciousness and Value*, Oxford University Press, 1990. In that place, the notion is employed in exploring certain issues in metaphysics, more particularly, certain issues about personal identity. On page 88 I said, "Indeed, it would be rather surprising if these ideas had little bearing on the proper treatment of examples in moral philosophy." As we now see, there's no such surprise.

second-order intuitions, is an instructively disturbing pattern: Even while the two first-order intuitions strongly conflict with each other, with one quite positive and the other clearly negative, the second-order intuition strongly conflicts with the very idea that, in the first place, there's *any* moral difference between your conduct in the two cases, let alone one that's so enormous.

All that's great grist for the Liberationist's mill.[8] But, for the Preservationist, there's an absolutely insoluble problem here. A completely untenable position, it turns out that Preservationism's no real alternative to Liberationism. Now, perhaps there's a view that, while not nearly as pure as Preservationism itself, somehow affirms only what's best in the spirit of that utterly hopeless position. At any rate, for expository and heuristic purposes, sometimes we might "make like" there is such a view and, so, I'll offer a name. To show how humble are its origins, I'll just make a change in spelling, leaving pronunciation alone. Thus, insofar as they can be said to have a position, those (almost) always taking our moral responses to cases at face value will be said to favor *Preservashonism*.

4. The Liberation Hypothesis and the Fanaticism Hypothesis

Boldly but sensibly, let's first articulate, and let's then evaluate, some clearly competing hypotheses about what's generating those disturbingly disparate first-order intuitions. At a key level of explanation, there are two leading candidates. Though both are vaguely framed, we can see them to contrast markedly:

(1) *The Liberation Hypothesis.* In addition to being influenced by our Basic Moral Values, often our moral intuitions on cases are affected by contrary psychological factors. While our Values encourage us to respond positively to conduct that clearly does most to lessen the serious loss befalling innocent others, often these contrary factors *inhibit* us from, or *constrain* us from, responding in that way. Indeed, often their influence is so great as to have us respond negatively. But, in certain several-option cases, there's material that *liberates* us from the influence of the constraining factors. And, by doing that, it *allows us to* respond positively to such loss-minimizing conduct, in accord with our Values.

8. Even to the hapless Negativist, whose wildly implausible view appears in a few footnotes, this comes as a bit of good news. As it turns out, in some sense at least, Preservationism's a less worthy alternative to Liberationism than preposterous Negativism. For a reminder about Negativism, it's obliquely introduced in note 17 to chapter 1.

(2) *The Fanaticism Hypothesis.* While certain of our Values encourage us to respond positively to conduct that does most to lessen the serious loss befalling innocent others, they're not the most central of our Basic Moral Values. Far more central are Values that ground highly constraining prohibitions against, among other things, seriously harming innocent others. So, in the several-option cases that prompt us to respond positively to conduct that (though it clearly does most to lessen the serious loss suffered) is seriously harmful conduct, it's *not* any liberating material, but it's only *morally disorienting* material, that's influencing our responses: Even as it detaches our intuitive moral thinking from our most central Values, the material has us be *fanatical* in our assessments of such loss-lessening but harmful conduct. And, by doing that, it *prevents us from* responding negatively to such harmful conduct, in accord with our Values.[9]

Toward seeing the contrast between these two hypotheses, recall the Switches and Skates. With its two "middle" options working effectively, that complex case promoted a positive assessment of your seriously harmful, but clearly loss-lessening, trolley-stopping behavior. Now, on the Liberation Hypothesis, this positive reaction is *in perfect accord with* our Basic Moral Values. By contrast, on the Fanaticism Hypothesis, the positive response is *in strong opposition to* these Values.

Which of the hypotheses figures in the better account of our puzzling pattern of response? At least to my mind, so far the Liberation Hypothesis holds a small edge. With further inquiry, will the edge disappear, or will it increase? In brief compass, here's some reason to expect an increase: Consider a small variant of the Heavy Skater, the *Heavy Skater's Foot*. In this case, all that's needed to stop the trolley is to interpose one of the big guy's feet so that, even as it's crushed off in the process, it serves to stop the vehicle. Much as with the original Heavy Skater, to this case, too, most first respond that it's badly wrong to send in the big guy. Is this negative judgment mainly generated by our Values?

By this point in our inquiry, many will suspect not. And, to further their suspicion, we need only consider the parallel small variant of the Switches and Skates, a *four-option* case where all that's needed to stop the trolley is the destructively crushing interposition of one foot of the heavy skater's. As almost all respond to this example, that's good to do.

9. Holding we do better to rely on responses to apt several-option cases than on reactions to their troublesome two-option counterparts, Liberationists endorse the Liberation Hypothesis. Holding that such Liberationists are morally no better than a bunch of fanatics, Preservashonists, let's heuristically say, endorse the competing conjecture.

Now, it's very, very plausible to hold that, with *this* several-option case, where what's taken is nobody's life but just someone's foot, there's (middle option) material that liberates us from the distortional stuff the case shares with its noted two-option counterpart, the Heavy Skater's Foot; much the same, it's far, far less plausible to hold *this* several-option example's additional (middle option) material gets us to respond as would an insensitive loss-lessening fanatic. But, there's no psychologically significant difference between how we're differentially affected by the two cases in this foot-featuring pair and, in the first instance, how we're differentially affected by the couple of cases where, to save six down the line, a skater's very life is taken. So, though we need to investigate much further, already we've reason to prefer the Liberation Hypothesis to the Fanaticism Hypothesis.

Clearer every minute, the conflict between the two conjectures has big implications for our puzzle of the Foot and the Trolley: As the Fanaticism Hypothesis urges, the best solution has the Foot's conduct be badly wrong; but, as the Liberation Hypothesis urges, the best solution has it be morally good.

5. Projective Separating and Projective Grouping

In deciding between the hypotheses, two main courses may be followed. In the chapter, I'll follow the one focused on thoughts favoring the Liberation Hypothesis. In the chapter's appendix, I'll follow the course focusing on thoughts favoring the Fanaticism Hypothesis.[10] As I'll there make clear, that other course is filled with futility.[11]

10. Well, since it places a proper perspective on the chapter itself, there's one form of the Fanaticism Hypothesis, the Numeric Form, that's usefully exposed at this early stage: When confronting those disorienting middle options, we're goaded into simply "going for the numbers;" it's just in that way that we're prevented from responding in accord with our Values. Unfortunately for the Numeric Form, we find the very same results when respondents confront apt multi-option cases where, on every single alternative, exactly one person's up for suffering a serious loss. Aptly paralleling the four-option case I've displayed, there's the *Non-numeric Switches and Skates*. Here, if you do nothing, the empty trolley will kill just *one* person (or, on a variant, it will take off both his legs). If you change switch A, that trolley will take off a whole leg, and also the other leg's foot, from the *one* guy who's "overlappingly" tied down to A's other track. If you change B, the *one* heavy passenger, in the light trolley, will lose just one whole leg in the derailing collision. But, you send in the heavy skater, and just a foot is lost. To this non-numeric case, most respond positively. Yielding similar results, many of the chapter's numeric cases have nice non-numeric variants.

11. Except to the most extreme Preservashonists, I doubt that those undermining arguments will be very interesting, however correct and cogent they may be. Largely, that's why they've been relegated to an appendix.

Toward showing how much explanatory power flows from the Liberation Hypothesis, I'll first observe how certain negative highly subjective factors, well placed under the head *projective separating,* serve to generate distorted moral responses to many particular cases. Then, I'll note that their positive counterparts, well placed under the head *projective grouping,* serve to liberate us from the sway of such pervasively distorting influences.

With a few vaguely framed speculations, I'll try to begin the job by striking chords deep within your mind: Divorced from morally relevant considerations, often we view the world as comprising just certain *situations.* Likewise, we view a situation as including just *certain people,* all of them then well grouped together within it; and, then, viewing all the world's *other folks* as being only in *other situations,* we view all of them as being *separate from* the folks in the first situation's group. Also dissociated from morality, often we view a certain serious problem as being a *problem for* only those folks viewed as being (grouped together) in a particular situation; and, then, we'll view the bad trouble as *not* any problem for all the world's other people. As with the world, so, too, with particular cases, both actual and hypothetical: Though not with all examples, with many we view some of the case's people to be in one situation, having that situation's problem, and view its other folks as beyond the purview of that horrid problem.

All too often, such projective separating serves to promote badly distorted moral reactions. In very general terms, here's why: When viewing just certain people as having the problem of what's taken to be just their situation, we tend to think that it's badly wrong to spare them the serious losses that might stem from *their* problem by imposing serious loss on *other* people, who *don't have that* problem. And, we tend to judge such impositions harshly, even when the number of these *other* people is *much smaller,* perhaps just one, and even when the *greatest* loss suffered by any of them is *much less* than the *least* loss that would be suffered by anyone who *has that* problem. But, those harsh judgments don't properly reflect our Values, much less morality itself. Rather, the wholesale assigning of people to situations, and the assigning of problems to people, hasn't any moral significance.[12]

By observing our response to an example, we may much better understand the thrust of those lofty speculations and, with luck, we might begin to confirm them:

12. Now, even quite often, we may make only such separations of folks into different groups as *are* morally appropriate. For instance, this may happen when we separate some vicious torturers from their innocent victims. But, of course, I'm addressing the many cases where there's clearly no moral ground anywhere around.

The Yard. Having started by sheer accident, an empty trolley is barreling down a track. Now, if you *do nothing about* the situation, your *first* option, then it will soon run over and kill six innocents who, through no fault of their own, are trapped down the line. (So, on your first option, you'll let the six die.) Regarding their plight, you have *one other* option: If you flip a remote control toggle, you'll change the position of a switch. Then, another heavy empty trolley will go onto the switch's lower fork and, instead of passing each other, there'll be a collision where both trolleys are derailed; they'll go down a hill, across a road, and into someone's yard, where they'll wreak fatal havoc on the yard's owner, asleep in his hammock, as well as many of his bushes. (So, on your second option, you'll save six lives and you'll take one.) On reflection, you choose this second option and, in consequence, the six are prevented from dying.

Especially with no presentational order to overcome, here most respond that your conduct was wrong.

With the Trolley, we respond positively to your deflecting conduct; with the Yard, we respond negatively. What explains the disparity? A lot of it's this: As he's down the hill, and across the road, and in his own yard, we see the Yard's napper not to be involved with the likes of tracks and their trolleys; so, we see him to be in a different situation from the six up the hill and on the track. So, we view the problem posed by a runaway trolley as only a problem for them, and not for him. So, we don't see the guy in his yard as "fair enough game" for a solution to the problem facing the six others.

As might be thought, with the Yard our positive response stems from a factor that's morally significant: The person killed was on *his own property.* But, common sense directs that won't have the Yard's conduct be worse than the Trolley's, let alone much worse. And, that's indicated by our reactions to the Yard's most instructive variants, like:

The Small Missile. Six Innocents are trapped on a certain trolley track that, not theirs, is owned by a conglomerate. As the company left that business long ago, trolleys don't run there anymore. Down the hill from this track, and across the road, there's someone in his own backyard, sleeping in his hammock. Accidentally, one of the army's very small missiles has been launched. If you *do nothing*, your *first* option, the missile will land where the six are and, upon impact, it will kill them. (So, on your first option, you'll let the six die.) Regarding their plight, you have *one other* option:

By pushing a remote control button, you can reroute this missile, but only in a certain way. Now, if you thus deflect it, then the missile will land in the noted yard and, upon impact, not only will it kill the yard's owner, but it will destroy his entire house and yard, full of furniture and bushes, respectively, but empty of other people. (So, on your second option, you'll save six lives and you'll take one.) On reflection, you choose this second option and, in consequence, the six are prevented from dying.

Sensibly, most respond that your conduct was good.

No concern about property rights, it's clear, did much to generate our negative response to the Yard.[13] Rather, _along with other_ factors, the fact that he was in his own yard encouraged us to _view the napper as separate from_ the six others. So, as we then viewed that case's people, the six had a terrible problem, which was just their problem, while the man in his hammock hadn't so much as a care in the world. Since we didn't view him as "fair enough game" for resolving what was a problem only for them, we responded negatively to your (resolving their problem in a way that involved) killing him.

Happy with that explanation, when noting a complementary account of the Small Missile, we'll be happier still: Partly because the projectile's high up in the air, and partly because it came from a source distant from them all, and partly for other morally irrelevant reasons, we don't see the missile as "strongly associated with" _any_ of the noted folks on the ground. So, though the missile more directly presents a problem for the six, that problem seems assignable enough to the one in his yard. Almost as much as each of them, he's seen as "fair enough game" for solving a problem that's "common enough" for them all. So, since there are six of them but just one of him, not only _is_ it true that, but it even _seems_ true that, the best solution is to make sure it's just him who's killed.

In a more complex way, much the same happened with the Switches and Skates. As our experience with the Heavy Skater showed, without the people in that case's middle options, it's very hard to group the skater, who's not on any track, but only on a path off to the side, together with the six tied to a currently dangerous track. But, with apt

---

13. Though much less instructive, it's worth noting that the "property rights ploy" receives lots of static even from relevant variants of the Trolley. Suppose that the one tied down on the fork's left-hand side, by the mustachioed villain, is the owner of that track (and, if you like, he's also the trolley's owner). As most rightly respond to this variant, you act well when you turn the trolley away from the six and onto the man who owns the track.

"intermediaries" available, we're helpfully encouraged to project a group whose members extend from the six on that track all the way to the single skater off to the side: (a) Partly because the six are on one side of a certain switch-track and the three are on the other side of that very same switch, we readily group the three with the six, thus projecting a group of nine. (Then, any of those nine is seen as "fair enough game" for the morally best solution of the problem that's so salient.) (b) Partly because they're involved with the same network of tracks as are those nine, and partly because both they and three of the nine are susceptible to death from trolley-involvement via just the change of a switch, we readily group the light trolley's two heavy passengers together with our projected nine and, so, we project a group of eleven people. (Then, any of those eleven is seen as "fair enough game" for best resolving the salient problem.) (c) Partly because he's also on wheels, partly because his whereabouts also can be determined by a remote control device, partly because he's also a heavy guy, and partly because those three facts also make him useful for preventing the empty trolley from killing folks tied down on the tracks, we readily group the heavy skater with the eleven's two heavy passengers and, so, finally we project a group of fully twelve people. Thus it is that, by encouraging us to be properly inclusive, this four-option case's material lets us see the heavy skater as the best solution to the moral problem posed by the moderately complex example, and lets us respond accordingly.

For having all its options helpfully specified and organized, the Switches and Skates lets us see that every single person whom the example's agent might affect has an equal ethical claim on her conduct. So, we're enabled to see that, for her to do best at rightly respecting each of the case's "patients", and for her to do best at according each of them all his weighty moral rights and claims, the agent must have it that there occurs what's, by far, the least serious suffering overall. But, it's not nearly often enough, I think, that we confront material that's so helpful toward seeing the true moral order of things. So, because we projectively separate some folks from others, it's much too often that some seem to have an enormous moral claim on our conduct while others seem to have hardly any at all.[14]

14. Compare the Liberationist approach with such occasionally brilliant, but perhaps wastefully brilliant, Preservashonist essays as Robert Hanna's "Morality *De Re*: Reflections on the Trolley Problem," in Fischer and Ravizza's *Ethics: Problems and Principles,* 1992, and Frances M. Kamm's "Harming Some to Save Others," *Philosophical Studies,* 1989. As I think you'll eventually agree, such wonderfully clever works show how, when it's wedded to a misguided methodology, much philosophical intelligence

In the chapter so far, I've placed six cases in display. With which did we confront so much liberating material that, rather than projectively separating, we engaged in good projective grouping? To a great extent, that happened with the Trolley and, in the present section, with the Small Missile. Not quite as much, but impressively still, it occurred with the Switches and Skates. By contrast, it didn't happen much with the Heavy Skater or, in this section, with the Yard. Finally, at the very bottom of the list, there's the Foot, where we engaged only in strong projective separating.

To a great degree, it was due to our projectively separating him so strongly from the neighbors that, in the Foot, we couldn't see the sports fan as "fair enough game" for a decent solution to a terrible problem that, as we viewed the case, was a problem only for them, not his at all. Now, with this, we've come a long way toward seeing how the solution of the chapter's puzzle lies with Liberationism. What's more striking, however, is the thought that, after another section or two like this, there won't remain any real contest between the fruitful Liberation Hypothesis and the conflicting Fanaticism Hypothesis.

6. Protophysics and Pseudoethics

Besides projective separating, many factors distort our responses to cases of ethically serious causal conflict. In this section, the focus will be on the peculiarly powerful factors of *protophysics*.

As our protophysical thinking would have it, there's much moral substance in five principles that not just ethically, but even physically, are absolutely empty: First, when serious loss will result, it's harder to justify moving a person to, or into, an object than it is to move the object to, or into, the person. Second, when serious loss will result, it's harder to justify changing the speed of a moving object, or changing its *rate* of motion, than changing the object's *direction* of motion. Third, when there'll be big loss, it's harder to justify speeding up an object than slowing down an object. Fourth, it's a lot harder to justify taking an object at rest and setting it in motion than to justify taking an object in motion and increasing its speed. Last on this list, a fifth protophysical generalization "explains" many of the instances where, apparently, the previous four fail to hold: Should serious loss result,

---

can be spent without correlative gains in philosophical insight. But, owing to my own biases, am I being unduly judgmental? In the fullness of time, it's others who should make that judgment.

it's harder to justify imposing a substantial force on an object than it is to justify allowing a force already present (just about) everywhere, like gravitation, to work on the object. From a brief discussion of a few examples, you'll get a good feel for these silly ideas.

First, recall the Trolley. In switching the vehicle from a track where six were roped to one with only one tied down, you neither imposed a substantial force on the object in focus, the trolley, nor did you set that object in motion. And, you didn't change in any way, much less did you increase, the object's rate of motion. Rather, you changed only the direction of its motion. Finally, not making anyone move into the object, you merely made the object move into a person. Largely for its featuring such weak protophysical factors, we're free to respond positively to the Trolley's conduct.

Now, recall the Switches and Skates. There's *more* resistance to (thinking well of) changing switch B, and moving people into a harmful object, than to (thinking well of) changing switch A, and merely moving the object into people. But, there's *not very much* more. After all, for overcoming that resistance, it's enough to see that there'll be one less death if you change switch B.[15] So, in our quick intuitive reasoning about the complex case, we'll think that, even as it's better to change switch A than be passive, it's better to change switch B than switch A.

Next, consider two closely related three-option cases, each obtained from the Switches and Skates by deleting one of that example's four options: (1) By deleting just its *third* option, the one with switch B and the lightweight trolley, we obtain *A Switch and a Skater*. In this example, you send in the heavy skater and, by harmfully using him, you kill him and save the six. Here, our response is negative. (2) By deleting just its *fourth* option, the one with the heavy skater, we obtain *Two Switches*. In this other three-option case, you send in the light trolley's two heavy passengers and, by harmfully using them, you kill those *two* and save the six. But, here, our response is *positive*. To thoughtful people, this *pattern* of response is remarkable. What explains these remarkably contrasting responses? As I'll suggest, most of the work's done by protophysical thinking.

15. For simple support of what's in the text, consider this: (1) First, (deleting from the four-option case both alternatives with useful heavy people, there obtains) the very minor variant of the Trolley where, rather than one, three are tied to the opposite track and, taking the active option, you *kill three* and save six. To this case, most respond *positively*. (2) Second, (deleting from the four-option case both the alternative with switch A and the one with the heavy skater, there obtains another two-option case, namely,) *A Single Switch and Two Trolleys;* taking the active option, you *kill two* and save six. To this case, most respond *negatively*.

When sending the passengers into a derailing collision, you were moving people into a harmful object, it's true, not merely moving such an object into people. But, then, you *didn't* go against any of the other noted "protophysical principles." First, you didn't change the speed of, but you changed only the direction of, people already in motion. So, second, you certainly didn't increase the speed of the people. And, third, you didn't take a resting person and put him in motion. By contrast, when sending in the heavy skater, you did even the last, and the worst, of all these "protophysically objectionable" things: You took a person who was at rest and, in a deathly direction, you put him in motion. Our fallacious protophysical thinking has a remarkable influence on our intuitive responses to cases.

But, as our positive response to the Switches and Skates showed, that influence can be overcome. In apt multi-option cases, "intermediate" material can liberate us from our primitive protophysical thinking. (Though their power is hardly unlimited, protophysical factors do have substantial influence. Indeed, that was why, in order to get most to respond positively when confronting our first fatal several-option case, I presented not just one, but two helpful middle options.)

Usefully, we've discussed both the factors of projective separating and those of protophysical thinking. In those discussions, perhaps I created the impression that each family of factors must work on us *independently* of the other. But, in fact, nothing I've said implies anything so simplistic. And, as I'll now make explicit, the psychological situation is actually much more complex. To see part of the picture, again recall the Heavy Skater. There, the only person you might harm was completely at rest. And, it's *partly because* he can become involved in the case's bad problem only by being *set in motion* away from his resting place that it's *so hard to group* the big guy together with the six already embroiled in that problem. So, often, certain distortional factors, like the factors of protophysical thinking, do at least some of their deceptive work *through encouraging the work of other* distortional factors, like the factors of projective separating.

7. A Few Further Funny Factors

While it's foolish to attempt a complete survey of them, it's useful to say a few things about other factors affecting our responses to cases of causing and preventing serious loss.

Featured both in the simple Heavy Skater and in the complex Switches and Skates, recall our awfully heavy guy. As specified, he was on roller skates. And, because they contained a certain device, his skates could be controlled by way of your distant dial. Of course, there was a good reason to specify those details: Wanting a contrast between a two-option case and its several-option counterpart that might prove most instructive, I wanted the number of the latter's middle options to be small. So it was that I chose to base a several-option case on the readily useful Heavy Skater. Let me explain.

Partly because its useful person was on wheels, and partly because you could distantly determine his placement by using a remote control to spin the wheels, with this example it's only *very* hard(!), and not *very*, *very* hard, to think well of your fatally using the big guy. There are many cases where it's harder to think well of your fatally using someone to save six others. And, obviously, here's one that differs from the Heavy Skater only trivially:

> *The Big Push.* Not on roller skates, there's no way for you to move the big guy by remote control. But, since he's standing on a slippery surface, there's a way for you to get the him in front of the trolley in time to save the six: From behind, you can push him onto the track, where he'll be crushed to death in stopping it. On reflection, that's what you do, and the six are spared.

To the Big Push, all untainted respondents react that your conduct was absolutely outrageous. Just so, here it's even harder to think well of your conduct than with the Heavy Skater.

Why the marked difference? While we won't find a complete explanation, of course, citing three new factors does much to explain the disparity.

First, there's this: In the Big Push, you *push someone.* Now, even without the likes of crushing trolleys, those words spell bad news about how to treat another person. In our minds, this may magnify the seriousness of your killing him.[16]

Second, there's this: When somebody pushes someone around, then, typically, and even stereotypically, it's a bad bully who's the agent. So, in the Big Push, your conduct fits a *negative stereotype.* That also gets us to think badly of that behavior. In the Heavy Skater, by contrast, there isn't such a strong mental connection to such a negative stereotype. Indeed, there the "psychologically closest" stereotype may

---

16. Perhaps, it's no coincidence that, in the Foot, this factor's pretty heavily at work. For, there, you *cut off someone's foot.* So, in the Foot, too, a very accessible, very negative description goes to work very quickly.

be the playfully innocent operation of remote control cars by harmless hobbyists, typically, quite nice kids.[17]

Third, with the Heavy Skater, there's quite a fair amount of *psychological distancing* between the agent's "most direct" behavior and, at the other end of the causal chain, the big guy's being crushed to death: As it appears, all you directly do is push a remote button; then, via some radio waves, skate wheels start turning way over there; then, a big guy who's strapped above those turning wheels is moved onto a track where he's crushed to death by a trolley. With the Big Push, there's much less distancing.[18]

Owing both to those and to still further distorting factors, the Big Push's four-option counterpart of the Switches and Skates, with just the same two middle options, doesn't get as many positive responses to its killing conduct as does the Switches and Skates itself. So, for a case that promotes widespread positive response to fatal Pushing conduct, we may need a *five*-option example, with fully three middle options.[19] Again, thus it was that, instead of the likes of the Big Push, I chose to employ the more readily useful Heavy Skater.

None of them morally significant, in this section we've noticed three new funny factors. If I wanted to expand the section enor-

17. Perhaps, it's also no coincidence that, in the Foot, this second factor's also at work. But, note that there it may work only to a moderate degree: First, there *was some* work done; for, there this very negative stereotype is readily applicable: the *knifing of people in parks*. But, second, and spoiling some of that work, there was this: As the knife but was a *laser* knife, we tend to think of *surgery;* and, typically beneficent, surgery provides a *positive stereotype*. But, third, there then also appears this *further negative* stereotype: the *scary fanatical scientist* who physically invades people to carry out his bizarre projects. Spoiling some of the spoiling done by the positive thought of surgery, this serves to reinforce the negative work first mentioned.

18. Perhaps, in the Foot the distancing factor also was at work, even if only modestly. How so? Well, because your knife worked by way of a remote control button, you operated on the sports fan from what even appeared to be *some* distance, even if a very small distance. By contrast, when a steel blade's typically used to slice off a foot from someone else, there's not even a modest amount of such psychological distancing.

19. As a matter of course, the extra option will find its place between the choice where you can send in a light trolley with two usefully heavy trolley-derailers and the one where you can shove in a single massive trolley-stopper. All of them essentially the same, the details of one such additional choice run like this: By using a remote control device, you can send in a single heavy skater who'll then be used fatally to stop the empty trolley. But, when using that remote control, even while you'll activate that big guy's skates, you'll also activate a device that gets a massive metal pole to topple over and slam into the ground. And, on its way to the ground, this pole will slam through, and sever forever, the left leg of yet another individual, distinct from everyone else in all our examples. (So, on this option, while you'll save the six, you'll take not only one person's life but also another's leg.) With the five-option case just sketched, most respond positively to your fatal Pushing conduct.

mously, perhaps I'd observe thirty-three more. Even then, I'd have exhausted little more than your kind patience and my limited intellect. By contrast, one thing I *wouldn't* have exhausted is the many ethically trivial factors that affect our intuitive moral reactions. At all events, let's now take stock: First, in our untutored responses to ethically intriguing examples, often we're strongly influenced by a highly *complex combination* of factors. Second, even when in such highly complex combinations, often the factors having the most psychological influence are those having the least ethical significance. Third, and finally, there's this: To learn a lot about the main moral realities, we needn't always pay much attention to most of, or even to many of, the factors involved in these great complexities. Rather, we may well learn most with a sensibly selective inquiry, aptly balanced and reasoned, into the operation of just a few of the many factors.

8. Using the Method of Combining to Overcome Protophysical Thinking

By exploring examples quite different from any featuring trolleys, we may find far broader confirmation for the Liberation Hypothesis, and for several more specific Liberationist thoughts about projective separating, about protophysical thinking, and so on.

Just as the trolley cases form a family, so do the examples next considered. We'll start with a couple of cases that have a great deal in common, including this: All the people present are enjoying the natural beauty in a great national park in the West of the USA. On a plateau, there's a bomb that's set to explode soon, at which time it will kill anyone then in its vicinity. From a much higher plateau, it's only very indirectly that you can do anything about the impending explosion. Alike in those respects and many others, the two cases are:

The Resting Bomb. Pretty far from a cliff, a bomb is *resting* on a plateau. As it happens, it's resting on a catapult. To get the bomb off the plateau, you must press a remote control button that activates the catapult. If you do this launching, then, even while the twelve on the plateau will be spared, the bomb will go over the cliff and into a deep canyon where, in a minute, it will explode and kill the two people on the canyon's floor. If you don't launch, the bomb will kill the twelve on its plateau. On reflection, you launch and save the twelve, but you kill the two down below.

The Rolling Bomb. Pretty far from a cliff, and parallel to the cliff's edge, a bomb is *rolling* on a plateau. As it happens, it will soon roll over a wide trapdoor. Under the trapdoor, there's a chute that ends in an opening about half way down the cliff. To get the bomb off the plateau, you must wait a few seconds and push a remote control button, which will open the trapdoor. If you do this opening, then, even while the twelve on the plateau will be spared, the bomb will go down the chute and into a deep canyon where, in a minute, it will explode and kill two people on the canyon's floor. If you don't open, the bomb will kill the twelve on its plateau. On reflection, you open and save the twelve, but you kill the two down below.

When confronted only with the Rolling Bomb, very many react to your conduct positively; with the Resting Bomb, not so many. So, it's harder to think well of your fatal launching than your fatal opening.

Reflecting no morally significant difference, the disparity stems from protophysical thinking: In the Resting Bomb, but not in the Rolling Bomb, you impose a great outside force on the bomb and, what's more, you thereby put in motion a harmful object that was at rest. In the Rolling Bomb, you merely affect the course of an object already in motion and, what's more, you *don't* impose any substantial force to do that. Rather, by imposing only a slight impulse, you allow gravitational force, already at work everywhere, to change the direction of a bomb already in motion. (And, while the bomb's rate of motion also is changed, it's only the change in its direction that makes any difference as to who's harmed.)

Toward confirming those thoughts, we should notice that, with the rolling bomb, it's just as easy to think well of your deadly opening conduct with three down in the canyon as it is with only two. For once that's done, we're set to employ another new method for ethics, which complements the Method of Several Options. This is the *Method of (Aptly) Combining.* Thinking to combine aptly the main aspects of both our two-option bomb cases, I'll offer this example with just three options:

The Two Bombs. On a plateau, there are twelve people and two bombs. If *both remain* on the plateau, then, in a minute, each will send a signal to the other, activating and exploding it. In that case, the bombs will kill the twelve. Now, if you do nothing about the situation, your *first* option, you'll let the twelve die. But, you have *two other* options: Only pretty far from one side of the plateau, where there's the First Cliff, one of the bombs is *rolling*. To get it off the plateau, you must wait a few seconds and push a remote control button, which will open the trapdoor on which the bomb then will be rolling. If you open, the bomb will go down a chute and into the First Canyon where, in a minute, it will explode and kill the *three* people on the canyon's floor. (So, on your *second* option, you'll save the twelve, but you'll kill the three.) Finally, there's this option: Only pretty far from the other side of the plateau, where there's the Second Cliff, the second bomb is *resting* on a catapult. To get it off the plateau, you must press a remote control button that activates the catapult. If you launch, the resting bomb will go into the Second Canyon where, in a minute, it will explode and kill the two people on that canyon's floor. (So, on your *third* option, you'll save the twelve, but kill the two.) On reflection, you choose this third option and, in consequence, the twelve are prevented from dying.

To your conduct in this case, most react positively. Nicely, that confirms our Liberationist suggestion.

9. Using the Method of Combining to Overcome Projective Separating

Based on material from previous sections, I'll now aim to construct cases useful for solving the chapter's central riddle, the puzzle about the Trolley and the Foot. With the Foot much in mind, first I'll construct this two-option example well suited for use with the Method of Combining:

The Leg. While here much is the same as in the Two Bombs, there are crucial differences: You *can't remove either* of the two bombs from the lower plateau. Rather, your only option to letting the twelve die from exploding bombs lies here: Near you on the higher plateau, a man is reading a nature magazine. Because he has a certain rare body chemistry, should that much of him, when well liquefied, come in contact with the resting bomb, a leg's worth of him will render that bomb totally inoperative. So, if that soon happens, then, since there won't be any signals sent between the two bombs, *neither* will explode and the twelve will be spared. But, how so? Using your laser knife, you must slice off one of this reader's legs and, liquefying it in your portable blender, you must place the product in a balloon. At hand, there's a chute running right to where the resting bomb is on the lower plateau. By placing the filled balloon in the chute, you must get it to smash onto the resting bomb and render it inoperative. (So, on your only active option, while you'll make one person lose one of his legs, you'll prevent twelve from losing their lives.) On reflection, you choose this active option and, in consequence, the twelve are prevented from dying.

As most relevantly fresh folks respond, your conduct was morally outrageous.

Presenting them with the cases side by side, I've asked folks for an intuitive moral comparison of your conduct in the Leg and your behavior in the Foot. As most react, your conduct in the Leg isn't the least bit better than your conduct in the Foot. Surely, that's some reason to think that, for indirect reasoning aimed at our central puzzle's solution, the Leg might prove well suited.

For progress toward such effective reasoning, we'll combine the Leg and the Two Bombs so as to obtain this four-option example:

> *The Leg and Two Bombs.* Even as you have *three* remote control buttons ready to hand, so, one opens a trapdoor, another activates a catapult, and the third operates your laser knife. So, in addition to letting the twelve die on the lower plateau, which is your *first* option, you have *three other* options: On your *second* option, you open the trapdoor and send the rolling bomb into the First Canyon, killing the three there and preventing the twelve from dying. On your *third* option, you launch the resting bomb into the Second Canyon, killing the two there and preventing the twelve from dying. And, on your *fourth* option, you push another button and, taking a leg from the nature lover on the higher plateau with your laser knife, you use the limb to prevent the twelve from dying. On reflection, you choose this fourth option and, in consequence, the twelve are prevented from dying.

To this case, most fresh folks react positively.

In addition to presenting just one of these two cases to some folks and just the other to others, to still other fresh subjects I've also presented both, side by side. When asking those in this third group for a moral comparison of your leg-taking conduct in the two-option example and your leg-taking in the four-option case, all strongly respond that there's no moral difference at all. And, evidently, this second-order intuition on these key cases is as clear as it's powerful.

Of course, from all our intuitions on this pair of cases, both first- and second-order reactions, there arises an inconsistency. How best to resolve it? By now, there's little question but that we'd best look to the Liberation Hypothesis: First, with the simple Leg itself, certain inhibitory material prevents us from responding in accord with our Values. Second, with the Leg and Two Bombs, there's additional material that liberates us from that badly inhibiting influence; so, when judging it positively, we much more accurately assess your conduct. Third, and quite as our second-order intuitions help secure, it's just such a positive judgment that's the correct assessment of your conduct in the two-option Leg.

10. Putting This Puzzle's Pieces in Place: A Short but Proper Path to a Liberationist Solution

At this point, it's a piece of cake to correctly employ our indirect strategy. For, first, this statement's well enough supported to be embraced and placed in display:

(1) Your conduct in the Foot is at least as good, morally, as your conduct in the Leg.

With that comparative premise in place, everything depends on the moral status of the conduct in the Leg.

We've just seen that, on the best account of the example, your conduct in the Leg is morally good behavior. So, second, this statement's also well enough warranted for some strong moral reasoning:

(2) Your conduct in the Leg is morally good behavior.

But, of course, from those two well warranted premises, we correctly reason to this conclusion:

(3) Your conduct in the Foot is morally good behavior.

As I hope you'll agree, we've conducted moral reasoning that's nearly as convincing as it's sound.

11. A Longer Proper Path to That Sensible Solution

A moment ago, I made this report: When asked intuitively to compare the Leg's behavior with the Foot's, folks found that the Leg's conduct wasn't any better than the Foot's. To make the report more complete, I must also relate this result: With a minority, there's the different response that, though the Leg's *outcome* was markedly worse than the Foot's, maybe the Leg's *conduct* wasn't *as* bad as the Foot's. In this section, I'll aim to show that this minor explanatory problem presents an explanatory opportunity that's more than minor.

To that end, I'll present a tough two-option case satisfying two conditions. First, to prompt an apt use of the Method of Combining, it's closely related to the cases most recently considered. And, second, to prompt a severe response from the noted minority, it promotes extremely strong projective separating of one person, who might suffer a useful serious loss, from others who'll each be spared a far more serious loss if, but only if, they benefit from the serious loss the first might suffer.

With that in mind, let's now have a "chemically useful" fellow be in the downtown area of a big city, a fair ways from our national park. And, rather than being directly under the same big sky as the twelve, let's have him be cozily seated in a fancy French restaurant, enjoying an elaborate dinner. With that background, I'll display this two-option example:

> *The Peg Leg.* It's not a matter of a few minutes, but it's a couple of hours, until, unless you intervene, the two bombs will send signals to each other and both will explode. If that happens, the twelve trapped on the lower plateau will be blown to smithereens. So, if you *do nothing about* the situation, your *first* option, the twelve will die. But, you also have a *second* option: Just a fair ways from the park's nearby entrance, somebody's having lunch in a fancy downtown restaurant. Now, if you jump in your nearby car, you'll be there in well under an hour. And, upon creating a diversion, you can quickly escort the gourmet, with your concealed gun placed against his ribs, from his table to your car. Rendering him unconscious for several hours, you'll drive him back to the plateau from whence you came. Using your laser knife, you'll take from this man just the lower part of his leg, from the knee down, which is all you need from him to deactivate the resting bomb. Liquefying just that, and sending it down the chute onto the bomb, you'll achieve

deactivation with a minute to spare. Shortly after, and well before he awakens, you'll make sure the man's well fitted with a good peg leg. (So, on your only other option, while you'll make one person lose half a leg, you'll prevent twelve from losing their lives.) On reflection, you choose this active option and, in consequence, the twelve are prevented from dying.

From fresh subjects confronted with this case, the response is extremely negative.

How does your conduct in the Peg Leg compare morally with your behavior in the Foot? Since the answer's crucial for this whole section, please give it your full attention: With almost all, there's the strong (second-order) intuition that the Peg Leg's outrageous conduct is at least as bad as the Foot's.

Now, by combining (the main aspects of) the Peg Leg with (those of) the Leg and Two Bombs, we obtain a *five*-option case that, especially for the noted minority, can be an ethical eye-opener:

> *The Peg Leg, the Leg and Two Bombs.* Much here's the same as with the Leg and Two Bombs, but there are these differences: Rather than its being a few minutes until the two bombs send each other signals to explode, it's a couple of hours. So, there are temporally longer analogues of that example's four options. As well, you have a *fifth* option: Featuring your car and a fancy downtown restaurant, it's the only active alternative in the (two-option) Peg Leg. (So, on this option, while you'll make one lose half a leg, you'll prevent twelve from losing their lives.) On reflection, you choose this fifth option and, in consequence, the twelve are prevented from dying.

To this complex case, most fresh folks respond positively.

How markedly that differs from the extremely negative response to the Peg Leg! What accounts for the blatant disparity? Again, we look to the Liberation Hypothesis. Along its lines, the shorter half of the explanatory story runs like this: When confronted with the two-option Peg Leg, the promotion of strong projective separating has us see the distant diner as being quite distinct from the troubled twelve in the national park. So, while they have an awful problem, it certainly isn't his problem. So, as we'll see the matter, no acceptable solution to *their* problem will have *him* suffer seriously.

Concerned with the five-option case, here's the start of the story's much longer half: Correctly, we see the three who might be killed by the rolling bomb to be in a group with the twelve already imperilled by the bomb. As well, we see the two who might be killed by the resting bomb to belong with the three and, thus, we group together the two, the three and the twelve. What's more, we rightly group the useful reader with the two below the catapult and, with that, we can see each and every one of these "park" people to have an equal claim on your behavior.

Further, there's this: Once we can see ourselves going in for such useful leg-slicing of such a nicely peaceable reader, we can group together with him almost anyone else who, through similar slicing, might be similarly useful in such complex life-saving activity. So, even as we'll see the reader grouped with all those others in the big park, we'll also rightly see him grouped with the one in the urban restaurant.

Finally, there's this: When seeing the urban diner grouped with the rustic reader, we also see him grouped with all those others we've grouped with the reader, including even the twelve on the lower plateau. So, we rightly see the diner as "fair enough game" for the morally best solution to the bad problem that's centered in that outdoors area. So, to this five-option example, we rightly respond that your active conduct was good behavior.

When realizing that this complex case's conduct is good behavior, we're in a position to assess properly the precisely similar conduct in the two-option Peg Leg. For, we can hardly doubt the accuracy of our strong (second-order) intuition that there's not the least bit of moral difference between that simpler case's conduct and the five-option example's behavior. So, now, it's only reasonable to think that, despite disorienting intuitions to the contrary, the Peg Leg's conduct also was good behavior.

Thanks to the explanatory problem posed by the notably difficult minority, we're now well along another clear path to the sensible solution of the chapter's central puzzle. Paralleling the route followed in the previous section, the next step along this path is to advance a proposition that, if anything, is even more well warranted than (1), that section's first premise:

(1+)   Your conduct in the Foot is at least as good, morally, as your conduct in the Peg Leg.

Paralleling the previous section's second premise, (2), on this path's next step, we access a proposition that, in this section, has been made very credible:

(2 +)   Your conduct in the Peg Leg is morally good behavior.

These two premises yield nothing less than the previous section's conclusion:

(3)   Your conduct in the Foot is morally good behavior.

So, even more than before, we have strong reason to accept this conclusion. (Putting the Liberationist solution of the chapter's puzzle in a way that's almost absurdly cautious and concessive, perhaps it's useful to say that, even as your *killing* conduct in the Trolley is *good* behavior, so your *non*-killing conduct in the Foot is, at the least, *acceptable* behavior.)

Never mentioning the Foot, I could have framed this chapter's puzzle in terms of the Trolley and the Peg Leg. And, had I done that, almost all the chapter's main points would have been made more briefly. But, for two good reasons, our start paired the Trolley with the Foot: First, though it's only slightly more contrived than the Foot, the Peg Leg's a great deal more complicated. Second, by starting with the Foot, I made it sensible to foreswear direct reasoning, and to seek a very indirect argument. Now, because our psychological tendencies are often distortional, it's important that, in basic ethics, we often engage in such indirect reasoning. And, by having us here do that successfully, I prepared us well, I trust, for the rest of the book.

APPENDIX
Two Forms of the Fanaticism Hypothesis

As we're seeing in the text, the best reason for forswearing the Fanaticism Hypothesis is the explanatory power flowing from its competitor, the Liberation Hypothesis. Still, to be fair, I should give some direct attention to thoughts meant to favor the Fanaticism Hypothesis. Here, I'll aim to be fair but brief.

Each suggested by a different friend of the beleaguered conjecture, I'll discuss two forms of the Fanaticism Hypothesis. First, and much as was tentatively suggested by Frances Kamm in an informal discussion, I'll discuss the hypothesis in its *Explosive Form*. Second, and much as was similarly suggested by Bruce Russell in writing not meant for publication, I'll discuss the *Distractive Form*.

A. The Explosive Form of the Fanaticism Hypothesis

To begin, let's consider these correct suggestions from Kamm: While most judge your conduct in the Trolley to be good, even they have a certain inhibition against making that positive judgment. And, there's the same inhibition against positively judging your going even just that far in the Switches and Skates. But, just as is appropriate with both cases, most are well able to overcome the inhibition.

Rather more doubtful, I think, are further propositions she proposed. First, and roughly put, there's this psychological conjecture: In overcoming inhibition against thinking well of fatal switching behavior, there usually occurs an explosive impulse toward judging well *almost any* conduct that lessens markedly the serious losses suffered by innocents overall. Now, whether or not this conjecture's plausible, it's acceptable to us Liberationists. By contrast, what we can't accept is a more ambitious proposition, that saddles us with a propensity to make incorrect moral judgments. Thus, to deny Liberationism, the initial conjecture must be expanded much like so: When then moved to think well of conduct that markedly lessens serious suffering, we *fail to be aptly affected by moral* considerations.

Yet, even while it's widely obliging, this initial conjecture is probably false. Nipping things in the bud, it suffices to see a single scenario that's already under our noses. By deleting just the third option from the four-option Switches and Skates, the one featuring the light trolley and its two heavy passengers, we obtain a three-option case that's well called the *Single Switch and the Skates:* In addition to letting the six die, your first option, here your only alternatives are to change a switch and kill three, your second option, and, third, to kill just the skater, by using him to stop the trolley. As with the Switches and Skates, you choose the "protophysically worst" option and, so, the six are prevented from dying. With presentational order well placed to the side, here most respond that your conduct was wrong.

With any well detailed development of the Explosive Form, however, even the very first step will imply that, to this immediately available three-option example, most will react positively. So, in its Explosive Form, the Fanaticism Hypothesis is a nonstarter.[1]

B. The Distractive Form of the Fanaticism Hypothesis

As with its Explosive Form, the start of the Distractive Form doesn't actually deny Liberationism. Put roughly, it's this: Before responding to a several-option case, first you make just certain pairwise moral comparisons of the behaviors specified in the example's options. So, while you *don't make any other* pairwise judgments, you compare the behaviors of *adjacent* options. So, early in the process leading to response, all the pairwise comparisons are much like this:

> *Moral Comparison of Adjacent Behaviors.* Because it will result in markedly less serious loss suffered by the example's innocent folks than will the behavior specified for the currently considered adjacent alternative, this markedly *more effective* "loss-lessening" behavior is *morally better* than that markedly *less effective* conduct.

Quickly (and unconsciously) making all such comparisons for an interesting several-option case, and making no others, you reason that, among the behavioral alternatives, the best is the one with the least serious suffering. So, then, you respond positively to that option's conduct.

1. Within the set-up of the Single Switch and the Skates, we may specify that, instead of taking the third option, you chose another. Of course, there'll be two alternative specifications. First, it may be specified that you took the first option: doing nothing about the situation, you let the six die. With this specification, most fresh folks respond that your conduct was at least pretty bad. Second, it might be specified that you took the second option: changing the switch, you saved the six and killed the three. As I've found, it's only with that specification that, to this three-option case, most fresh folks don't respond negatively, but make a positive response. While I won't make a big deal of the matter, this confirms the point made in the text.

To move toward something that conflicts with the Liberation Hypothesis, the ideas about mediating comparisons must be expanded much like so: In various several-option cases, you confront more pairwise comparisons than you can accurately manage, and you see certain adjacent options in a way that obscures morally weighty differences between them. And, since your thought's then not aptly affected by what's morally weighty, your response *fails* to reflect your Values.

When we encounter many more alternatives than the two faced with a two-option case, there might be, even fairly often, such distraction as to foster judgmental error. But, since the Switches and Skates has *only two more* options, with that case it's pretty unlikely. And, then, there's this to consider: By deleting the example's fourth option, which features the heavy skater, there's yielded a case with *only one more* option than the minimum for choice found with all two-option cases: In the *Switches and Trolleys,* as we may call the three-option example, your only alternatives are, first, to let the six die, and, second, to change a switch and kill the three, and, third, to change another and reroute the two passengers into a fatal collision. As with the Switches and Skates, here you choose the option where you do most to lessen serious suffering; so, with the Switches and Trolleys, you save the six and kill the two rerouted passengers. Now, to this case with just *one middle option,* most react *positively.*

But, to the otherwise identical case that just *lacks* that single middle option, a two-option case well called the *Single Switch and Two Trolleys,* most fresh folks make a *negative* reaction. Already, things look bad for the Distractive Form.

Easily, we see things go from bad to worse. From just above, recall the three-option Switches and Trolleys. Now, for finding any troublesome distortion, here only one of the case's two adjacent option-pairs is at all promising. Of course, it's not the pair with, first, doing nothing and, second, changing switch A; so, it's the pair with that second option, changing switch A and, third, changing switch B. But, if judging *that* pair is so deceptively difficult for you, what morally weighty difference might you be failing to appreciate? Let's consider an obvious candidate: When you change B, you *very harmfully use* some people as means to achieve your end of saving others; but, when you change A, you never use any folks in any way at all.

By supposing that's actually a morally weighty difference, we'll see how, with any candidate difference, we can so accommodate it as to test the Distractive Form: When a course for conduct is said to have a certain morally horrible feature that's often badly obscured, or overlooked, or whatever, we'll *redescribe* the behavioral option so that, if there really ever is any distortional obscuring, or whatever, it will be forced to give way and, at least in this event, there'll be a more accurate assessment. So, by explicit and redundant reference, for instance, we may emphasize the candidate in question. Applying such a general procedure to what's at hand, we obtain a helpfully redescribed version of the (three-option) Switches and Trolleys, with the "morally most suspect" option put with words like these:

> Finally, on your *third* option, you'll flip a remote control toggle and change the position of another switch, switch B. Then, a very light trolley that's rolling along another track, the Feed Track, will shift onto B's lower fork and, instead of letting them safely bypass the speeding empty trolley, what you'll make happen to the light trolley's heavy passengers is this: Not only will that trolley deliver the heavy folks to where they'll be a useful means to your loss-lessening end, but, to save the six, you'll use the two in a way that's sure to kill them. On reflection, you choose this third option and, while the two are fatally used to save just three times their number, the six are prevented from dying.

Now, the allegedly weighty difference *won't* be obscured, or over-looked, or whatever. Yet, there's precious little difference, if any at all, between the quite positive responses made to this version of the example and those made to the plain old Switches and Trolleys. And, with that, things look about as bleak for the Fanaticism Hypothesis's Distractive Form as for its hopeless Explosive Form.

5

BETWEEN SOME HARDER ROCKS AND ROCKIER HARD PLACES: ON DISTORTIONAL SEPARATING AND REVELATORY GROUPING

For most still skeptical of the main Liberationist thoughts encountered, this short chapter should seal the deal. Happily, the brief exploration of projective separating's pervasive power will feature, in its second and largest part, cases that are even more amusing than they're psychologically amazing. Less amusingly, in the chapter's first two sections, we'll observe, and explain, two strangely opposite psychological phenomena.

1. A Strange Psychological Phenomenon: No Threshold

In this section, there'll be presented what's well called the *Phenomenon of No Threshold*. To get set to see its strangeness, I'll stress this sensible deliverance from our moral common sense: Even with *psychologically very constraining* cases, like the Foot, there's a reasonable limit on how many innocent folks must *each* suffer an *enormously serious* loss without its being acceptable, and even good, to spare them all through conduct imposing on only *one* a loss that's *much* less serious than what each of the many would suffer. In fewer words: Even with such cases, there's a decently low threshold.

With a wide infinity of cases, however, the intuitive reactions of most fresh folks are to the effect that there's *no* threshold at all! To see that, most of what's needed comes with confronting:

> *The Enormously Needed Foot.* In addition to the sixty neighbors, a billion other innocents have similarly contracted the deadly disease. Down to the last one, they can be saved only by an antidote that's made by mixing with water a liquefied foot's worth of the sports fan; (so there'll be enough antidote for all, the two substances should be mixed in a proportion of about one to fifty million). Being civil, you ask the fan to give up a foot to save so many lives. But, he refuses to cooperate. More impressed by the imperilled billion than by the refusal, you remove a foot, you make the antidote and, in short order, the billion are prevented from dying.

When intuitively responding to this case, how do fresh subjects assess your behavior? In making a rapid judgment, most experience some psychological conflict, but none that's paralyzing. And, while it's true that many respond that your severing conduct was good, even more react that it was bad behavior. These negative reactions are instances of No Threshold.

By this point, most will find No Threshold an awfully fishy psychological phenomenon. But, many won't fully realize just what it is that's found so strange. Indeed, some may ask themselves a question like this: "In such a purely quantitative extension of the Foot, is there *ever* a number of people's lives so large that, according to our intuitive reactions, taking the sports fan's foot *isn't* bad?" With simple variants of the Enormously Needed Foot, we'll give the question a treatment that's clarifying.

To begin, let's suppose that, provided they're biologically fertile, and most are females, and so on, to ensure a long future for intelligent life on earth, only five thousand folks are needed. And, let's suppose you and the sports fan must be among their number. With that, we're set to confront two complementary variants of the Enormously Needed Foot: First, we'll suppose that there are now *exactly five billion five thousand* on earth and, none of them needed for a long future for humankind, exactly five billion have the deadly disease. To this case, most respond that, when taking the fan's foot to save the "unneeded" five billion, your conduct is wrong. Second, we'll suppose, instead, that there are now exactly *six* billion five thousand alive on earth, with exactly six billion both so unneeded and in such terrible trouble. To this other case, just as many respond negatively. So, what we see is that, according to most fine folk's responses to such constraining cases, the very lives of a *billion* innocents count for *nothing*! With that pattern of response observed, we see that our recent question gets this answer: "No; there'll never be a large enough number of people's lives." So, it's clear that here's a phenomenon that's ever so properly called *No Threshold*.[1]

Does No Threshold reflect a remarkable feature of our Basic Moral Values; or, is it a remarkable indication of the distortional power of projective separating? Initially, the latter thought's far more plausible. On reflection, the big difference only increases: Just as there are many in our culture circle with whom No Threshold is often instanced, there are many others with whom it's seldom instanced. It's hardly plausible that, with the decent members of our own society, those great individual differences are stemming from great differences regarding deep moral commitment. Rather, they're just reflecting big differences in how much, or how little, a person's projective separating affects her responses to cases.

2. Another Strange Psychological Phenomenon: Near Tie-breaker

Already evidently bizarre, No Threshold seems stranger still when taken together with another strange psychological phenomenon, the *Phenomenon of Near Tie-breaker*. To see a simple instance of this strangely opposite phenomenon, we need only encounter this minor variant of the Trolley:

> *The Tie-breaking Foot.* Because he became drunk last night, a trolley worker didn't rightly set the line's switches today. So, instead of being set as it's supposed to be, a certain switch-track is set in such a way that a certain empty trolley, now stationary but soon to be rolling fast, will be routed away from the main line onto a side-

---

1. To a dramatically different variant of the Enormously Needed Foot, there's a *widespread positive* response: Suppose that, except for you and the fan, everyone on earth has the dread disease and, if you let things run their course, then, starting in just a few decades, there won't ever again be any people on earth; with that in mind, you take his foot and save humankind. In light of what's been lately observed, this positive assessment of your foot-slicing conduct is an interesting reaction. But, however interesting, it's *not* a sign of any *threshold*.

track. The work of a mustachioed villain, on this side-track there are twelve people wholly tied down and, as well, there's tied down just one foot of a thirteenth, the greatest part of her safely away from the track. Also the work of that villain, on the main track just below this switch, just twelve whole people are tied down. You have precisely two options: If you do nothing about the situation, your first option, then, on the side-track, twelve will lose their lives and one will lose a foot. If you push a remote control button, your second option, you'll change the switch-track to its proper setting and, while it's the twelve on that main track who'll then die, nobody else will be harmed. You take this more active option.

Here, most fresh folks respond that your conduct was good. As I think you'll agree, it's fine to give the name *Near Tie-breaker* to the psychological phenomenon the positive reactions instance.[2]

While few do both in the very same breadth, in the fullness of time many do these two things: On the one hand, exemplifying No Threshold with (enormously many cases like) the Enormously Needed Foot, they'll react that, even if being passive means a billion folks will soon lose their lives, you mustn't take a foot from just one. On the other hand, exemplifying Near Tie-breaker with (enormously many other cases like) the Tie-breaking Foot, they'll react that, just for a net gain of saving a single foot, it's good to kill a dozen fine folks, provided that, in the bargain, you prevent a dozen from getting killed. There's little reason to think this bipartite response pattern reflects a deep or decent moral commitment.[3]

With more reason than ever, we listen to Liberationism: Rather than reflecting some marvelously great moral importance that's to be

2. Judging just by examples in the family of trolley cases, there doesn't seem to be a similarly widespread psychological phenomenon that, equally aptly, might be called "*Mere* Tie-breaker": Instead of having an additional innocent's foot placed on the main track, we can have something whose loss wouldn't be truly serious, like the favorite teddy bear of a young child. To this variant, not nearly so many respond positively, or even leniently.

3. In this note, I'd like to provide a helpful perspective on the problem posed by the strange phenomena lately encountered and, on the other hand, the puzzle that focused the previous chapter's discussion: In a nice use of "acute", while people's negative responses to the Foot and their positive reactions to the Trolley pose an acute philosophical puzzle, a *far more acute* puzzle can be posed with the contrasting intuitions to the Enormously Needed Foot and the Tie-breaking Foot. So, why didn't I use *that* puzzle to focus the prior chapter's discussion? The reason's about as simple as it's sensible: Even as it's best first to present readers with a *highly accessible* enigma, the puzzle of the Foot and the Trolley is *much more accessible* than the parallel problem, just lately encountered, that's much more acute.

found in letting an isolated innocent keep both his feet, our harsh reaction to (the likes of) the Enormously Needed Foot reflects nothing so much as the powerful influence on our intuitive moral thinking that, all too often, flows from our engagement in projective separating. By contrast, even as we're there encouraged to group together all whom the agent might affect, it's only with (the likes of) the Tie-breaking Foot that our intuitive response accurately reflects our Values.

As is clear, things are now better than ever for the Liberation Hypothesis. And, we're clearly struck by the thought that our projective separating promotes *grotesquely* distorted responses to cases.

3. A Causally Amorphous Egoistic Puzzle: Introducing Dr. Strangemind

Again, recall the Envelope: Not actually causing anything much at all, in that case you *allowed* **there to be more** *serious loss suffered than if you'd behaved better.* As those roundabout words remind us, there your consequential allowing conduct was causally amorphous; there wasn't even a single person whom *you* let suffer.[4] Taking a cue from that, we'll explore cases where, on one of the two options, you *cause there to be more* serious loss suffered, but where there *isn't* even a single person whom *you* make suffer. By examining such cases of *causally amorphous harming,* we may see how vast is the domain where our ability to group folks together equitably is limited by our propensities with projective separating. In the vast domain, we'll observe, and explain, some astonishing phenomena.

To that end, it's useful to introduce the lunatic Dr. Strangemind, an eccentric *multi-billionaire* who's as powerful as he's insane. Lacking any moral sensibility whatever, this invulnerable madman vigorously pursues his prime passion, the horrific activity he's named *Realistic Social Psychology,* or RSP, a field in which he's the sole investigator. In his RSP experiments, the magnate's assisted by many henchmen; each of them a decent guy, they've all been made, by the clever Strange-

4. Let me remind you of the note offered in chapter 2, when introducing a distinction between causally focused aid and causally amorphous aid. That chapter's note 14 consisted of these concessive words: "On one logico-metaphysical view, there can't be casually amorphous relations. Though it appears false, it just might be true. If so, then, this distinction marks no real difference. But, of course, it might well be false. And, since I should see if Liberationism prevails even on a "worst case scenario," I'll suppose that, in the Envelope, any aid would be causally amorphous." For the present discussion, reasonably similar words are appropriate.

mind, to be greatly deceived. As well, in each of his horrific RSP studies, Strangemind utilizes many cleverly enticed experimental subjects and, in each case, you'll be one of them.

In the upcoming series of Strangemind examples, I'll start with a pair where the choice is between acting in your own financial interests and acting in the much more serious interests of others. Being more complex, the second of these two "egoistic" examples is best seen after confronting the first:

> *The Gold Card.* Strangemind has lured you to a luxurious suite of offices. But, these aren't really the offices of a law firm involved with the will of a wealthy distant relative recently expired; rather, the suite is the loony tycoon's psychological testing lab. Though you've just been once deceived, Strangemind makes it clear that, for participating in this experiment, nothing else like that will happen to you. At the beginning of your experimental trial, you're presented with a "gold" plastic card, and have precisely two options: If you leave the card on the table before you, your first option, that's the end of the matter. But, if you pick it up, your second option, that's far from the end of the matter. Rather, having both a "positive" and a "negative" side, the situation will be this: Positively, the magnate will give you a million dollars. Negatively, in Cambodia, where the abundance of land-mines means much daily leg loss, he'll strangely ensure that tomorrow there'll be more foot loss: Besides you, there are 199 other subjects in today's RSP experiment. While you're in the *second* hundred, out of the first, you're informed, at least ten picked up the card, but not all did. At the day's end, the tycoon will tally the total number of cards lifted. From a list of a hundred thousand fully normal Cambodian children, just that number will be selected, randomly and simultaneously. Tomorrow, his henchmen will slice a foot off each selected child. (As the deceived employees think, by slicing off a child's foot, they're saving her life.) As Strangemind stresses, if you pick up the card, there won't ever be *anyone* whom *you* make lose a foot; it's only that, due to your behavior, there'll be one *more* child who, at the hands of henchmen, loses a foot. You pick up the card and, so, one more does lose a foot.

As everyone responds to this case, your conduct was abominable. Now, in the Envelope, your donating would have meant your incurring an *actual cost.* But, in the Gold Card, those not picking up the card incurred only an *opportunity cost.* Partly because it makes just such closer contact with the Envelope, it's useful to confront this yet more complex example:

> *The Bank Card.* Not a gold card, there's a green plastic card with the word **BANK** inscribed in black and, underneath, the words **Stop Withdrawal of $100.** If you don't pick up the card, nothing much happens. But, if you do, there'll ensue this situation with both a positive and a negative side: Negatively, matters are precisely the same as in the Gold Card. Positively, matters are less grandiose but more complex: Already arranged by Strangemind, there's been placed on your checking account, well-stocked with well over $1000, an electronic withdrawal order for $100; unless the order is soon rescinded by the tycoon, it will go into effect first thing tomorrow morning, when the banks next open. Now, if you pick up the card, he'll rescind the order, and there'll be no decrease in your account. You pick up the card and, so, tomorrow one more child loses a foot.

Here, too, everyone responds that your conduct was outrageous.[5]

According to our Primary Values, does the Envelope's self-interested conduct merit a lenient appraisal while the Bank Card's merits a severely negative judgment? Posed by that question, it's no easy problem that's well called the *Causally Amorphous Egoistic Puzzle.* For at least these three reasons, this puzzle is at least pretty difficult: First, consider all of the "initially promising" factors that differentiated the Envelope from the Vintage Sedan. All of them place the Bank Card with the Envelope, not the Vintage Sedan. Second, since all the Cambodian children's needs are always completely inconspicuous to you,

---

5. Mindful of the caution signal raised in the just previous note, these words still seem well worth addressing to readers conversant with the literature of contemporary moral philosophy: It may be of considerable interest to compare our cases of causally amorphous aiding with some famous cases found there, and our cases of causally amorphous harming with others.

For aiding, compare an Envelopey case where you *do* send UNICEF $100 for ORT with one that, based on work of Jonathan Glover's, Derek Parfit prominently displays on page 76 of his justly acclaimed *Reasons and Persons,* Oxford University Press, 1984: In the *Drops of Water,* each donor puts a pint into a water-cart, and the whole is doled out, equally, to many thirsty men. On each drinker, each donor has an *imperceptible* effect. Still, on a drinker, a donor does have an (actual, genuine, determinate) effect. But, with your $100 UNICEF donation, there's *no* (actual, genuine, determinate) effect on any needy child.

For harming, compare the Bank Card with Parfit's *Harmless Torturers,* prominently displayed on page 80 of the book. There, each torturer has an imperceptible effect, but an (actual, etc.) effect, on each victim. But, when you lifted the Bank Card, there was *no* (actual, etc.) effect on any victim.

that fact also places the Bank Card with the Envelope, not the Sedan. Third, there's this: Near chapter 2's outset, we noted five factors favoring a *more severe* judgment for the Envelope's conduct than the Sedan's; for example, while you had *at least thirty more* innocents suffer in the Envelope, in the Sedan *only one more* suffered than if you'd have behaved better. And, while some of these factors also favor a *stricter* judgment for the Envelope's conduct than the Bank Card's, *none* favor a stricter judgment for the Bank Card's behavior. Being hard, this Egoistic Puzzle might well prove instructive.

4. A Causally Amorphous Altruistic Puzzle: Strangemind's Terribly Ghastly Ingenuity

To complement that Egoistic Puzzle, it will be instructive also to encounter a *Causally Amorphous Altruistic Puzzle*. To that end, it's useful first to confront a card case that has much in common with the Account, a familiar altruistic example. So, here's an altruistic variant of the Gold Card:

> *The UNICEF Card.* On the table before you, there's a white plastic card with the bold inscription, **UNICEF,** in light blue block letters. If you don't pick up the card, then nothing much happens. But, if you do, what happens has both a positive and a negative side: Positively, the tycoon will soon make many anonymous contributions to UNICEF, clearly earmarked for ORT in Africa and totalling a million dollars; consequently, in the next month thousands fewer African children will die. Negatively, in the Asian country of Cambodia, tomorrow one more child will lose a foot to a henchman's knife. You pick up the card and, so, while thousands fewer African children die this next month, there's one more Asian child who loses a foot.

Especially among the relevantly untainted, almost all react that your conduct was wrong.

The UNICEF Card well may be called a *wholly amorphous* case: If there's to be less serious loss befalling folks overall, you'll be amorphously involved in *causing* serious loss to some, in Asia, and you'll also be amorphously involved in *aiding* some, in Africa, who'd otherwise suffer seriously. For another step toward an Altruistic Puzzle, let's confront a case where it's *only in causing* loss that you'll be amorphously involved. And, for the step to be substantial, let's have the folks whom you might aid have dire needs that are highly salient to you:

> *The Heart Card.* On the table before you, there's a white card with a symbolic red heart at its center. If you don't pick up the card, nothing much happens. But, if you do, what happens has both a positive and a negative side: Positively, the tycoon makes sure that, instead of dying soon, there'll be a long life for each of sixty horribly diarrhetic Ethiopian children that, big as life, for a minute you see vividly on Strangemind's closed-circuit TV. Negatively, in the Asian country of Cambodia, tomorrow one more child will lose a foot to a henchman's knife. You pick up the card and, so, sixty fewer young Africans die soon and, tomorrow, one more Asian loses a foot.

To this case, almost all fresh folks respond negatively.

For the Altruistic Puzzle, we'll pair the Heart Card with a novel wholly amorphous card case. Because the example's pretty complex, before placing it in display, I'll provide some background. Strangemind takes a cue from Ed McMahon and the Publishers Clearinghouse Sweepstakes: From an original list of a hundred thousand very healthy African children, just two hundred kids have *already been selected,* at random, by the loony tycoon. Now, except insofar as these "finalists" may be indirectly helped by the subjects participating in yet another RSP experiment, tomorrow each of the two hundred children will have a foot sliced off by henchmen and, as well, a hand. For the feet and hands of these African children, the only hope is that, among the two hundred subjects participating in a certain RSP experiment, many pick up the card before them. For, the greater the number of subjects leaving the card on the table, the greater the number of young Africans who'll soon lose a foot and, in addition, a hand. But, as a matter of course, the greater the number picking up their cards, the greater the number of young Asians who'll lose just a foot. With that background in mind, we confront:

> *The Lesser Loss Card.* Many things here are the same as in the Heart Card, but not all: This time, there's a card with the words **Lesser Loss** boldly inscribed. You have two options: (1) If you pick it up, then, of the two hundred subjects in this experiment, the number picking up the Card, N, which you know to be greater than zero but less than 200, will be *higher by one* than if you don't. At the day's end, from the 200 young African finalists already

randomly selected, N True Winners will be chosen at random. While the magnate's henchmen won't even so much as touch any of these True Winners, from each of the *other* finalists, the 200-N Leftover Losers, a henchman will slice off both a foot and a hand. So, on this option, while you'll be lessening the losses in Africa, you'll be increasing, though to a *lesser degree*, the losses in Asia. (2) If you *don't* pick up the card, then, even as the number of subjects picking it up will be *lower by one* than if you do, the number *not* picking up the card, which must be 200-N, will be *higher* by one. Then, at this day's end, Strangemind will randomly select precisely *that* number of young Cambodians and, tomorrow in that Asian country, from each of these 200-N Opposite Losers, a henchman will slice off just a foot. You pick up the card and, so, while there's one more child who loses a foot in Asia, in Africa there's one less child who loses both a foot and a hand.

To this case, most respond positively. How dramatic is the difference between our negative reaction to the Heart Card and our positive response to the Lesser Loss Card!

With that dramatic difference, there's the first "half" of our Altruistic Puzzle. And, with the four thoughts we'll next consider, there's enough of the puzzle's other half.

First, consider the serious losses that, in these two card cases, you knowingly have it that others will suffer. On the negative side, the two cases are the same; in each, one more person will suffer the loss of a foot. On the positive side, by contrast, the Heart Card's conduct fares far, far better than the Lesser Loss Card's: In the Heart Card, you have it that fully sixty fewer people will suffer the loss of their lives, but, in the Lesser Loss Card, you have it that only one fewer will suffer nothing more than the loss of a hand and a foot. Taking full stock of this whole key consideration, of both the positive and the negative, it's quite fishy that, while we respond favorably to the Lesser Loss Card, we respond unfavorably to the Heart Card.

Second, on this negative, harming, causing side, the two cases are perfectly congruent in every relevant evaluative respect; matters certainly aren't morally worse in the Heart Card than in the Lesser Loss Card. Not that the particulars must be mentioned, but, for good measure, here are some salient specifics: By contrast with the likes of the Foot, in the Lesser Loss Card you didn't harmfully use anyone and, along other such "quasi-Kantian" lines, you also didn't do anything morally objectionable. But, of course, all that's just as true of the Heart Card! So, taking fuller stock, it's *very* fishy that, while we respond positively to the Lesser Loss Card, to the Heart Card we respond negatively.

Third, since the Lesser Loss Card is causally amorphous with both options, had you there *not* picked up the card, you *still wouldn't* have failed to prevent *anyone's* serious suffering. By contrast, since the Heart Card's amorphous only with its passive option, had you *there* not picked up the card, you *would* have failed to prevent the serious suffering of sixty vitally needy people, each of whom you've seen to be in vital need. When taking stock at this stage, it's very *strangely* fishy that, though responding positively to the Lesser Loss Card, to the Heart Card we respond negatively.

Fourth, not only are the needy people whom you aid highly salient to you in the Heart Card, but, relatedly, so is the great depth and urgency of their vital needs; so, there's not the least chance that, for an engagement in futility thinking, you might underrate the moral importance of preventing them from suffering most seriously. (By contrast, in the Lesser Loss Card there's nobody whose dire need is even the least bit conspicuous to you.) And, with your knowing many legs are violently lost there every day, why are you so down on the Heart Card's lifting behavior, whose only significant black mark is that, on just one of these days, just one more Cambodian loses just one foot? With our responding negatively to the Heart Card and positively to the Lesser Loss Card, there's a perplexing Altruistic Puzzle.

5. A Sensible Liberationist Solution of the Altruistic Puzzle

For an account that best resolves this perplexing puzzle, we'll want an explanation flowing from the Liberation Hypothesis. The account's leading idea will be that, rather than anything with much moral weight, it's the peculiarly varied working of projective grouping and separating that explains this extremely puzzling pair of intuitive reactions.

In the Lesser Loss Card, almost everything helps us group together, quite properly, everyone who, as a consequence of what's going on in Strangemind's present experiment, is vulnerable to suffer a serious loss. As the main matter then appears, there's a *mathematically secure connection* between the number selected to be harmed in the Asian land of Cambodia and, on the other side of the salient situation's conceptual coin, the number selected in Africa. Just so, there seems a strikingly strong connection between those to be harmed by henchmen in Cambodia, whomever they may be, and, on the coin's other side, those to be so harmed in Africa, whomever *they* may be. We see the 100,200 "experimentally vulnerable" children as all being in the same (salient Strangemindian) situation and, so, we see each of them as "fair enough game" for the morally best solution to the bad problem that's common enough for them all. About your conduct in this case, our most operative thought is that it's an instance of *making the best of a bad situation*. So, with the Lesser Loss Card, we respond positively to your card-lifting conduct.

With the Heart Card, by contrast, we *don't* group together the people in African Ethiopia, whom you might save from terribly serious harm *never* flowing from a Strangemindian cause, and anyone in Asian Cambodia. Rather, we see the Heart Card's potential victims as belonging to, or as forming, two quite separate groups; some sixty of them form one of the groups, whose boundaries never get out of Africa, and the other 100,000, all in Asia, form the other group. So, we see the sixty starving Ethiopians to be in *one* particularly bad situation, with just their "pretty natural" problem, and we see the 100,000 healthy but randomly vulnerable Cambodian kids as being in only quite another bad situation, with just *their* "Strangemindian" problem. So, our tendencies with projective separating have us think that, as part of any solution to the *Ethiopians'* problem, it's badly wrong to increase the serious suffering of folks in the *Cambodian* group.

Disclosing our tendencies with distortional projective separating and revelatory projective grouping, what's just been related provides most of the solution to our extraordinarily perplexing Altruistic Puzzle. Those potent tendencies do more than all other factors combined. For good measure, briefly I'll expound most of what little remains to be said: With the Lesser Loss Card, even the case's folks in Africa faced trouble that was very dramatic and exciting; being randomly selected for a visit from severing henchmen is exciting stuff. At least to some degree, that helps respondents think well of conduct that has fewer kids get such terribly exciting visits and, so, with the Lesser Loss Card, that also encouraged a positive response. By contrast, the Heart Card's Africans faced *much less* exciting trouble; to the likes of us, who've for so long been well aware of so much deathly African starvation, the starving to death of just another sixty Africans *isn't* exciting or dramatic. So, it's no wonder that, to the Heart Card, we make a response that's not well rooted in our Values.

6. A Similar Solution for the Egoistic Puzzle

Happily, the most sensible solution for the chapter's Egoistic Puzzle is a Liberationist account that, overall, is very like the Altruistic Puzzle's.

By contrast with the Envelope, with the Bank Card there's a thought like this: Along with what will happen to some young Cambodians on Strangemind's long list, what happens to *us* 200 experimental subjects depends on, or is part of, the outcome of the RSP experiment in progress. And, it's in a conspicuously strong way that your future (financial) status is intertwined with the future (anatomical) status of Cambodian children on Strangemind's list. So, you projected as salient a single group comprising both the Cambodian children and the experimental subjects, yourself included. Thus, you saw all concerned, Cambodian youngsters and experimental subjects alike, to be embroiled in a single Strangemindian situational problem.

Vaguely thinking I may have used some conceptually illicit trick to capture "your own perspective," some might not clearly understand what I've just advanced. To make things clearer, I'll provide an indirect line of thought that's obviously free of tricks. To begin this line, consider the *Ethiopian Bank Card*, a case that's a very minor variant of the Bank Card: In this example, Strangemind's assigned each of his 200 experimental subjects, including you yourself, a different well-to-do adult Ethiopian. As with each of the case's 199 other subjects, the choice with which the tycoon confronts you has this be the positive side of your picking up your card: The withdrawal order Strangemind's placed on your assigned Ethiopian's account will be rescinded and, rather than having her lose $100 dollars, you'll have her financial assets be perfectly preserved. Of course, just as with all our other card cases, here the negative side of your picking up the card is the increase in foot loss, by one, in Cambodia tomorrow. Suppose that, knowing all this, you pick up the card. We respond that, barring insanity, your conduct was morally outrageous.

Next, consider the perfectly parallel *All-American Bank Card*: Instead of assigning each of his 200 well-to-do American experimental subjects a well-off Ethiopian adult, Strangemind assigns each a different well-off *American* adult. Naturally, we respond just as negatively to your lifting behavior.

Finally, notice this: Even as far as the force of explanation goes, again nothing changes when we move to consider the *Reflexive All-American Bank Card*, which is, of course, just the original Bank Card itself: To each of his 200 well-off American experimental subjects, the well-off American adult Strangemind assigns is that very subject herself. So, now, readers should have a good understanding of the present account's most novel material.

By adding material that's fairly familiar, I'll finish expounding a Liberationist solution to our Egoistic Puzzle: When confronting the

Bank Card, you realize that, as compared with the truly serious loss that will be suffered by one more Cambodian child if you pick up the card, the loss you're liable to suffer, for leaving it on the table, is a trivial loss. So, since you don't think of the Asian kids as having a problem that's quite separate from what might here happen with your finances, but view their prospective loss and yours as just two sides of the same situation, you realize that, if you lift the card, your conduct's bad behavior.

As I've just explained, our negative reactions to the Bank Card are largely generated by, and are good indicators of, our Basic Moral Values. Though not new, it's useful to hear a few words to explain why, going against these Values, we respond so permissively to the Envelope's conduct: By contrast with the Bank Card, in the Envelope there's nothing much to help you see yourself as belonging in a group with the world's very vulnerable children. To the contrary, when confronting that ubiquitous case, you view whatever happens to them as quite separate from whatever losses you might incur. So, as often happens, the ground's well laid for futility thinking, and kindred fallacies, to hold sway. And, of course, in the Envelope there's nothing to liberate us from fallacious forms of thinking. So, seen several times over, we respond that it's all right to keep your bank balance high and let more little Third Worlders die.

With both our Altruistic Puzzle and our Egoistic Puzzle given satisfying Liberationist solutions, things look about as good as can be for the Liberation Hypothesis, and about as bad as possible for any significantly differing alternative. As well, it's clearer than ever that, for any approach to ethics that's even remotely like Preservashonism, there aren't any significant prospects. More specifically useful for what's directly upcoming, we've seen clearly how our proclivities with projective separating might get us to think, almost all the time confidently, that there's nothing really wrong with your enjoying an affluent lifestyle while, each month and every year, you let more little Asians and Africans die.

6

LIVING HIGH AND LETTING DIE RECONSIDERED: ON THE COSTS OF A MORALLY DECENT LIFE

It's time to consider the cost, for a well-off adult like you and me, to live a morally decent life. By the chapter's end, we'll see reason to conclude that, compared with any ordinary estimate, the cost is enormous.[1] At the same time, we'll see reason to feel fortunate that, though living in this perennially rotten world, we needn't literally give our lives, or even our legs, to lessen others' serious suffering.

Wanting some agreement with many readers, I'll first offer argument for thoughts that, while pretty demanding by ordinary stan-

1. In the contemporary literature, prominent treatments of cost include: Bernard Williams, "A Critique of Utilitarianism," in J. J. C. Smart and B. Williams, *Utilitarianism: For and Against,* Cambridge University Press, 1973, and "Persons, Character and Morality," in B. Williams, *Moral Luck,* Cambridge U. P., 1981, Susan Wolf, "Moral Saints," *Journal of Philosophy,* 1982, Samuel Scheffler, *The Rejection of Consequentialism,* Oxford University Press, 1982 and *Human Morality,* Oxford U. P., 1992, Thomas Nagel, *The View from Nowhere,* Oxford U. P., 1986, Peter Singer, *Practical Ethics,* Cambridge U. P., 1979 and Shelly Kagan, *The Limits of Morality,* Oxford U. P., 1989. For a very recent contribution that excels in its discussion of earlier writers, see Liam Murphy, "The Demands of Beneficence," *Philosophy and Public Affairs,* 1993.

The "hard line" for which I'll argue is similar to those taken by Singer and by Kagan. So, this chapter's arguments offer some support for their views and, correspondingly, they undermine the various "softer" lines advanced, variously, by the other authors.

133

dards, are far less so than those argued subsequently. Of course, even at the chapter's end, we'll be most confident of its least demanding conclusions.

1. A Pretty Demanding Dictate

For a well-organized discussion, it's useful to start with a statement that's no more than pretty demanding. So, I'll display this proposition, which has both moral and nonmoral aspects:

> *A Pretty Demanding Dictate.* On pain of living a life that's seriously immoral, a typical well-off person, like you and me, must give away most of her financially valuable assets, and much of her income, directing the funds to lessen efficiently the serious suffering of others.

Both in actual fact and according to this Dictate, one key part of what determines how much someone must contribute comprises *nonmoral* truths. Some of these nonmoral propositions concern the particular circumstances of the individual in question, including facts about the agent's financial status and prospects, facts about whatever dependents she may have, and so on. Others concern the things that, during the next few years, any of us can do to lessen, efficiently, the serious suffering of innocent people, including facts about how we can direct funds to UNICEF, OXFAM, and CARE, and so on. Of course, the other key part of what determines someone's cost comprises moral propositions. So it might be that, as moral precepts join with relevant nonmoral truths, for typical well-off folks it's determined that the cost of living a morally decent life is at least what's signalled with the Pretty Demanding Dictate.

Of course, hardly any of us does that. To the contrary, each year only a minute minority give even a thousand dollars to any cause, or program, anywhere near as vitally effective as, say, UNICEF's campaign against vaccine-preventable diseases. The vast majority don't willingly give even a single dollar toward any such extremely important end. But, of course, when assessing the common conduct, we commonly judge that it's not so much as wrong at all. Between our lenient judgments and what our Dictate implies, there's a huge gap. So, to argue convincingly for the Dictate, a great deal must be done. Indeed, were I to attempt it without benefit from what's already been disclosed in the book, there'd be little chance that, in the space of just this chapter, I'd enjoy even a modest success.

Accordingly, I'll here rely heavily on central truths already discovered: At least since chapter 3's discussion, we've been aware that, rather than flowing from our Values, our lenient response to the likes of the Envelope stems from distortional mental tendencies, like our fallacious futility thinking. And, as we've learned in chapters 4 and 5, each of us adds fuel to those crazy flames when, as commonly happens, she projectively separates herself from almost everyone else. For behavioral judgements that accord with our Values, we must protect ourselves from such misleading proclivities. Moved by that thought, I'll start an argument for the Pretty Demanding Dictate by constructing an "instructively liberating" example.

2. An Argument for This Dictate from the Consideration of Three Cases

At this point, most will find boring even the suggestion that we consider yet another case featuring a potentially lethal rolling trolley. But, surprisingly, several such cases are each bound to engage even the most jaded readers.

For one engaging case, I'll provide this background: Having worked hard throughout his adult life, Robert R. Roberts, the successful 70-year-old engineer, has amassed $3 million. Selling his house and other financially valuable assets, Bob's taken to renting a little apartment and, with all but $3,000 left in an account for emergencies, he's put the rest of his wealth into his retirement fund. Fully committing the fund to just one excellent investment, for the bargain price of just under $3 million, Bob's become the owner of one of the world's few mint-condition Bugatti automobiles; during the short time before his planned retirement, it certainly can be expected to appreciate at over 20% per year. As with the very few other owners of these terribly rare cars, Bob's unable to insure his Bugatti. But, during the last fifty years, no occurrence with these cars was more than modestly costly for the Bugatti's owner. So, both for the joy of owning the vehicle and for the great prospects of appreciation, Bob's quite willing to shoulder the slight risk. To be sure, in the unlikely event that great damage befalls his Bugatti before he's sold it, instead of a comfortable retirement Bob will have a hard time just making ends meet for the remaining 15 to 20 years he can expect to live: After working hard and saving scrupulously for the next 5 years, after which he'll have to retire, in his last 10 to 15 years he'll also have to watch every penny. With that background provided, we're set to encounter:

> *Bob's Bugatti.* On a rural road near the garage where it's securely kept, Bob's gone for a careful drive in his Bugatti. At a certain point, he spies a shiny object. To inspect it, Bob parks his car in the only place from where, directly, he can proceed on foot for a close encounter, a parking place that's just ten yards beyond the end of a certain trolley track. As it develops, when Bob walks over to the shiny object, he finds it's a switch that can be set in two ways. And, as Bob observes, there's a trolley up the line that's barrelling toward the switch's fork. As the shiny switch is set, the trolley will go down the fork's opposite side, not the branch leading to a spot near Bob's Bugatti. But, as Bob sees, on that side there's a young child trapped on the track. As he knows, Bob has two options: If he does nothing about the situation, the child will be killed, but he'll enjoy a comfortable retirement. If he changes the switch's setting, his second option, then, while nobody's killed, after rolling down the vacant branch and beyond that track's end, the trolley will totally destroy Bob's uninsurable Bugatti, wiping out his entire retirement fund. Bob chooses the first option and, while the child is killed, he has a comfortable retirement.

When confronting this engaging example, everyone responds that Bob's conduct was monstrous. Doubtless, the severe reaction accurately reflects our good Values.

Next, we'll encounter another example that features the completely unhelpful conduct of a financially successful 70-year-old. In *Ray's Big Request from UNICEF*, our protagonist is the able accountant, Raymond R. Raymond. Now, we'll suppose that, both morally and materially, at this case's start Ray's situation is, in all relevant respects, just the same as Bob's when starting the previous example. At any rate, after he's clearly informed how much each thousand of his dollars can do for the world's neediest children, it's requested of Ray that he give 99% of all of his material assets, including both what's in his retirement fund and what's not, to UNICEF's efficient life-saving programs. In such an event, with only five financially productive years left before his long retirement, Ray would be left with only $30,000 to his name, a far cry from his $3 million. Understandably, Ray does nothing toward meeting his Big Request and, so, thousands more children die than if he'd met it. To this example, fresh folks respond with a lenient judgment of Ray's behavior.

Before giving a Liberationist account of our responses to the two cases, it's worth noting some differences between Bob's Bugatti and Ray's Big Request. Complementing each other, here are two salient disparities: First, as surely as $30,000 is ten times $3,000, the cost to Ray of meeting his Big Request from UNICEF is *much less* than the cost to Bob of behaving helpfully when his Bugatti's future was at stake. And, on the other side of the ledger, while Bob's behaving unhelpfully, rather than in his saliently helpful way, meant that only one more child soon dies, Ray's behaving unhelpfully, rather than in *his* saliently helpful way, meant that *thousands* more children soon die.

Dovetailing nicely with a Liberationist account of our divergent responses to the two cases, there's also this salient divergence between the examples: In Bob's case, it was psychologically *easy* for a normal protagonist to behave in his most salient helpful manner, even when fully aware of the great cost of his so behaving; indeed, while it was hard *not* to do that, Bob did it anyway. In Ray's case, by contrast, it was psychologically *very hard* to behave in his most salient way (and, in the wake of succumbing to that great difficulty, it was pretty hard to behave at all helpfully.) But, morally, what can that difference mean? Clearly, it won't mean any elevation in the moral status of Ray's bad behavior. So, (unless we shift the context set to prevail for most of our inquiry, which there's now no reason to do) it's correct to say that, though it was much more difficult for Ray to behave decently, still, even as both failed morality completely, Ray's terribly consequential conduct was no better than Bob's behavior.

Before confronting this argument's third, and final, case, it's worth sketching a sound Liberationist account of our divergent responses to those first two examples: Why do we respond so leniently to Ray's badly unhelpful conduct? Unlike the child in Bob's Bugatti, the dire needs of the kids whom Ray might serve to help were entirely inconspicuous to the protagonist in question; and, unlike the exciting trouble in which Bob's trapped child was embroiled, the troubles embroiling UNICEF's potential clients were as unexciting to Ray as they are to you and me. Thus, while there was available to Bob more than enough to break the grip of his futility thinking, there was nothing to break the grip of Ray's futility thinking. Quite automatically, we give Ray a pass on the matter of his Big Request; but, we don't give a pass to Bob when, instead of a child's life, he chose to preserve his own comfortable retirement.

While what's just been said is adequate to the task, the field's here so fertile for Liberationist fruit that, so far, we've just been warming up. To seal the deal, I'll really turn up the heat. First, consider Bob's Bugatti: Just as the endangered child's plainly trapped in the salient trolley track territory, so, by way of his retirement fund's precarious placement, Bob's prospect for a nice future is also plainly placed in that same salient territory. Further, with the two-fold fork creating a conceptual coin with the child's life on one side and Bob's comforts on the other, it's blatantly obvious to Bob that this is the morally relevant situation: If he chooses one side of the fork for the trolley's path, he's a winner and the child's a big loser; if he chooses the other side, there's an opposite outcome. So, even as he groups himself with that child, Bob clearly sees his retirement fund as fair game for the solution to the pressing problem that, well enough, concerns them both. But, even while seeing that clearly, Bob *still* let there be such serious suffering. Because we appreciate all that well, to Bob's Bugatti we respond harshly. Next, consider Ray's case: In keeping with his habits of thought, Ray saw himself as quite separate from the distant needy UNICEF children and, so, he saw their terrible troubles as not being any problem concerning him at all. Thus, he certainly didn't see his assets as fair game for helping to solve any such pressing global problem. Because we also habitually think like that, to Ray's Big Request we respond leniently.

From those two hypothetical examples, we turn to the actual case of us typical well-off Americans. Now, most of us aren't as well off as I had Ray be. But, to comply with the Pretty Demanding Dictate, we need part with only 51% of our assets, while Ray was asked to part with 99% of his. Right off the bat, and at the least, it's not *much* more costly for us to comply with that Dictate than for Ray to comply with his Big Request. And, on a most reasonable reckoning, for most of us it's actually *less* costly to comply with the Dictate: Since Ray's fully 70 years old, there's only five more years, we've supposed, when he can earn significant income. But, as I'll realistically enough suppose, most readers are, like me, between 30 and 60 years of age. Because we're over 30, we can expect that, in the years soon upcoming, we'll be enjoying a significant income, part of which is to be placed aside for our eventual retirement. And, because we're not yet 60, we can expect that, in most of our future years, it will continue. So, even after parting with 51% of what we've got, we'll be better off than old Ray would be, had he complied with his Big Request.

Since there'll be great preventable problems for millions of poor children for years to come, there'll be widespread application for the remaining part of the Dictate, the clause requiring an able earner to part with "much" of her continuing income. Year after year, hardly anyone gives even one percent to anything that's in UNICEF's moral league, and most give nothing. So, on any reasonable interpretation of the term, this "much" is well satisfied with twenty percent of an able earner's income. So, the cost to us of complying with the Dictate is less than the cost to Ray of complying with his Big Request. On balance, then, our failure to comply will be at least as badly wrong as old Ray's failure.

Is there anything to be said for the thought that our failure's really not so bad as Ray's? There's little more than this: First, old Ray was made to be particularly well-informed about what each thousand dollars given to UNICEF could mean for the lessening of serious suffering; whereas most others don't have such definite information so plainly laid out before them. And, second, it was actually requested of Ray to give almost all he had to UNICEF's best programs; whereas none of us is ever asked by UNICEF, or by anything of the like, to part with anywhere near as much.

Though such considerations might do a bit, they can't do much to give our conduct a better behavioral record than Ray's, or than old Bob's poor showing. After all, with almost all giving UNICEF nothing, several million of us have already been that well informed. And, with nearly every well-off individual, actually being asked for most of her assets will be as entirely unproductive as was asking old Ray to part with nearly all of his. Far from there being any serious fault with the Pretty Demanding Dictate, we must conclude, there'll be just such a fault with our behavior, unless we make a big move to do at least as much as that Dictate demands.

3. Two Principles of Ethical Integrity

The foregoing argument can be complemented by reasoning that supports, as well, statements far more demanding than that Dictate. In this section, I'll lay the foundation for the reasoning. To that end, we'll consider two precepts in the family, *Principles of Ethical Integrity*, beginning with:

> *The Reasonable Principle of Ethical Integrity.* Other things being even nearly equal, if it's all right for you to *impose losses on others* with the result that there's a significant lessening in the serious losses suffered by others overall, then, if you're to avoid doing

what's seriously wrong, you *can't fail to impose equal or smaller losses on yourself,* nor can you fail to accept such losses, when the result's *an equal or greater* significant lessening of such serious losses overall.

When there's no fussing over niceties of formulation, this precept is embraced by anyone with even a modicum of moral decency. For, even if it's the only way there'll be much less serious suffering overall, the precept never says we may impose losses on others; rather, it says only that, *if* we may do so, then it's on the condition that, in the assigning of such necessary losses to people, we mustn't favor ourselves over others. So, since this Principle is eminently fair and sensible, when moving to a weaker precept I go well out of my way to seek nearly universal agreement.

As it will turn out, to argue for "very costly" conclusions, we needn't use the unobjectionable Reasonable Principle. Instead, we can make do with a logically far less ambitious member of its family:

> *The Weak Principle of Ethical Integrity.* Other things being even nearly equal, if it's all right for you to impose losses on others with the result that there's a significant lessening in the serious losses suffered by others overall, then, if you're to avoid doing what's seriously wrong, you *can't fail to impose much lesser losses on yourself,* nor can you fail to accept such lesser losses, when the result's a *much more* significant lessening of such serious losses overall.

To make vivid this maxim's lack of ambition, I'll offer these words: How can you give big hits to others to lessen losses significantly, but forgo taking a much *smaller* hit, yourself, to lessen serious losses *much more* significantly?? In its central thrust, the Weak Principle's a completely compelling moral maxim.

Because they can't be disturbed by the fruit of distorted moral thinking, no matter how habitual, these Principles are fit to figure in good moral arguments for costly conclusions: It's perfectly all right that they make not the slightest provision for the prospect that those up for suffering seriously can have needs entirely inconspicuous to you, and to any other potential benefactor, or that, to the well-off, their troubles might be boring. Indeed, since they make no provision for any of our distortional proclivities, these Principles are open to treating a vast range of cases.

Since few Preservashonists know what's been disclosed by our inquiry, many will think that, from this vast range, plenty of pairs each mean a genuine counterexample even to the Weak Principle of Ethical Integrity. So, when thinking of the obvious pair comprising the Envelope and the Trolley, they'll have thoughts like these: "In the Trolley, you impose on another the loss of her life just so that six more folks don't lose theirs and, as our reactions show, that's all right. Yet, as our reactions also show, in the Envelope it's all right for you to refrain from imposing on yourself a loss of only a hundred unneeded dollars, though that means over thirty more folks will soon lose their lives! So, while they may be initially appealing, the least bit of sensitive reflection shows these simplistic Principles to be hopelessly inadequate precepts." But, as we've learned in this book, it's only in such futile objections to the fair-minded maxims, and it's not in the Principles of Ethical Integrity, that there's anything simplistic or hopelessly inadequate.

4. A More Principled Argument Also Yields More Highly Demanding Dictates

Toward arguing for more costly conclusions, we can turn the tables on that futile Preservashonist thinking. To expedite the matter, I'll combine the Trolley and the Envelope into one longish example, *From the Trolley through the Envelope*: In May, you switch the path of a nearby runaway trolley and, while imposing the loss of his life on one, you have it that five fewer suffer so seriously. In June, while failing to impose on yourself the loss of $100, as UNICEF's appeal then requested, you have it that thirty more kids soon die, perhaps in July.

According to even the Weak Principle, your conduct, spanning May and June, was seriously wrong. And, though our intuitive reactions to the temporally extended example are lenient responses, by now we know that reaction's hardly derived from our Values. A matter for more serious consideration is that, consistent with even the Weak Principle, there are two very different approaches. First, there's the approach that Liberationists favor: While May's conduct was at least all right, June's was seriously wrong. Second, and found appealing by certain absolute pacifists, there's this approach: While May's killing conduct was wrong, it's at least open whether June's unhelpful conduct was acceptable behavior.

Though we do best to reject this second approach, some can feel some sympathy for the view. Thus, we're happy to realize that, for drawing costly conclusions with Principles of Ethical Integrity, we needn't call on cases where one person imposes death on others. Instead, we'll do well with almost any case where you impose on another both a large nonserious loss and also a serious loss much less than the loss of life. For one step in that direction, we'll first consider this case, where the only loss imposed is a large nonserious loss:

> *Your Destruction of Bob's Bugatti.* Even while it's you who's spied a shiny metallic object, it's Bob who's parked his Bugatti in the aforementioned place for another reason, namely, to get a close look at some unusual wild flowers growing near the end of the fork's short branch. While you're examining the shiny switch, Bob's scrutinizing the wild flowers. Knowing Bob's fine financial situation and your poor one, still you bear him no malice. But, spotting the approaching trolley, you're aware that, unless you turn it onto Bob's multimillion-dollar auto, it will kill the young child trapped on the switch's long branch. You choose the more active option and, while that ensures a very uncomfortable retirement for Bob, the child is spared.

As almost everyone responds here, your conduct was good. And, we're only a short step from this variant where, in addition to that large nonserious loss, you impose a certain serious loss:

> *Your Destruction of Bob's Bugatti and His Leg.* Generally the same as just before, the situation here is this: On the fork's long branch, *two* little kids are trapped. And, while looking at the wild flowers, Bob gets his foot caught in the short branch's track. So, if you switch the Trolley away from the children, it will take a leg off Bob, irrevocably, moments before it destroys his Bugatti. You choose the more active option and, while that leaves Bob with just one leg and little for his retirement, the children are spared.

As most respond to this example, your conduct was good.[2] No doubt, that's a proper reaction.

From Principles of Ethical Integrity, we're well set to reason for Highly Demanding Dictates. For the reasoning to be cogent, it's not important that you, or I, ever actually impose any serious loss on anyone else or, really, any loss at all. Rather, all that's wanted is an

---

2. For the Highly Squeamish, there will be a negative response to this latest case. Not that it's necessary to do so, but, still, it may be worth pointing out that even most of these Highly Squeamish won't respond negatively to the more lop-sided case where there are *twenty* trapped kids opposite Bob's leg and car. As the text will show, even with this lop-sided case serving as a (very ecumenical) pivot point, the main arguments go through without a hitch.

accurate moral assessment of certain loss-lessening behavior, whether it's actually been emitted or whether it's only been imaginatively considered. And, with our consideration of Your Destruction of Bob's Bugatti and His Leg, we've got what's wanted. So, let's reason.

In Your Destruction of Bob's Bugatti and His Leg, as your conduct was good, it was certainly all right. So, even from just the Weak Principle, we can conclude that, if it's needed for there to be as much as *three* fewer children dying soon, it's seriously wrong for you not to impose just a *non*serious loss on yourself, however large, like almost any financial loss. Now, as we all know, by imposing on yourself as large a financial loss as you can, and easily aiming the funds toward efficient vital programs, you'll lessen serious suffering to a *far* greater extent than that. So, it's seriously wrong not to send to the likes of UNICEF and OXFAM, about as promptly as possible, nearly all your worldly wealth.

Without bothering to spell out the "more principled argument" in laboriously explicit terms, we've again reasonably reached the Pretty Demanding Dictate and, this time, far more Demanding Dictates, too. Leaving most of the matter for subsequent sections, I'll close this with words that help place things in an appropriately practical perspective: Covered by a Principle's "Other things being even nearly equal" clause, there's the point that, when contributing promptly to save lives soon, you shouldn't badly impair your ability to contribute, in the future, to save lives later. For most, this won't mean much more than keeping yourself presentable enough to prosper. For a few, it means much more: Perhaps by legally binding himself to do so, or perhaps in another effective way, a successful entrepreneur must commit his profits to a judicious mix of efficient business investment and efficient lessening of serious suffering; then, he'll do all he can to lessen the serious suffering of others, taking good account of both the shorter and longer terms.

5. A Decent Principle of Aiding: Being Appropriately Modest about Lessening Early Death

When discussing the Envelope and the View that Ethics is Highly Demanding, in chapter 2, we considered some principles about aiding folks in vital need. At that early stage, my aim was very unambitious and, so, the modest goal was easy to meet: Rather than your horrible behavior in the Vintage Sedan, it was the Envelope's unhelpful conduct that violated even highly *undemanding* precepts about what to do for folks in vital need. To further the present discussion, it's useful to recall the penultimate precept there displayed. For, while the chapter's last maxim, Very Cheaply Lessening Early Death, was *obscenely* lenient, nothing *that* bad was true of:

> *Pretty Cheaply Lessening Early Death.* Other things being even nearly equal, if your behaving in a certain way will result in the number of people who *very prematurely lose their lives* being less than the number who will do so if you don't so behave and *if even so you'll still be at least reasonably well off*, then, first, it's morally required that you behave in that way and, second, it's even seriously morally wrong for you not to so behave.

As I'll remind you, full compliance with "Pretty Cheaply" is much more costly for the very rich than for the many others who are only rather well-to-do; after all, with this "leveling" precept, even a full billionaire's compliance will turn her into someone who's just reasonably well off. But, for reasons recently observed, that's no serious objection to the maxim. Indeed, for a precept that's not just literally correct, but that's also usefully informative, Pretty Cheaply doesn't go far enough in the decently altruistic direction. So, for better guidance, we'll want an aiding precept that's at least as demanding as:

> *Being Appropriately Modest about Lessening Early Death.* Other things being even nearly equal, if your behaving in a certain way will result in the number of people who *very prematurely lose their lives* being less than the number who will do so if you don't so behave and if even so you'll still be at least *very modestly* well off, then it's seriously wrong for you not to so behave.

Because full compliance with it will leave you only very modestly well off, at the present time in the actual world, it's costly even for us, who aren't billionaires, to comply fully with this decent maxim.

Because that's so, some will wish to object to the maxim: "However it's formulated, won't this principle be inordinately and hopelessly vague? After all, even relative to just one particular agent at just one particular time in her life, how well off must she be to be only *very modestly* well off? Even granting all that relativization, without *much* more help we *still* won't understand this maxim at all well. So, where's the help that's sorely needed? Most likely, nowhere to be found."

That assessment's far too pessimistic: When saving just two trapped kid's lives, you made Bob become not only a guy in a bad financial fix, but a man with just one leg. Still, he was otherwise in pretty good shape: After all, he was able to see well and hear well, and he was able to get around pretty well with the aid of nothing more than ordinary crutches, and he lived in a country with lots of freedom, and lots else, to be enjoyed, and so on. So, even then, Bob's a great deal better off than very many other people. For just one example, he's much better off than the millions of deeply impoverished Third Worlders who, as they didn't get enough Vitamin A when very young, as children became completely and permanently blind. With a properly global perspective in force, then, it's plain that a person at Bob's level is *at least* very modestly well off. Well, then, as long as you're doing even just a little better than old Bob, you'll *certainly* be at least very modestly well off. So, for almost any application of Being Appropriately Modest, we may take old Bob's one-legged level as a (generous enough) lower bound of how much of a cost you must incur to comply, well enough, with that modest proposition.

For a decent upper bound, what's a correspondingly workable idea? At least for someone who's typically whole and healthy, like well over 90% of my readers, this rough but tough rule will work well: By sending funds to the most efficient loss-lessening programs, you must incur financial losses up to the point where going further will be unproductive, overall, in lessening serious losses. So, anyone who owns and enjoys a nice home is far above a decent upper bound. And, with rare exceptions, so is anyone who owns a nice car. And, when it's mainly just for pleasure, someone who takes a costly vacation is also living far too high. No doubt, you can go on quite well enough with this.

For serious attempts to comply with the decent precept, you know plenty well enough what you must do. So, though there may be a great difficulty in doing decently well by Being Appropriately Modest, it's not with our understanding of the precept that the difficulty lies.

When beginning the book, I had us suppose that there's only a very small cost, for the well-off likes of you and me, in efficiently saving a distant child's life or, more precisely, in the causally amorphous moral equivalent. For psychological reasons, it was then good to do that. But, as recent developments have shown, for a well-to-do adult, like you or me, it's badly wrong not to provide vital aid even if it costs *many thousands* of dollars to lessen by just *one* the number of distant children who'll die young rather than live long. So, if there weren't available more efficient means of lessening serious suffering, it would be required of each of us, very strongly, to contribute greatly to "unappealingly costly" life-saving activities, say, vitally effective costly pediatric surgery, whether performed in India or in Indiana.

6. Currently Common Lifesaving Costs, Important Efficiencies and Irrelevant Probabilities

As far as morality's concerned, nothing really depends on whether you can mean that a couple of thousand more, or whether you can mean only that a couple more, of the world's vulnerable children survive to live reasonably long and healthy lives. In either case, you're *strongly* required to forgo your mere comforts and have it that fewer die young. With that established, now's the time to make good a promise made near the book's outset: We'll look hard at the real dollar cost, to each of us well-off Americans, of causally amorphous lifesaving in places not only with low incomes, but with high childhood mortality rates.

Many countries in sub-Saharan Africa fill the bill, well over twenty. A few populous Asian nations present even more cheap chances. All together, we've got salient sites for several hundred million under-five kids. Now, for this book's discussion, we should consider children, in those dangerous places, who are relevant analogues of the imperilled child in the Shallow Pond: As that first and central case is boringly understood, the child certainly isn't an infant (whose crazy caretaker put her in the water for the fun of it); rather, he's maybe two, maybe three, maybe even four years old. So, for an Envelopey parallel, we look at imperilled Third Worlders in that age-range. To be *nicely conservative*, let's take a toddler who's just barely two years old and, so, we'll take on the *highest* relevant cost.

What's the (average additional) cost of taking a typically sick two-year-old, in the likes of Pakistan or Nigeria, and turning him into an adult? Well, even in wealthy and peaceful Switzerland, a billion bucks can't *guarantee* that a *healthy* toddler will see his majority. So, our question becomes: What's the cost of taking our poor, sick two-year-old kid and, by paying his health bills this year, and even in each of his other most dangerous years, giving him a high chance to become a twenty-one-year-old, a chance that's over ninety percent? Now, since the bulk of our targeted two-year-olds have already gotten their vaccinations, about 80% of them, we (probably and boringly) *won't* be paying the $17 *that* standardly costs in our bargain basements. Much more conservatively than boringly, however, we're assuming that, in every one of their relevant early years, our target kids all need considerable health care. Even so, all we'll pay for is a few years of "caring for the sick child." Net of overhead, leakage and waste in his region's health care delivery system, in our bargain basements that currently runs a bit over $12 per year; conservatively, I'll round up to $13 per annum.[3] But, what about those gross associated costs? Well, according to the experts, they add 20% to the local expense. So, again rounding upward, the local cost rises to $16 per year.

Once the children are 5, and they're in even moderately good health, they'll have over a 90% chance of becoming 21-year-olds; by the age of 5, they're no longer so very vulnerable to the big-time Third World child-killers. Well, since they've already lived through their first and second years, for our targeted kids that means paying sick-care coverage for just their third, fourth, and fifth years. Multiplying the 3 years by $16, we find a local bill of $48. Being nicely conservative, let's also pay for a fourth year, so that our two-year-olds become *six*-year-olds, with a chance of becoming 21 that's *well* over 90%; paying another $16, there's a local bill of $64.[4]

Though that's the whole *local* bill, *we're* not local. And, we won't soon go to Pakistan, or Nigeria, to get our money into an effective slot. So, we should ask about the possibility of further costs. Well, though it won't make a difference to our calculation, I still think I should tell you that, with annual donations to UNICEF's Committee *under* $5000, sometimes funds earmarked for a certain sort of intervention—for ORT, or for Integrated Management of the Sick Child—won't be used in precisely the way requested. But, anyhow, who cares whether *my* dollars go toward supplying *ORT* and *yours* toward furthering *vaccinations*, or *yours* to ORT and *mine* to vaccinations? Since it costs money to keep track of what goes where, and that money can otherwise be spent on *more* ORT *and more* vaccinations, no right-thinking person cares.[5]

3. For the figures used in my calculations, and for the associated figures mentioned but properly not used, my main source, and very kind source, is José-Luis Bobadilla, MD, PhD, Senior Health Specialist, Population Health and Nutrition Department, The World Bank. Seeking an up-to-the-minute expert, I was kindly given Dr. Bobadilla's name and phone number by Dr. W. Henry Mosley of The School of Hygiene and Public Health, The Johns Hopkins University.

4. With young male children, who are most young children, these impoverished Third World youngsters will, I'm told, have a greater chance of reaching their majority than the male six-year old kids in the far richer neighborhood of Harlem, just six miles uptown from my own truly rich neighborhood in downtown "money-makin' Manhattan."

5. For those who feel bad about the fact that earmarks aren't always honored with small donations, or even not-so-small donations, recall a theme of chapter 3: Putting together the truth about futility thinking and the obvious truth about the "multiply suspect" Small Marina, we can see there's no serious wrong when, to have fewer children die, someone misleads others who are perennially well-off. That's true whether the misleader is me or whether it's a writer hired by a UNICEF affiliate.

Anyway, since we've seen that, to the likes of UNICEF, such well-off folks as us must contribute *more* than $5000 annually, what may be true for some smaller donations has no bearing on our current calculation. Well, then, for a nice round number, let's suppose that, with OXFAM and others also getting hefty chunks, you send the Committee $10,000, as that's all you can now afford to send there. We'll also assume that, because no relevantly more specific earmark can be honored, your note says, "Where it will do most good, use for the care of sick children under six years old." And, third, let's conservatively suppose that, because fully half your money will be "wasted" on caring for children in their *first two* years, only *half* will be spent on kids in their *next four* years. With only half your donation helping sick two-year-olds become healthy six-year-olds, the unit cost of saving our *targeted* children rises to $128 a head.

Since the U.S. Committee has various domestic expenses, not all the money sent to the group goes overseas. Can we ignore these associated costs? Well, the Committee's assured me that, with less finicky donors willing to pave the way, all of your earmarked $10,000 can go abroad. So, in our calculations, the associated costs *can* be ignored. But, instead of quibbling over a few dollars, let's not be free-riders here; let's do our "fair share in shouldering costs." When that's done, the $128 we've figured rises, I can assure you, to about $188. Finally, to be duly conservative cost-sharers, we'll round up to an even $200.

Going by that even figure, we might say that, for your $10,000, you can do the moral equivalent of saving 50 toddlers. Then, again, we might possibly fail to take full account of money spent on toddler care that, despite best efforts, fails to see treated tykes through to their sixth birthday. Still, since *most* of those proportionately *few* tykes won't even see their *third* birthday, this can't decrease much your figured 50. Indeed, it's terribly conservative to put forth a final reckoning as low as this: Forty more toddlers saved for $10,000 donated. Not an incredible moral bargain; instead, that's a credible bargain.

But, we've already learned that, for the likes of us, a morally decent life is bound to be terribly costly. So, who are we to lust after moral *bargains*? Indeed, to any right-thinking person, earmarking money for a "bargain" intervention is costly nonsense: Just as some inadvisably "adopt" certain distant children, others will *inadvisably* "adopt" certain interventions.

While our most recent reasoning highlighted a useful lesson, that encounter with the Real World isn't crucial to any of the book's main points. Here and now, that's clear from arguments offered earlier in this advanced chapter. Had I made you confront certain complexities early in the book, even in the first two chapters it would have been clear from such complementary considerations as these: Beyond our straightforward Shallow Pond and Vintage Sedan, there are probabilistic versions of the cases. So, in one such version of the Pond, your chance of saving the drowning youngster, should you make a good attempt, is only 50 percent. (That's *much* less than UNICEF's chance, when it makes a good attempt, of saving a typically targeted toddler.) Knowing there's that chance the kid will die *anyway*, you pass him by. Obviously, that's abominable behavior. And, with a "50% version" of the much more costly Sedan, your unhelpful behavior also is outrageous. What's more, within the relevant range, compounding probabilistic complexities doesn't change matters: Further suppose that, whether or not his leg's saved, our chancy trespasser has only a 50% shot at living even three more years; so, even if you help him, there's only a 25% chance he'll enjoy *both* legs for any *long* time. Still, it's horribly wrong not to aid.

Anyway, before we beat this horse to death, let's move on.

7. Special Obligations and Care for Dependents

For many well-to-do folks, the strong general requirement to give vital aid may conflict with certain strong moral duties that, in each agent's case, concern only a very few people to whom she's specially related in a morally most weighty manner. As I'm suggesting, it's possible that, in some cases, you'll have special obligations strong enough to outweigh your great general obligation to lessen the number of children dying painfully and prematurely. So, you might face two serious questions: To which few people, if any, do you have such enormously strong obligations? And, with your benefiting them meaning there'll be more distant children horribly dying, for each of these few, what is it, really, that you must do? We'll take them in turn.

For the vast majority, there are only a very few people to whom we might have obligations so strong that, at this late stage, are worth mentioning. For you, the special circle might include your parents, or your children, or your spouse, or, perhaps, someone to whom you're related in much the way that, typically, folks are related to parents, or children, or spouses. Without trying to put a fine point on things, that's about it. So, typically, you won't have such strong obligations to almost all your friends and benefactors, or to members of your family that aren't extremely close, or to people to whom you've made promises, and so on.[6] With no need to give the first question an answer that's precise or complete, we turn to the second.

When your children are still young, you might have a very strong obligation to see that their basic needs are met, including, perhaps, the need for an adequate education. But, beyond thoughts of costly toys and garments, that *doesn't* mean you may send them to expensive private schools; rather, even if it means your moving to a different neighborhood, you should see to it that they attend, free of charge, an adequate public school. For, by not spending thousands annually on tuition, you'll send thousands more to the likes of UNICEF and, thus, you'll see to it that fewer vulnerable youngsters die painfully and prematurely.[7] And, when they're older, it's nearly certain you should spend only what's needed for them to attend a reasonably good public institution of higher learning, not a socially more prestigious private college. And, for almost all of us with children, by the time they've become adults, we should no longer provide them financial assistance.

For the vast majority of well-to-do adults, a person's spouse requires far less from her financially than her young children. So, it will serve no good purpose for me to spend many words detailing someone's duties to her spouse, or to another most significant other. And, except if they should be infirm, it's little indeed that you should spend on your parents. Indeed, even if they are infirm, usually it won't cost much to do just what's morally decent. In sum: For most of us well-to-do folks, no consideration flowing from strong special obligations will change the moral picture much and, for most of our lives, we must give most of what comes our way to lessen distant serious suffering.[8]

8. More Than Merely Material Costs

For expository purposes, so far I've explicitly considered only the financial costs, or the merely material costs, of living a morally decent

6. For the weakness of the moral obligations created by (almost all) promises, contracts, and so on, recall chapter 2's discussion of cases like the Small Marina, the Large Deposit, and so on.

7. One thing your children *won't* learn much about in any school is, I'm afraid, our good Values. But, partly for your reading this book, they'll learn much from you.

8. It may be worth noting that, because I had them be seventy-year-olds, the properly boring suppositions for old Bob and Ray had them quite free of strong special obligations. So, boringly, if they had kids, by now their children would be on their own. And, while they had parents, the properly boring supposition is that these parents have been dead for years; and so on. But, for most of us, there's no substantial difference between our own situation and those of Bob and Ray.

life. But, in the previous section, we made an implicit move toward a fuller consideration. For, not just in more tender ways, but also by getting them goods and services with our dollars, we want to do a lot for our nearest and dearest. Right there, we see that it's in more than a merely material way that our situation's unpleasantly demanding. Having just been explicit about some more than merely material costs of a decent life, in brief compass I'll try to do a lot more.

Though most well-off people like being paid well, that's not the main motive for engaging in the work we do. This is especially true, I think, of most of this book's mature readers who, no doubt, are academic philosophers. Since we professors have many friends on the faculties of universities, or other institutions devoted mainly to teaching or research, my discussion of work will focus on that vocation. But, as will become apparent, all the main points apply, as well, to other occupations.

Because we enjoy our academic positions, many of us earn significantly less than if we did work that, though we'd enjoy it less, is much more remunerative. For example, a senior professor specializing in corporate law could leave her intellectually fulfilling post at a major university's prestigious law school, earn far more at a top corporate firm and, while being less fulfilled, also donate the lion's share of her much higher income toward helping save distant youngsters' lives. If she did all that, how bad would things be for our able lawyer? Well, not only would she be better off than old one-legged Bob, hobbling about barely making ends meet, but she'd be far better off than the many millions who're each much worse off still. So, at the least, she'd still be very modestly well off. So, for many able academic lawyers, it's seriously wrong not to exchange their present posts for much more lucrative jobs and, then, to contribute about as much as they can toward the morally most imperative ends. Even if somewhat less dramatically, much the same holds true in the case of many able academic economists, and for many in the mathematical sciences, and the natural sciences.

Closer to home, what's a decently behaved academic philosopher to do? Since most readers are likely to be in that position, or to be preparing for it, I should give this at least a brief discussion: Those not yet very well established should seek employment in fields where there's markedly more money to be made. Now, since he's not well equipped to earn much more doing something else, and it's hard for an old dog to learn new tricks, it's just possible that the well-established philosopher may best stay in his post. But, even if that's actually so, things certainly won't be nice or easy for the old philosopher; rather, he'll have to change the focus of his work so enormously that, in short order, he'll enjoy little intellectual satisfaction. For example, on one of the few paths morally open to him, not only must he forever forsake the philosophically central site of metaphysics for the relatively peripheral domain of applied ethics, but, in the far less central field, he'll mainly produce writing that, in aims and effects, is more socially beneficial than it's philosophically revealing.

This leads to another area that's important to consider. My reference is to the *political activity* that, on behalf of the world's worst-off innocents, well-off folks may be strongly obliged to pursue vigorously. Since such activity certainly isn't something many of us enjoy, doing a lot of that amounts to another big cost that's more than merely material. Now, though there's much to say about how such morally imperative politicking might be done most effectively, it's only in other books that this large topic can be adequately addressed. Here, it's enough to emphasize that, in more than merely material ways, for most academics, this worldly engagement will be enormously costly.

9. Extremely Demanding Situations

Toward lessening the serious suffering of others, no serious loss on my part, in over fifty years of life, could have done as much as a well aimed check for, say, just $500. This has been true even while, during all the past thirty years, many mere financial losses on my part, a few quite large and many not so large, could have saved many lives or, better, could have meant the causally amorphous moral equivalent. Less than a century ago, such a proposition about giving money and saving lives would have held true of hardly anyone. But, nowadays, it holds true of many millions of well-off adults. By contrast, the question of when morality might require one to impose on himself a serious loss, like the loss of life or limbs, has little practical bearing for most of us and, for most, it may be taken mainly as a theoretical question.

Since we've recently observed several variants of the Trolley, it may be most efficient to explore our theoretical question by thinking further about that case, and about a few further variants. So, first, recall our positive response to the Trolley's killing conduct. As will again be agreed, that's an accurate reaction; so, at least in such a situation, it's fine for you to kill one and save six. But, then, an apt application of the Reasonable Principle of Ethical Integrity yields the thought that, with a choice between letting a trolley fatally crush six others and getting it away from them onto yourself, you must sacrifice your life for theirs. So, we face a troubling "trilemma" comprising our verdict on the Trolley, the Reasonable Principle, and, third, that tough conclusion. In the face of it, what shall we think?

Shall we think that, despite initial appearances, we should reject our positive verdict on the Trolley? To all appearances, that's just an *ad hoc* maneuver. And, at most, it serves only to relocate the trilemma's problem: First, even if saving six lives doesn't seem impressive enough to warrant taking one, there'll be *some* non-grandiose number, perhaps sixty will do, that has precious few remaining serious about this quasi-pacifist approach. And, second, there's a bitter pill to swallow when, in relevantly parallel cases, what's called for is a lesser serious sacrifice, as with having it that a rerouted trolley rolls over, and cuts off, your right arm and leg.

Alternatively, we can focus on the Reasonable Principle. Here, we might try to deny great sacrifices by looking to employ the Principle's initial clause, "Other things being even nearly equal," whose point is to allow for weighty moral exceptions. But, that won't be to any avail. For, rather than licensing folks to favor themselves, the clause will be triggered only if your electing a great sacrifice conflicts with your meeting weighty moral obligations. For instance, as long as you have dependent children, it *might* be that, with only a few strangers to be saved by your taking your life, you should spare yourself for the kids' sake. But, even if that's so, it won't mean much comfort: First, at some times in adults' lives, almost everyone's free of such terribly strong special obligations. And, second, even when they do have needy dependents, in the most salient parallel cases, almost all will be required to sacrifice a couple of large limbs to a trolley's crushing wheels. So, that clause won't allow any easy exceptions. And, verbal niceties aside, the rest of the Principle is unexceptionable.

Finally, we may take the hard way, straight through the trilemma: Even though moral failure would be very understandable, and even if it would be worse than pointless to blame the agent, in cases like the "Egocentric Trolley," you must sacrifice your life for a very few others. To support that thought, various ideas work well. But, for a brief discussion, we'll stay in the realm of trolley examples.

Following a novel suggestion from Keith DeRose, we'll consider a couple of new, but simple, several-option trolley cases. Simpler than its partner in one obvious way, we'll begin with this mere three-option case, which features a three-fold forking switch: On the fork's "rightmost" branch, toward which the switch accidentally happens to be set, fully thirty young children are trapped. So, if nothing's done, you'll let that many kids be violently killed. But, you have two more active options: On one of them, you turn your dial one setting to the left and, thus, you change the switch's setting so that the trolley will fatally roll down the next to rightmost branch, where six little kids are trapped. On the other, you turn the dial to the left as far as it will go and, thus, you change the switch so the trolley will fatally roll down the fork's leftmost branch, where only you are trapped.

About this case, some might say it's all right to let the thirty little children die; but that hardly seems a good answer. And, others might say that it's all right to kill the six young kids; but that also seems implausible. Though not a self-evident proposition, the most plausible view is the one remaining: Just as it's wrong to let the thirty little kids die and it's wrong to kill the six, so it's wrong not to sacrifice yourself for the thirty.

As Liberationism sensibly has it, matters aren't substantially different in a situation that, while otherwise precisely the same, just lacks the option with thirty children. So, whatever our initial reaction to the case with just a *two*-fold fork and just six little kids in deathly danger opposite you, the most plausible position is this properly parallel proposition: It's wrong not to sacrifice yourself for the six.

Simpler in another obvious way, our case's companion is this six-option example, which features a six-fold forking switch: On the fork's "rightmost" branch, toward which the switch accidentally happens to be set, *six* young children are trapped. So, if nothing's done, you'll let that many kids be violently killed. But, you have five more active options: On one of them, you turn your dial one setting to the left and, thus, you change the switch's setting so that, instead, the trolley will fatally roll down the next to rightmost branch, where *five* little kids are trapped. On another, you turn your dial two settings to the left and, thus, you change the switch so that, instead, the trolley will roll down the branch that's one step further to the left, where *four* little kids are trapped; and so on. On the last option, you turn the dial to the left as far left as it will go and, thus, you change the switch so that the trolley will fatally roll down the fork's leftmost branch, where only you are trapped.

About this companion case, some might say it's all right to let the six little children die; but, that doesn't seem a good answer. And, others might say that it's all right to kill just a very few of the trapped young kids; but that also seems implausible. Though not self-evident, the most plausible position is the remaining proposition: Just as it's wrong to let the six little kids die and it's wrong to kill a few, so it's wrong not to sacrifice yourself for the six.

Paralleling the previous Liberationist reasoning, an equally sensi-

ble line here yields a logically more ambitious conclusion: First, matters aren't substantially different in a situation that, while otherwise
precisely the same, just lacks the options with more than two children.
So, whatever our initial reaction to the case with just a two-fold fork
and just *two* little kids in deathly danger opposite you, the most plausible view is this: Though it may be very understandable, and worse
than pointless to blame, still, it's wrong not to sacrifice yourself for
the two.

Serious thought about many different cases apparently shows
that, with a forced choice between your life and the lives of just two
children, it's badly wrong not to sacrifice your life for theirs. How far
can this tough line be taken? Suppose provisos are made for whatever
few morally weighty considerations require them. Within those wide
bounds, might such a strong result hold whenever there's forced on
you the choice between your own life and the lives of two youngsters?
As I suspect, but can do little more than suspect, the answer is "Yes."
Now, for present purposes, we needn't show that to be so, nor even
make more progress in that direction. Rather, it's enough to have
made this modest thought reasonable to accept: In many possible
situations, you morally must give your life to spare two others.

In the actual world, hardly any of us affluent folk, and especially
us old philosophers, will ever be in such extremely demanding situations. Our realization of that fact can have a beneficial effect on the
attitudes we have toward the costs, in the actual world, of living morally decent lives: Were we to live in a world far more dangerously
unpredictable than this actual world, then, to live a morally decent life,
a fair number of us would have to suffer losses far, far greater than any
we need actually suffer. And, so, for all of us, the chances of suffering
such a grave loss, on pain of failing to be decent, would be very considerable, far greater than the minute chance we actually face. So, in such
a dangerously demanding world, those who cared greatly about being
decent would live terribly fearful lives. In a certain sense, then, we may
well feel fortunate that, to live morally decent lives, hardly any of us
need actually sacrifice her own life or limbs, or even live in much fear
of doing so.

Insofar as that realization has this beneficial effect on our attitudes, we may be more open to paying what, in this reasonably safe
and secure world, are the costs to well-off folks of living morally decent
lives. And, if anything much in the way of behavioral change ever
comes from that, then, from exploring our mainly theoretical question, there may come practical benefits. Of course, these benefits won't
come to us philosophical explorers; on the contrary, they'll come from

us, and perhaps from our friends and acquaintances, to those who really need to be benefitted.

10. Morality, Publicity and Motivating Morally Better Behavior

According to full-fledged Liberationism, fully spelled out, our conduct falls far short of what morality requires. As should be clear enough even initially, and as the next chapter will make much clearer still, that's no problem for the Liberationist view.

At the same time, many might think there's something badly wrong with publicizing requirements that hardly anyone, myself included, will even come close to satisfying in the next several decades: When publicizing this trying Liberationist line, don't I do something that *discourages* folks from doing more to lessen distant suffering? In closing the chapter, I'll try to put the question in proper perspective.[9]

Just as it's not aimed at the general public, nor even the fraction of it that reads a goodly number of nonfiction books, so it's unlikely this volume will be read by more than a few folks, or by anything like a representative sample of well-off people. For, in addition to the few who know me well, its audience will be, almost entirely, some academic philosophers, a few of their students, and a very few others whom they know. From my admittedly limited experience with people in such a small selective group, exposure to this Liberationism, even full-fledged and spelled-out, has had a small positive effect. Though that's an effect that's small, it's also an effect that's positive. So, it's likely that, for the rest of its small audience, too, this essay will serve to *encourage* morally better behavior.

At any rate, it's my hope that, fairly soon, there'll be written for the public a reader-friendly book that, by presenting just a few main Liberationist themes, will promote, in many readers, conduct that's well-aimed at lessening distant suffering.[10]

Especially as its intended audience wouldn't be philosophically sophisticated, in such a book it would be badly counterproductive, I'm

---

9. For a related discussion, see R. M. Hare, *Moral Thinking,* Oxford University Press, 1981.

10. Recently, Peter Singer wrote a book aimed at the general public, in his native Australia, on the personally positive aspects of leading a genuinely more ethical life. This popular work, *How Are We to Live?*, Reed Consumer Books, 1993, became an Australian bestseller, climbing to number 8 on that country's nonfiction list. Would that a book even remotely like that be a bestseller in a country as wealthy, populous and powerful as the United States of America!

well aware, ever to so much as suggest even a moderately high standard, rather than a standard rather more readily reached, for people's voluntary contributions toward efficiently lessening serious suffering. But, come to think of it, among Liberationist propositions, those suggesting a high standard for such contributions are scarcely the most important to omit in such a widely aimed work. It's far more important to exclude mention of positive Liberationist verdicts on conduct that, in our intuitive responses to cases, almost everyone judges negatively. Thus, in a truly public forum, it would be foolhardy to discuss such cases as the Account and, if anything, worse still to discuss the likes of the Foot. So, in a book that's aimed more at promoting moral behavior in the many than at promoting moral understanding in the few, there's an enormous amount of Liberationist material that should be omitted.[11] And, as bears repeating, while thoughts about high standards for aiding conduct will appear on the list of Liberationist propositions to omit, they certainly won't be at the top of the table.

There's no bad deception here: Just as reasonable Liberationists are more confident that we each must make a significant contribution to lessen distant serious suffering than that we ought to steal from affluent others toward the vital end, so, too, we place more confidence in that first proposition than in the thought that we must make contributions that, to each of us, are enormously costly. And, when addressing the public, rather than the scholars to whom this work's mainly directed, it's best, quite generally, to put forth just the Liberationist ideas in which we reasonably place a lot of confidence.

11. For some related ideas, see Henry Sidgwick, *The Methods of Ethics*, London: Macmillan, 1907; and, then, Derek Parfit's discussion of "esoteric morality" in *Reasons and Persons*, Oxford University Press, 1984.

7

METAETHICS, BETTER ETHICS: FROM COMPLEX SEMANTICS TO SIMPLE DECENCY

By now, I've made about all the substantive moral judgments in the book. Like the harsh assessment of the Vintage Sedan's conduct, many aren't unusual. Many other assessments I've made, like my severe judgment of the Envelope's conduct, are so unusual as to be jarring. As I've often noted, in *some* sense or way, those jarringly unusual judgments conflict with ever so many much more ordinary assessments that were made, and will be made, by almost everyone else. As I'll now note, they're similarly at odds with many judgments I've made, and many that, in everyday life, I'll be making.

These jarringly unusual judgments fall into two main classes. First, as occurred with the Envelope, I've judged behavior to be seriously wrong that, in everyday life, we judge to be not wrong at all. Second, as occurred with the Account, and the Foot, I've judged conduct to be good that, ordinarily, we judge to be wrong. Regarding both disparities, it first seems that there must be a contradiction between the book's judgments and what's ordinarily maintained. And, it seems this may well undermine the book's unusual moral judgments. But, both appearances may be deceptive.

First, in the noted disparities, there may be no real contradiction, but only the appearance of inconsistency. As it's this reconciling line I think most promising, most of the chapter will pursue it: Though I'll eventually give a reconciling account for the second class of jarringly unusual judgments, I'm more concerned, for obvious reasons, to do that with disparate judgments of conduct like the Envelope's.

With all my noted disparities, I aim for reconciliation through providing an account of morally useful terms on which they're so selectively flexible as to be aptly accommodating. By applying the semantic account to my disparate judgments, I might show they're actually consistent with each other.

As I expect, many will eventually agree that, with this semantic approach, there's impressive success. But, many others won't be much impressed. Especially interesting to them, perhaps, but most important for us all, there's this to be said: In all the *most important* senses, or ways, it's the book's Liberationist judgments, not those of everyday life, that accord best with morality. This remains true, even if there's *some* sense, or way, in which it's our ordinary ethical judgments that do better, as has been allowed, by your author, at least since chapter 2's second section. So, whether or not you agree with much of what this chapter newly offers, you should continue to agree with that most important truth. Especially in the book's last section, not only will that point be rightly stressed, but, with your cooperation, I'll have you put it to unequivocally decent use.

1. Diverse Judgments of the Envelope's Conduct: Two Main Considerations

Toward a reconciling account of my discrepant judgments of the Envelope's conduct, we'll be guided by two main considerations, both brought to prominence in the second section of the second chapter.

First, there are these: In a case as "unstimulating" as the Envelope—where there's No Apparent Conflict between unhelpful conduct and (even our Primary) Values—for normally decent folks, it's psychologically hard to be *aware of what's morally most relevant*. And, since it's *very* hard to be aptly moved by such awareness, it's so hard to *behave* decently. By contrast, in such a "stimulating" case as the Sedan—where there's an Obvious Sharp Conflict between unhelpful conduct and (even our Primary) Values, it's hard *not* to be aware of what's what morally. And, since it's hard *not* to be moved by such awareness, it's hard *not* to behave decently.

Second, there are considerations stemming from my method of inquiry: When making severe judgments of the Envelope's conduct, I ignored, or downplayed completely, features raising questions in the domain of our Secondary Values; just so, I had everything that determined the judgment's truth, or its acceptability, be wholly in the domain of the Primary Values.[1] In sharp contrast, when making lenient judgments of the conduct, in daily life, I may *play up* such epistemically oriented, motivationally complex considerations.

Important for my reconciling aims, the two considerations are closely connected. And, to further the aims, we'll do well to heed:

> *The Schematic Suggestion.* (i) By my then playing up (the moral significance of) only those aspects of the conduct that closely connect with our Primary Values, and by my then playing down all of the aspects that closely connect with our Secondary Values, in this book I had my judgment of the Envelope's conduct be severe. (ii) By my then playing up (the moral significance of) the psychological difficulty of our engaging in such helpful conduct as the case calls on from us, which connects closely with our Secondary Values, in everyday life I have my judgment be lenient.

Now, in this Suggestion, there appears something that's at least a lot like an inconsistency. Quite possibly, that's a sign we're now near the neighborhood of the reconciliation wanted. For the sign to be a good one, of course, the Suggestion shouldn't actually be inconsistent. So, in the next several sections, I'll show how it may be completely in the clear.

2. Preparation for an Introduction to a Selectively Flexible Semantics

A sensible treatment of my disparate judgments of the Envelope may proceed by way of a semantics that, for its being flexibly selective, has the apparently opposed assessments be completely consistent. Far from any *ad hoc* proposal, the approach should reconcile, as well, many other discrepant moral judgments. Happily, we'll observe an approach that does all that, and a lot more, too.

Recall chapter 3's primary puzzle cases, the Yacht and the Account. What made the examples intriguing may be usefully put like this: For each moral dimension closely concerning our Primary

---

1. For those who think that positive substantive moral judgements aren't ever *true,* some other preferred term can be used throughout, like *acceptable,* and adjustments can be made accordingly. The semantic matters considered here are distinct from questions about the relation between truth and morality, and from similar time-honored issues.

Values, in both cases everything *pointed in the same direction,* toward a *positive* assessment of the agent's behavior. For instance, as your conduct flowed from altruistic motivation in both the Yacht and the Account, along the dimension of (operative) *motive* matters favored a positive judgment in both cases. And, as your conduct resulted in there being fewer lives lost in both cases, with nobody suffering seriously at all, along the dimension of (actual) *consequences* the same was true.

As with those puzzle cases, in real life often all the Primary aspects of some conduct point in the same direction; sometimes they all point toward a positive judgment and sometimes all toward a negative evaluation. But, often it's the opposite that's true, with things pointing positively along some dimensions and negatively along others. Again confining our focus to (actual) consequences and (operative) motive, we'll consider this: With the best intent in the world, sometimes a person may strive to aid someone in serious trouble and, even against all reasonable expectations, the conduct flowing from his good will makes things far worse for the other. For instance, trying to pry a boulder off someone's thigh to save her leg, even a properly careful would-be benefactor might, through no fault of his own, cause the rock to roll onto the woman's chest and kill her. How do we morally judge this behavior?

At times, we seek to further certain purposes and, so, we stress the agent's good motive and ignore the bad consequences of his conduct. (When professing his official philosophy, perhaps Kant was doing this.) At these times, we'll rate highly well-intentioned conduct resulting in the loss of an innocent life.

At other times, we seek to further certain other purposes and, so, we stress the conduct's actual consequences and ignore the good motive issuing in the behavior. (When professing their official moral philosophy, perhaps certain Utilitarians did this.[2]) At these other times,

---

2. Employing morally useful terms to highlight some conduct's intentions is no private property of Kantians, nor have Utilitarians a monopoly on using these terms to feature the consequences of conduct: Consider a well-made solemn promise. Suppose that, in the prevailing circumstances, it's best for the agent to keep this promise. Trying her best to keep it, and being well-intentioned in her behavior, through no fault of her own she may not succeed in keeping the promise. (As an extreme case of this, certain wholly unpredictable events at the level of quantum physics may so upset matters as to foil her well-aimed attempt to keep the promise.) Did this agent conduct herself well, or not? At times, we may stress her fine motives, perhaps ignoring completely the unfortunate upshot. Then, we'll give her behavior a high moral rating. At other times, we may highlight the bad consequence only, the unkept promise, and ignore the agent's fine intentions. Then, we'll give her behavior a low moral rating. So, the main point is a very general proposition.

we'll give a low rating to well-intentioned conduct resulting in the loss of an innocent's life.

With which of the two very different assessments is there a moral judgment that's correct, or more nearly correct? Since matters of moral judgment are far more complex than this question presupposes, it has no single straightforward answer: Sometimes it's correct to give some well-intentioned conduct a low moral rating and, equally, sometimes it's correct to give that same conduct a high one. Apparently paradoxical, how can my suggestion offer the least bit of sense, much less a worthwhile idea? Shortly, I'll show how. But, first, I'll raise related questions.

As well as noncomparative moral assessments, we often make comparative moral judgments of behavior, as when we say, for example, that Jim's conduct on Tuesday was (morally) better than his behavior on Monday. (In an important sense, these comparative assessments might be the most basic moral judgments of our conduct.) Anyway, with these judgments, there's a parallel divergence: Stemming from better motivation, one piece of behavior may have worse consequences than another. At times, we'll stress only the motives involved and, then, we'll judge the first morally better than the second. At other times, ignoring the motives entirely, we stress just the consequences and, then, we'll judge the second to be better. Also appearing opposed, perhaps these judgments also are compatible.

Third, we also characterize conduct morally by placing it in one of these three "deontic categories": (a) what's morally forbidden, or wrong; (b) what's (at least) morally permitted, or all right; and (c) what's (as much as) morally required, or the (only) right thing to do. Stressing the conduct's motive and ignoring its consequences, we may judge some well-intentioned disastrous behavior to be all right. Highlighting only the consequences and downplaying the motive completely, at another time we may judge the same conduct to be wrong. Perhaps, both judgments are completely correct.

All appearing paradoxical, how can these suggestions offer sensible ideas?

3. Rudiments of a Context-Sensitive Semantics for Morally Useful Terms

To answer that question, there'll be provided a *multi-dimensional context-sensitive semantics* for moral talk and thought. In this section, I'll only introduce its rudiments. Yet, even this sketch will show the

semantics to have very unobvious key features, some of them somewhat unintuitive.

For a good reason, however, that's no problem for my project. The
point is that, in our *non*moral thought and talk, there's the same pervasive situation: First, between a nonmoral judgment someone makes at
a certain time and one she makes on another occasion, often there's a
disparity that, at a first philosophical glance, has the judger endorsing
a pair of statements that flatly contradict each other. And, second, for
a sensibly reconciling treatment of these apparently opposed nonmoral judgments, what's wanted is a multi-dimensional context-
sensitive semantics for terms that *aren't* so centrally useful in so much
moral talk and thought.[3] So, with an attempt to offer such a semantics
for terms that *are* so useful morally, I'm just taking an approach
already notably successful and looking to extend its range.

In that spirit, I offer this "extending" hypothesis: As is true of so
many other terms, many of the terms that figure centrally in our moral
judgments have a certain *indexical* aspect to their semantics and, for
that reason, they are *sensitive to the contexts* in which they're used or
understood. Commonly occurring in our thought and talk, these
terms include many with both moral and nonmoral proper uses, like
"right," "all right" and "wrong," "acceptable" and "unacceptable,"
"good" and "bad," and "better" and "worse." Finally, there are the very

3. On the general matter of contextual semantics, the seminal work is David
Lewis's "Scorekeeping in a Language Game," *Journal of Philosophical Logic*, 1979, reprinted in his *Philosophical Papers*, Volume 1, Oxford University Press, 1983. Although I
was being too much of a radical about the matters, a fairly early discussion of context-
sensitive semantics, and of its salient polar opposite, context-invariant semantics, is the
main theme of my *Philosophical Relativity*, University of Minnesota Press and Basil
Blackwell, 1984. Quickly becoming much more conservative, a bit later there appeared
my lengthy paper, "The Cone Model of Knowledge," *Philosophical Topics*, 1986; focusing on the semantics of knowledge attributions, this remains the fullest discussion, to
date, of a semantics for such sentences that's as usefully multi-dimensional as it's
context-sensitive. Noting certain deep commonalities between many epistemic assessments and, on the other side, many moral judgments, in my "Contextual Analysis in
Ethics," *Philosophy and Phenomenological Research*, 1995, I provide a context-sensitive
semantics for many morally useful terms. Not wishing to bite off more than I could chew
well, the semantics there provided was meant to apply only to judgments about certain
simple situations. So, there, I had no need to deploy a multi-dimensional semantics.
In this book, however, there certainly is that need. So, complementing the multi-
dimensional semantics I gave for epistemically useful sentences in "The Cone Model of
Knowledge," here I'll provide a *multi-dimensional* context-sensitive semantics for many
morally useful sentences.

Employing a context-sensitive semantics for epistemically useful terms, in his excellent essay, "Solving the Skeptical Problem," *Philosophical Review*, 1995, Keith DeRose
makes some real progress in epistemology. That bodes well for our prospects.

few *specifically moral terms*: "ethical" and "moral", their adverbial forms, their antonyms, and so on.[4]

In morally assessing your conduct, I may utter, or just think to myself, such widely useful words as these: "Your behavior was good." Then, I'll assess your conduct along this contextually sensitive line: With respect to the standards *prevalent in this very context* (of use or understanding), your behavior rates highly. Now, since "good" *isn't* a specifically moral term, in *non*morally assessing your conduct, I also may use those same words, "Your behavior was good." Then, I'll again assess your behavior along that same general contextually sensitive line. With that being both times the same, the difference lies in this: When making the moral judgment, I set a context, or manage to remain in a context, in which it's *morality* that's implicitly selected as the prevalent standard; in making the nonmoral judgment, I set a context in which it's something *other than* morality that's selected as prevalent, say, some rules of diplomatic protocol. Now, it's well worth mentioning that, both in the moral and in the nonmoral case, we can select the prevalent behavioral standard(s) explicitly. For the moral case, that can be done by standardly saying, "Your behavior was morally good," or something else prolix and, typically, pompous. Rationally preferring to be nicely efficient judges, we generally eschew qualifiers like that "morally," and, so, we have contexts determine the prevalent standard(s).

We've noticed just one way that, for having morally useful terms with a context-sensitive semantics, we can morally assess conduct efficiently. (So, for a reader-friendly exposition, from now on I'll often write "moral terms" instead of the longer "morally useful terms.") But, for present purposes, it's this related matter that's much more important: Because the moral terms have a *multi*-dimensional context-sensitive semantics, in making moral judgments they may be used to play up just certain of the morally significant aspects of some conduct (or some agent, or whatever) and, in the process, to play down all the other significant features. So, when happily making a moral judgment with the words, "Your behavior was good," beyond having it that morality's selected as the standard, we may select which of its ethical dimensions *count* (much) in reckoning how well your conduct conforms to morality.

---

4. Except for the words in this last group, the morally useful terms are usually used in utterances that have nothing to do with morality. Of course, that's *right,* as any *good* linguist can tell you. But, those facts about usage aren't important for the matters under consideration. For, here, we're concerned with the terms as standardly used in making moral judgments.

This variability can provide reconciliations for apparently conflict-ing behavioral assessments. In the simplest and most extreme case of that, there's set a context where only *one* dimension of the conduct judged gets weight in determining the behavior's moral status. So, with one correct use of "Your conduct was good," I'll set a context where, as is then proper, your conduct's motive is the only dimension of the behavior that, in reckoning its moral status, has any weight. Then, my judgment will be correct so long as the conduct flowed from an extremely good motive, *no matter what* the consequences of the behavior. And, with a different correct use of the same terms, "Your conduct was good," I'll set a context where, as is *then* proper, your conduct's *result* is the only dimension that, in reckoning its moral status, has any weight. So, then, my judgment will be correct so long as the conduct resulted in extremely good *consequences,* no matter what the *motive* for the behavior.[5]

With that understanding, we may see how a multi-dimensional context-sensitive semantics can deal with the previous section's appar-ent contradictions. Recall the conduct aimed at saving someone's leg that, against all odds, resulted in that person's death. With a use of "good" that sets a context where motives count for everything, we can correctly give it a high moral rating. And, with a use of "bad" that sets a context where consequences count for all, and motives count for naught, we can correctly give it a low one. In parallel, there's treated the corresponding comparative moral judgments.

Since it may be instructive, I'll say a bit more about reconciliations for apparently opposed deontic characterizations of common conduct: In morally assessing your behavior, I may employ such widely useful words as "What you did was all right." When that's done well, I'll have assessed your behavior along this contextually sensitive line: To be correctly considered acceptable in this very context, what you did was at least close enough to being in complete conformity with the stan-dard(s) prevalent in this very context (of use, or of understanding). But, then, there's set a context that, for correctly classing your conduct as morally acceptable, does much more than select morality as the standard; the context also determines what's (at least) *close enough,* then and there, to complete conformity with morality.

Before applying such a flexible semantics to my jarringly disparate moral judgments for the Envelope's conduct, I'll note two possible

---

5. At these other times, often it's apt to say, "Even if it was for the wrong reason, you did the right thing." And, though a little less colloquial, often it's also apt to say, "Even if it was done for a bad reason, what you did was good."

limits on the correct employment of the morally useful terms. As I'll also notice, there may be parallel limits on the application of many nonmoral terms.

First, in just one breath, we can't correctly use some moral terms in a manner that, then and there, opposes our use of others; rather, that first use places limits on those other uses. So, we don't make a correct moral judgment by saying, all at once, "Your behavior was good; and her conduct was seriously wrong; and her conduct was better than your behavior." But, of course, with nonmoral judgments, the central story is the same. For a well-worn but useful example, consider our standard use of "flat," in the central, geometric sense of the term.[6] In just one breath, we can't correctly use "flat" in a manner that, then and there, opposes our use of closely related terms. So, we don't make a correct judgment by saying, all at once, "Your land is flat; and her land is bumpy; and her land is flatter than yours."

Second, perhaps our use of moral terms isn't so potent that just any conduct at all can correctly receive a high moral rating; or just any behavior rightly be rated low. For example, no matter what context of judgment "good" is properly used to set, perhaps a deed correctly classed as malevolently motivated murder without even the slightest chance of issuing in any good result can't ever be correctly judged as conduct that's morally good.[7] So, though we can correctly use the moral terms quite variously in making ethical judgments, that might happen only within certain limits. Here, too, there's nothing that's peculiar to moral terms: To be sure, though a croquet field may have many small ups-and-downs, when saying "That's flat," I'll set a context where those little irregularities are properly ignored and, thus, I'll correctly characterize the land as being flat. But, even with the most lenient contexts for "flat" set, it might be that *some* land can't *ever* be correctly so characterized, as with, perhaps, the Himalayas.

Both in the moral sphere and in nonmoral spheres, with a context-

---

6. Taking a quite opposite and very radical semantic line, in my paper, "A Defense of Skepticism," *Philosophical Review,* 1971, there's the first salient treatment of this "absolute term" in the philosophical literature. In his "Scorekeeping in a Language Game," 1979, Lewis provides the first contextually sensitive treatment for this morally unimportant term.

7. The point I've just made has nothing to do with the alleged necessary truth of "Behavior that's murder is behavior that's morally bad." That's fine since, contrary to widespread opinion, that's no necessary truth: Suppose that, well after he did many terrible things, but well before he was able to do his worst, the horrible Hitler was murdered by a prescient, benevolent and heroic assassin. Then, it will be extraordinarily *easy* for us to set a context where *that* behavior, though a clear case of calculated murder, will be correctly reckoned morally good.

sensitive semantics there's a lot that can be thought, and said, without any real paradox or contradiction. Yet, as we've also seen, that's not to say that anything goes.

4. How This Semantics Can Reconcile My Disparate Judgments of the Envelope's Behavior

With the aid of such a nicely flexible semantics, I'll aim to provide a reconciliation for the disparity between my harsh judgment of the Envelope's behavior, made in the book, and, made in daily life, my lenient judgment of the same (salient sort of) behavior. As a start toward that end, let's note two main contrasts between the two judgments.

On one hand, if our proposed semantics is to have the judgment come out correct, something like this should be said about my lenient ordinary assessment of such horribly consequential behavior: As the context then has it, first, just certain of morality's dimensions are prevalent and, second, the score ordinarily achieved on these dimensions *doesn't* count as a low score; rather, it counts as a *passing* score. Thus, conduct like the Envelope's correctly gets reckoned as morally acceptable. So, my lenient ordinary judgment of such unhelpful conduct is correct.

On the other hand, something like this should be said about my severe Liberationist judgment of the behavior: When I made such a negative assessment, I established an unusual context. In this quite different context, first, certain other dimensions were the prevalent aspects of morality and, second, the scores ordinarily achieved on these *other* dimensions *did* count as low scores. What's more, the context had it that, along the other dimensions, the passing lines *weren't* low. Thus, conduct like the Envelope's correctly got reckoned as morally unacceptable. So, then, my severe Liberationist judgment of that same unhelpful conduct also is correct.

In its general form, that's the account I should give. But, I've yet to supply details. Toward that end, we'll begin with a cue taken from (i), the first part of:

The Schematic Suggestion. (i) By my then playing up (the moral significance of) only those aspects of the conduct that closely connect with our Primary Values, and by my then playing down all of the aspects that closely connect with our Secondary Values, in this book I had my judgment of the Envelope's conduct be severe. (ii) By my then playing up (the moral significance of) the psychological difficulty of our engaging in such helpful conduct as the case calls on from us, which connects closely with our Secondary Values, in everyday life I have my judgment be lenient.

So, when severely judging the Envelope's conduct, in the book I set a context where the moral dimensions selected were just those that connect closely with our Primary Values, not our Secondary Values. Now, when just these dimensions count in judging conduct, the Envelope's behavior gets a score that's even lower than what's correctly reckoned for the horribly unhelpful likes of the Vintage Sedan's. And, along the dimensions then selected, the context set lines that, for moral acceptability, were too high for the Sedan's conduct to pass, let alone the Envelope's lowly behavior.

While that was easy, it's time to make some headway with the hard part of the account I'm aiming to offer: For my lenient ordinary judgment of the Envelope's unhelpful conduct to be correct, what must that judgment's context do? As the Schematic Suggestion's (ii) directs, we look to the province of our Secondary Values. And, from there, we'll star a complex moral dimension to the effect that, as fully aware as she ought of what actually are her good Values, and of their true bearing on the nonmoral facts of her situation, an agent should be so moved by this awareness that her conduct accords well with those fine Values and, so also, with morality. For convenience, I'll call this dimension of conduct its *Secondary Star*.

Before proceeding with this attempt to reconcile, it's useful to recall, from chapter 2, a few thoughts about the contrast between the Primary and the Secondary Values. Having no monopoly on matters of motivation, what the Secondary Values alone do concern is, rather, the *unobvious* things someone *ought to know about her Values*, and *those* motivational matters most closely connected with those unobvious things. Perhaps only a helpful heuristic, the distinction may harbor a great deal of arbitrariness or, perhaps, indeterminacy. For one thing, there's this large area for that: (1) Through causing doubts as to what's really the case in certain moral matters, a person's social setting may make it hard for her to know much about the matters and, so, she may know far less than what, at bottom, she ought to know. (2) Insofar as she knows what's what morally about the matter, the setting may make it hard for her to be moved much by what she does know and, so, she may be moved far less than what, at bottom, she ought to be moved. For both reasons, (1) and (2), someone may fail to behave decently. Of a particular failure, often we may ask this: Did it derive (mainly) from a failure of awareness; or did it derive (mainly) from a failure of will?

Often, it may be arbitrary to *favor either* factor, (1) *or* (2), and also to say they're *equally* responsible. So, in offering this contrast, between Primary and Secondary Values, I don't pretend to mark a deep difference. But, I do suggest that, by discussing moral matters in its terms, we may make philosophical headway. So, let's try to do that with our so-called Secondary Star.

Toward the reconciliation I'm seeking, perhaps a useful step is taken with this idea: When leniently judging the Envelope's behavior in the book, my context selects the conduct's Secondary Star as the prevalent dimension for reckoning the moral status of the behavior. But, for a simple reason, such a step can be only a bare beginning: On anything that's even remotely like any absolute scale for scoring along that dimension, any plausible reckoning will have the Envelope's conduct get a very low score, scarcely higher than what's gotten when the Primary Values' dimensions are selected as prevalent. So, following our Suggestion further, we must suppose my context had it that, instead, a different scoring scale is the prevalent measure. Let's pursue that idea.

For normally decent people, with (cases saliently like) the Envelope it's psychologically so *difficult* to have their conduct's Secondary Star amount to anything significant. With such a sadly unstimulating case as that, no one can reasonably expect, from us normal folks in these present times, conduct much better than such disastrously unhelpful behavior. So, in line with these sad facts about normal decency and psychological difficulty, perhaps my context had a suitable "socially adjusted scale" be the standard for scoring some conduct's Secondary Star and, thus, for rating the conduct itself.

Here's a reason for thinking that's so: Even according to such a socially adjusted scale, with the Sedan, the conduct's Secondary Star gets a low score and, thus, with that case, the agent's conduct rightly receives a low rating. After all, in cases saliently like the Sedan, we decent folk already can be expected to engage in helpful conduct, and even to do so "for the morally right reason." Just so, with such stimulating cases, *our actual helpful* conduct's Secondary Star gets, on just about any scale, a high score, as does the behavior itself. So, it's fair to say that, according to a suitable socially adjusted scale, the Secondary Star of conduct in the Sedan gets a low score, as does that jarringly blatant unhelpful behavior.

At this point, we may complete the reconciliation we're seeking: When making my lenient ordinary judgment of conduct like the Envelope's, not only does my context select the conduct's Secondary Star as the dimension that's prevalent, but it selects just such a socially adjusted scale as the measure for scoring its Secondary Star. So, along that presently prevalent Secondary dimension, the commonly unhelpful conduct gets a score that's *not* low. Finally, along that prevalent dimension, my context sets *such* a low passing line that the behavior itself gets correctly classed as all right.

With a multi-dimensional context-sensitive semantics, we've reconciled my severe Liberationist judgment of the Envelope's behavior and my lenient ordinary judgment of the same behavior.

5. Reconciling My Other Disparate Judgments: Stressing a Conservative Secondary Value

Noted in the preamble, there's this other disparity to be addressed: As with the Account's conduct, and the Foot's, in the book I judge *positively* much behavior that, in my everyday life, I'll continue to judge *negatively*. For the chapter's main work, what's left is to offer a nice reconciliation of that disparity.

Even without complex semantic proposals, it's easy enough to explain how, in the book, I can correctly make positive moral judgments of such enormously helpful, extremely well-intentioned pieces of behavior. What's far more difficult to explain is how, even after becoming aware of Liberationism's main truths, my everyday negative judgments of such successful altruistically aimed conduct can possibly be correct: As inspection seems to reveal, the compassionate conduct comports well both with our Primary Values and also with our Secondary Values. For example, rather than being badly affected by habitual futility thinking, in the Account you saw what really mattered most morally and, for that right reason, you conducted yourself accordingly. So, as it certainly seems, that conduct's Secondary Star scores high on *any* apt scale and, so, the conduct itself must get a high rating.

With such bleak prospects, what's even a semantically sophisticated Liberationist to do? With a plea for your patience, I'll pursue a pretty esoteric idea: With these positive judgments, I make a *radical* departure from our ordinary thinking about conduct like the Account's and, especially, the Foot's. If only because my Liberationist judgments conflict blatantly with norms long upheld by so very many apparently sensible folks, a reasonable recognition of our *epistemico-ethical fallibility* may counsel that we not place much trust in my radically positive assessments. Now, providing that, in certain areas of morality, her society's *Prevailing Moral Norms*, or *Norms*, are *tolerably* decent, as our society's *might* be in the area of stealing, and might *well* be in the area of serious harming, perhaps there's a certain moral importance in an agent's having her conduct, in those moral areas, conform to those Norms. And, then, there may be a moral dimension that, for it's being selected as prevalent by many of our common contexts, can mean correctness for our harsh ordinary judgments of such *radically* righteous conduct as the Account's and, especially, the Foot's.

With this hypothesized conservative moral dimension, there's something positive and also something negative. Since it's the positive part that might further a reconciliation for the disparate judgments under discussion, I'll focus on it first, reserving remarks on what's negative for the next section.

Positively, there's this to be said for doing well by the posited Secondary Value: Insofar as you make sure your conduct conforms well to your Norms, you'll engage in the sort of modestly unimposing behavior that, for almost all decent people, may be appropriate for most everyday situations. This modest conduct is behavior that's held in check, above all, by the thought that any given mortal is a fallible thinker, perhaps as likely as most others to be mistaken not only in many nonmoral matters, but also in quite a few moral areas.[8] (In those moral areas, there may be a great divergence between how well some conduct does by our Basic Moral Values and, on the other hand, how well it does by our Prevailing Ethical Norms. So, even if the Foot's conduct does well by our Values, it may do badly by our Norms.)

By aptly employing the moral terms, I'll hypothesize, I may set contexts where what's relevant for rating certain conduct morally concerns just its conformity with our Norms, not its agreement with our (Primary) Values. When judging in that conservatively modest way, I may correctly judge the Account's conduct to be bad behavior, even while correctly judging the Yacht's conduct to be good. For, it may be that, according to our Norms, while it's good to steal when that's needed to lessen suffering that's salient or exciting, one mustn't steal when it's needed to lessen suffering that's as obscure as it's boring.

Whatever further details may still be wanted, it's along this line, I suspect, that there's the best chance for reconciling my positive Liberationist judgments of the Account's conduct, and even the Foot's, with the negative judgments of my daily life. While that's my suspicion, I'm certainly not very confident in the matter. By contrast, I'm more confident that, in the previous section, there was provided a pretty good

---

8. The points I'm now making have nothing whatever to do with anything even remotely like Rule Utilitarianism, or so-called levels of moral thinking, or anything that may be good with "ordinary morality," or any relation there might be between the moral status of behavior and, on the other side, any morally useful rules of thumb.

reconciliation of my disparate judgments of (conduct like) the Envelope's unhelpful behavior. Still, since I'm less concerned about this section's featured disparity, and reasonably so, I'm reasonably content, for the time being, with its ambitious but tentative explanatory proposal.[9]

6. This Conservative Value and Barriers to Moral Progress

Just before, I said I'd reserve for this next section remarks regarding what's negative in having one's behavior guided by one's Norms. In brief, it's that, insofar as we do well by such a conservative Value, we may fail to make moral progress. Since that's a serious possibility, it's worth some discussion.

Toward a usefully broad perspective, recall the slaveholding of old Virginia that, in another connection, we discussed in chapter 1. Now, let's consider some disruptively rebellious conduct, only or mainly hypothetical, that's the antithesis of that perfectly lawful and widely accepted slaveholding: At risk to themselves, a few well-off white folks, who'd already set free all their slaves, stole slaves from some of the many wealthy whites, like Washington and Jefferson, who continued in the immoral practice. In successful cases of such stealing, the benevolent thieves sent the blacks far north, even into Canada; at first supported by their rebellious benefactors, there the freed slaves had good lives.

Far from acting in accord with their Norms, the thieving rebels acted oppositely. Even when acknowledging that, we'll now judge their conduct positively. As we may suppose, however, in old Virginia most judged the rebellious activity to be wrong. And, in that likely event, there'd be social reinforcement of badly prevalent attitudes and, thus, there'd be reinforced a barrier to moral progress.

As suggested in the previous section, when I still make negative judgments of conduct like the Account's stealing, as I may in daily life, my judgments may be correct. As there explained, I then set contexts

---

9. Though most able philosophers of language will be clear about what are, and what *aren't*, the points I've pursued in this section, and many able epistemologists will be, too, many able ethicists may fail to be clear. Perhaps especially for them, I emphatically repeat the previous note's message: The points I've just made have nothing whatever to do with anything even remotely like Rule Utilitarianism, or so-called levels of moral thinking, or anything that may be good with "ordinary morality," or any relation there might be between the moral status of behavior and, on the other side, any morally useful rules of thumb.

where what's relevant for rating behavior is the agent's conforming her conduct to our Prevailing Ethical Norms. But, in this matter, as in many others, our Norms may conflict with our Values: Against the good Values, the Norms may badly have it that, when it's to lessen serious suffering that's as boring as it's obscure, one mustn't steal anything of value. So, we should ask: Even if I thus manage to have my harsh everyday judgments of such stealing come out correct, when making those judgments won't I myself then do something to reinforce a barrier to moral progress? Yes, I will. So, there may be something immoral about my making the conservatively oriented moral judgments. Even so, those judgments may be true, or correct. And, since it's all too common for people to do wrong when saying something that's right, as may happen with someone's gratuitously telling another hurtful truths about her, here there's no mark against my reconciling semantic account.

7. How a Broad Perspective Supports the Chapter's General Approach

When thinking about judgments of slaveholding, we uncover material that confirms the chapter's main suggestions. Here, I'll explore just two small sets of these judgments.

First, we'll consider a *morally modest* slaveholder and, by contrast, an *egoistically persistent* one, both of whom lived, and died, some centuries ago. Now, though he himself thought slaveholding to be seriously wrong, our modest man lived in a society whose vast majority believed the practice to be perfectly all right; mainly because he was just a reasonably conservative fellow, he went along with the widely accepted practice and, until his death, he owned slaves. By contrast, our persistent man lived in a society where, even though it was still legal, and profitable, too, the vast majority knew slaveholding to be badly wrong and, so, hardly anyone still engaged in the practice; happy enough to go against that widespread moral belief, which he himself shared, our egoist persisted in profitably owning slaves, until the day he died, a wealthy man.

When considering the conduct of these two slaveholders, we typically judge the persistent egoist's conduct to be morally much worse than the morally modest man's behavior. No doubt, this typical judgment is correct. But, how to account for its correctness? As it appears, the best way lies in the area we've recently explored: Though there's precious little difference between how well the two did by our Primary

Values, our egoist did far worse by our Secondary Values than did our morally modest man. Now, when making our typical judgment, we may set a context where the scores on certain Secondary dimensions count heavily, while scores on Primary dimensions carry little weight, if any at all. Then, since he scores much lower on those Secondary dimensions, it may be correct to say that the persistent profiteer's conduct was far worse than the morally modest man's bad behavior.

Second, let's consider a situation in which our modest man is discussing the morality of slaveholding with an ardent abolitionist who's arguing that, to be morally decent, the uneasy owner must stop his slaveholding. Rather than trying to compare himself favorably with any egoistically persistent owner, we'll further suppose, our modest slaveholder fully agrees, both in thought and even in speech, with the moral activist addressing him. As it certainly seems, here his negative judgment of his own considered conduct is completely correct. Now, how to account for *its* correctness? Again, the best way apparently lies in the area lately explored: In making his staunch statements, our abolitionist set a context where, as was perfectly proper, scores on Secondary dimensions carry little weight, if any at all, while scores on certain Primary dimensions count heavily. So, since he sensibly stays in the abolitionist's set context, and he gets low scores on those Primary dimensions, it's correct for even our modest man to say that his considered conduct is horrible behavior.

To get good accounts of both sets of moral judgments, we'll want to use much of the semantics that's been featured in this chapter. Or, so it certainly appears. As I'll suggest, that speaks well for the chapter's general approach to reconciling my disparate moral judgments.

In closing this section, I'll first note that, had our morally modest man even so much as tried to move out of the tough context our abolitionist set, perhaps in an attempt to have his conduct seem not so bad, we'd rightly take a dim view of his mental, or judgmental, activity. Based on that notable fact, I'll also note that, should we similarly move out of the tough Liberationist contexts this book's set, it's a similarly dim view that would be rightly taken of our mental, or judgmental, activity.

8. From Complex Inquiry to Some Simple Decency

As I'm well aware, this chapter's suggestions raise many questions that the book leaves with no answer. For a couple of nearby examples, there are these: Placing aside a few sophisticated Liberationist philosophers, when most folks make lenient judgments of (conduct saliently like) the Envelope's fatally unhelpful behavior, do *they* set contexts that have *their* judgments come out correct? And, when ordinary Old Virginians made lenient judgments of slaveholding conduct, did they set contexts that had *their* judgments come out correct? Left unaddressed, it's not easy to give these questions, and many others, satisfactory answers. Is this strong reason to think that, in its attempt at reconciliations, the chapter's accomplished next to nothing? Hardly; indeed, on balance, there's more reason to think that a fair amount has been achieved. But, however that may be, there's nothing about any of these semantic matters, I'm sure, that's nearly as important as the thoughts expressed toward the end of the chapter's preamble, which help place all the issues we've discussed in a proper perspective: While there may be *some* sense, or way, in which our ordinary moral judgments accord better with morality than do my Liberationist assessments, in the most important senses, and ways, it's the reverse that's true.

Of course, with certain moral matters, I'm *more confident* of Liberationism's superiority than with others and, so, with those other matters, my Liberationist belief *isn't that* confident. So, though I do think you behaved well in the Foot, that thought's not as confident as my belief that you behaved well in the Account. And, though *pretty* sure of the latter judgment, I'm still more confident that the Envelope's conduct is wrong.

With that much in mind, it's fair to have the book's end pose a Real World situation that's even easier for you to confront responsibly than the one posed at its start. So, here are:

Three Helpful Toll-free Numbers

CARE:	1 - 800 - 521 - CARE, easily dialed as: **1 - 800 - 521 - 2273**
Oxfam America:	1 - 800 - OXFAM-US, easily dialed as: **1 - 800 - 693 - 2687**
U.S. Committee for UNICEF:	1 - 800 - FOR - KIDS, easily dialed as: **1 - 800 - 367 - 5437**

By phoning, it's extremely easy, for almost any well-off American adult, to make an unrestricted contribution of $10, or $50, or $100, to CARE, or Oxfam America, or the U.S. Committee, or even to all three. If you have an active Visa, or MasterCard, or American Express Card—and, almost all of us have at least *one* of them—it's easy as pie.

So, with phone and card at hand, you'll decently make good use, I hope, of the information. And, if you do, then some important good will come from your reading this book and, less directly, from my writing it. For that, I think, my hope is reasonable. After all, though this Liberationist study's left big gaps in our ethical understanding, it's increased our moral awareness, I trust you'll agree, to a considerable extent. And, with even just that much of a gain, we've considerable cause to break with the behavioral inertia that's as horribly consequential, for very vulnerable people, as it's dreadfully preserved by parochial concerns.

BIBLIOGRAPHY

Ahmed, Fauzia. "Cyclone Shelters Saving Lives," *Oxfam America News*, Summer 1994.

Alden, John R. *George Washington*, Louisiana State University Press, 1984.

Bennett, Jonathan. (1) "Morality and Consequences," in S. McMurrin, ed. The Tanner Lectures on Human Values, Volume II, University of Utah Press, 1981.

———. (2) *The Act Itself*, Oxford University Press, 1995.

Cullity, Garrett. "International Aid and the Scope of Kindness," *Ethics*, 1994.

DeRose, Keith. "Solving the Skeptical Problem," *Philosophical Review*, 1995.

Downs, Hugh. "Polio Isn't Dead Yet," *The New York Times*, June 10, 1995.

Fischer, John M. and Mark Ravizza, eds., *Ethics: Problems and Principles*, Harcourt Brace Jovanovich, 1992.

Foot, Philippa. "The Problem of Abortion and the Doctrine of the Double Effect," *Oxford Review*, 1967, reprinted in Fischer and Ravizza.

Franke, Richard W. and Barbara H. Chasin. *Kerala: Radical Reform as Development in an Indian State*, Institute for Food and Development Policy, 1989.

Galloway, J. H. "Brazil," *The World Book Encyclopedia*, Volume 2, 1988.

Grant, James P. (1) *The State of the World's Children 1993*, Oxford University Press, 1993.

———. (2) *The State of the World's Children 1995*, Oxford University Press, 1995.

Hanna, Robert. "Morality *De Re*: Reflections on the Trolley Problem," in Fischer and Ravizza, eds., *Ethics: Problems and Principles*, Harcourt Brace Jovanovich, 1992.

Hare, R. M. *Moral Thinking*, Oxford University Press, 1981.

Hazarika, Sanjoy. "New Storm Warning System Saved Many in Bangladesh," *The New York Times*, May 5, 1994.

Jefferson, Thomas. *Thomas Jefferson: Writings*, Merrill D. Peterson, ed., The Library of America, 1984.

Kagan, Shelly. *The Limits of Morality*, Oxford University Press, 1989.

Kamm, Frances M. (1) "Harming Some to Save Others," *Philosophical Studies*, 1989.

———. (2) *Morality/Mortality*, Volume 1, Oxford University Press, 1993.

———. (3) *Morality/Mortality*, Volume 2, Oxford University Press, 1996.

Lappé, Frances Moore and Rachel Schurman. *Taking Population Seriously*, Institute for Food and Development Policy, 1988.

Lewis, David. "Scorekeeping in a Language Game," *Journal of Philosophical Logic*, 1979, reprinted in David Lewis, *Philosophical Papers*, Volume 1, Oxford University Press, 1983.

Murphy, Liam. "The Demands of Beneficence," *Philosophy and Public Affairs*, 1993.

Nagel, Thomas. *The View from Nowhere*, Oxford University Press, 1986.

The New York Times, January 5, 1993, "With Hint of Scandal, New Social Values Are Sold."

The 1993 Information Please Almanac, Houghton Mifflin, 1993.

Parfit, Derek. (1) "Innumerate Ethics," *Philosophy and Public Affairs*, 1978, reprinted in Fischer and Ravizza.

———. (2) *Reasons and Persons*, Oxford University Press, 1984.

Patterson, Orlando. *Slavery and Social Death*, Harvard University Press, 1982.

Population Division of the United Nations Secretariat. *World Population Prospects: The 1994 Revision*, United Nations, New York, 1995.

Quinn, Warren S. (1) "Actions, Intentions and Consequences: The Doctrine of Double Effect," *Philosophy and Public Affairs*, 1989, reprinted in Fischer and Ravizza.

———. (2) *Morality and Action*, Cambridge University Press, 1993.

Rachels, James. "Active and Passive Euthanasia," *The New England Journal of Medicine*, 1975, reprinted in Fischer and Ravizza.

Rawls, John. "Outline of a Decision Procedure for Ethics," *Philosophical Review*, 1951.

Scheffler, Samuel. (1) *The Rejection of Consequentialism*, Oxford University Press, 1982.

———. (2) *Human Morality*, Oxford University Press, 1992.

Sen, Amartya. "Population: Delusion and Reality," *The New York Review of Books*, September 22, 1994.

Sidgwick, Henry. *The Methods of Ethics*, Macmillan, 1907.

Singer, Peter. (1) "Famine, Affluence and Morality," *Philosophy and Public Affairs*, 1972.

———. (2) *Practical Ethics*, Cambridge University Press, 1979; Second Edition, 1993.

———. (3) *How Are We to Live?*, Reed Consumer Books, 1993.

Smart, J. J. C. and B. Williams, *Utilitarianism: For and Against*, Cambridge University Press, 1973.

Taurek, John. "Should the Numbers Count?," *Philosophy and Public Affairs*, 1977, reprinted in Fischer and Ravizza.

Thomson, Judith Jarvis. (1) "Killing, Letting Die, and the Trolley Problem," *The Monist*, 1976, reprinted in Thomson (3) and in Fischer and Ravizza.

———. (2) "The Trolley Problem," *The Yale Law Journal*, 1985, reprinted in Thomson (3) and in Fischer and Ravizza.

———. (3) *Rights, Restitution and Risk*, Harvard University Press, 1986.

———. (4) *The Realm of Rights*, Harvard University Press, 1990.

Unger, Peter. (1) "A Defense of Skepticism," *Philosophical Review*, 1971.

———. (2) *Philosophical Relativity*, University of Minnesota Press and Basil Blackwell, 1984.

———. (3) "The Cone Model of Knowledge," *Philosophical Topics*, 1986.

———. (4) *Identity, Consciousness and Value*, Oxford University Press, 1990.

———. (5) "Contextual Analysis in Ethics," *Philosophy and Phenomenological Research*, 1995.

United Nations Development Programme. *Human Development Report 1993*, Oxford University Press, 1993.

Williams, Bernard. (1) "A Critique of Utilitarianism," in Smart and Williams.

———. (2) "Persons, Character and Morality," in A. Rorty (ed.) *The Identities of Persons*, University of California Press, 1976, reprinted in Williams (3).

———. (3) *Moral Luck*, Cambridge University Press, 1981.

Wolf, Susan. "Moral Saints," *Journal of Philosophy*, 1982.

World Bank. *World Development Report 1993*, Oxford University Press, 1993.

INDEX OF CASES

In initial occurrences, definite and indefinite articles are omitted.

INDEX OF PERSONS

INDEX OF SUBJECTS